KU-201-199

The Communication of Politics

Ralph Negrine

SAGE Publications
London • Thousand Oaks • New Delhi

© Ralph Negrine 1996

First published 1996

All rights reserved. No part of this publication may be
reproduced, stored in a retrieval system, transmitted or utilized
in any form or by any means, electronic, mechanical,
photocopying, recording or otherwise, without permission in
writing from the Publishers.

SAGE Publications Ltd
6 Bonhill Street
London EC2A 4PU

SAGE Publications Inc
2455 Teller Road
Thousand Oaks, California 91320

SAGE Publications India Pvt Ltd
32, M-Block Market
Greater Kailash – I
New Delhi 110 048

British Library Cataloguing in Publication data

A catalogue record for this book is
available from the British Library

ISBN 0 8039 7738 7
    0 8039 7739 5 (pbk)

Library of Congress catalog card number 96–070158

Typeset by Mayhew Typesetting, Rhayader, Powys
Printed in Great Britain by Biddles Ltd, Guildford, Surrey

The Communication of Politics

2

4

LIVERPOOL
JOHN MOORES UNIVERSITY

LIVERPOOL JMU LIBRARY

3 1111 00767 1058

Contents

Acknowledgements

The author and publisher would like to thank the following for their kind permission to reproduce copyright material: plates 2.1 and 2.2 Her Majesty's Stationery Office; plates 5.1 and 5.2 the *Daily Mail* (a division of Associated Newspapers Ltd), London; plate 5.3 the *Daily Mirror* (of Mirror Group Newspapers), London; and plate 5.4 Rex Features, agents for News International.

Many people helped in the making of this book. My thanks to the Nuffield Foundation and to the University of Leicester for their financial assistance at various points in the last five years. My thanks also to the many librarians who answered my queries, and to my colleagues at the Centre for Mass Communications Research who helped in many different ways. I would also like to thank Stelios Papathanassopoulos and Professors Peter Golding, Jeremy Tunstall and Colin Seymour-Ure for their thoughts on earlier versions of some of the material found here.

I would also like to thank the Nuffield Foundation for funding the research on the British Aerospace–Rover Group takeover in 1988. Their financial assistance was invaluable and enabled the work to be carried out. That research features at various points throughout this book, in particular in Chapters 1, 2 and 4.

I would also like to thank the Research Committee of the University of Leicester for their financial assistance, which enabled me to pursue the idea of specialisms in journalism. Their financial help enabled me to carry out many interviews. The research findings appear at various points, in particular in Chapters 3 and 5.

A shorter account of the BAe–Rover takeover can be found in R. Negrine (1992) 'Parliamentary select committees and the media: a case study of the British Aerospace takeover of the Rover Group', *Parliamentary Affairs*. 45(3): 399–408.

Earlier, shorter and somewhat different, versions of Chapter 3 can be found in R. Negrine (1995) 'Reporting British Parliamentary select committees: A case study in the communication of politics', in D. Paletz *Political Communication Research*, USA: Hampton Press.

A version of Chapter 4 can be found in R. Negrine (1993) *The Organization of British Journalism and Specialist Correspondents* (Discussion Papers in Mass Communication), Leicester: University of Leicester.

A much shorter version of Chapter 5 can be found in R. Negrine (1995b)

'The "gravest political crisis since Suez": the press, the government and the pit closures announcement of 1992', *Parliamentary Affairs*, 48 (1): 40–56. Oxford: Oxford University Press.

Finally, a shorter version of Chapter 7 can be found in R. Negrine and S. Papathanassopoulos (1996) 'The "Americanization" of political communication: A critique', *Press/Politics*, 1 (2). Cambridge, MA: 1–91. Harvard University Press.

Preface: The Communication of Political Information

The role of the mass media within the political system has long been a subject of intense debate. Indeed, discussions about the 'freedom of the press' and the ways in which such freedoms can be achieved have continued to play an important part in recent reconceptualizations of 'the mass media and the democratic process' (See Keane, 1991; Lichtenberg, 1990).

A common purpose behind such attempts to reconceptualize the role of the mass media has been to move beyond the simple and traditional statements and assumptions about what the media ought to do and to construct a contemporary agenda for exploring the mass media. In the process, such attempts have had to meet head-on the many criticisms of the mass media which have been voiced throughout the last quarter of a century, and to confront the challenges posed by contemporary developments. They have had, for example, to take on board

- studies of media coverage of politically or socially controversial issues which have readily exposed the limitations of the mass media (see Schlesinger, 1978; Golding and Middleton, 1982);
- analyses of the media's relationship to those who wield political and economic power which have stressed the former's dependency on the latter (Schlesinger, 1990; Gandy, 1982);
- criticisms of the idyll of the free market place as a guarantor of press and broadcasting freedoms which have highlighted, to the contrary, the potential for a restriction of diversity (Golding and Murdock, 1991);
- evidence which points to the growing professionalization of the sources of information leading to increasingly strategic and planned communication for the purposes of controlling the flow, and hence, 'impact' of information (Blumler, 1990; Manheim, 1994).

But they have also had to give some thought to

- the changing national and global political and socio-economic environments which, in their own ways, raise some significant issues about the nature, and distribution, of political power in the present and in the future. For instance, do the processes of 'globalization' – of politics, of systems of communication – shift power away from more locally bounded territorial spaces (that is, nation-states)? Do they redistribute power? Do they redistribute the source and locations of communication power away from national to international communication systems (Sreberny-Mohammadi, 1991; Keane, 1995; Garnham, 1995)?

- the potential importance of systems of communication, such as the Internet, which allow for more direct, uncontrolled, and individual/group communication in direct contrast to the mass forms of unidirectional communication (i.e. television, newspapers) which currently take up a vast proportion of the leisure time of populations.

Thus, whilst the objective of creating, in John Keane's words, a form of media and communication which 'should enable [citizens] to live democratically' (Keane, 1991: 126) unites diverse critics of the mass media, the way to arrive at this objective is open to considerable debate. Does the possibility of a 'plurality of public spheres' contain within it the potential for making it easier to 'monitor the exercise of power from a variety of sites within state *and* social institutions' and so increase the 'likelihood that its exercise is rendered more accountable to those whom it directly or indirectly affects' (Keane, 1995: 20), or does it simply reduce the potential for accountability because it disperses the power of opposition and organization? If the latter, should not the aim be to shore up the forces which enable those in power to be held accountable, namely those institutions of communications which provide the 'necessary information and imagery to allow equal and full participation in the social order' (Golding, 1990: 98)?

How one decides between these two positions – if, that is, one has to decide – has a bearing on some of the major themes which are explored in this book. In essence, if the aim is to encourage active participation in 'defining the public good or general interest and then ensuring its political enactment' (Garnham, 1995: 23) and/or to hold those in power to account, some means must be found by which a proper amount of information which facilitates this achieves widespread circulation. Without a proper amount of information – however defined in detail – citizens and publics are unable to pass judgement on events or their causes.

As noted above, media analysts have long been aware of some of the professional practices of policy actors and journalists which constrain the media's abilities to fulfil their 'duties' as channels of communication which lend support to the democratic process. As Philip Schlesinger observed, a concern with practices and source–journalist relationships 'inevitably takes us into the broader questions about the nature of information management in society by a variety of groups in conditions of unequal power and therefore unequal access to systems of information production and distribution' (Schlesinger, 1990: 82).

But while these sets of concerns with the structures and organization of the mass media and journalistic practices clearly contribute significantly to our understanding of the ways in which the mass media work within democratic polities, I wish to argue that they represent approaches which often ignore both the nature of the specific political contexts within which they work and the nature of the information *per se* that they work with. In other words, they greatly simplify some of the other very real problems with which the mass media have to contend and which, in turn, force us to reflect on their roles within democratic polities.

By focusing on a number of different case studies, this book examines some of the problems faced by the media and by journalists in their efforts to create an 'informed' citizenry and by citizens to become 'informed': on the one hand, the work of the media and journalists is in part bounded by their relationships to those in government and the imperatives of governing, and, on the other hand, the work of the media and journalists is made immensely more difficult by the nature of the information available to them which is often so ambiguous that it cannot easily be interpreted and explained. In this respect, the extensive attention that will be paid to questions of 'information' *per se* in this book will complement more traditional approaches to the study of the role of the mass media in the democratic process, which often completely ignore this question. This particular orientation to the subject takes us away from 'Grand Theories' about the mass media and democracy in order to remind us of the context within which they operate and the sorts of information they work with. Similarly, it forces us to look more carefully at the way news organizations operate as a means of exploring their adequacy in communicating complex, subtle and abstract ideas. It does not assume that a proper amount of information – diversity, plurality, accuracy – is something that can be achieved simply through the creation of adequate structures of communication. The day-to-day activities of journalists, of media, in trying to make sense of events and their causes are equally important considerations.

Having explored these issues, it may then be possible to return to the more general questions concerning the means by which active citizen participation can be engendered, discussions of the 'general interest' can be opened up, and those in power can be held more accountable.

Although no specific answers to these questions are offered in the book, the orientation to the subject adopted here places a great deal of emphasis on two factors which implicitly inform a considerable amount of the discussion (and which have a bearing on the questions posed immediately above). The first of these factors is the continuing importance of socio-political activity within a physically defined territorial space. In spite of the globalization of communication systems and of political fora, political activity of the sort which has a direct and visible effect on the lives of citizens emanates from the nation-state. The second factor is an extension of the first, namely, that the media can still inform individual, local and national concerns even though they may be part of international corporations. There is then a strong justification in focusing on national contexts or specific examples as a way of introducing more general questions and more general issues.

About this book

The remarks above set out the overall orientation of this book. Each of the following chapters develops a number of themes about how the mass media work and how this helps, or hinders, our particular constructions of an improved media structure for a democratic society. Though the book draws on a series of case studies from contemporary British politics, it also incorporates a considerable amount of material from other political systems, most notably the United States. In this way, it is hoped that the themes developed here can be applied more generally. And if there is a common theme running through these chapters it is the complexity of the links between the media, the institutional political world and the public as each generates and confronts information for use and for consumption.

The general background to these ideas – especially as they relate to the whole question of information – can be found in Chapter 1. Particular attention is paid to the ways in which different strategies are employed to generate information for mass media use, as well as the different levels of information to which the mass media have access. One important suggestion in this chapter is that the mass media often do not make the most of the available information for a variety of reasons.

One aspect of this argument is taken up in the second chapter, which focuses exclusively on 'leaks' and the ways in which 'leaks' say something about routinized journalistic activity. In Chapter 2, one argument is that 'leaks' reveal as much about in-fighting as about journalism itself. 'Leaks' are seen as releases of information which sabotage the normal patterns of information management because they subvert 'normal' practices. However, they also highlight the limitations of everyday journalistic practices and, more critically, the paucity of information available within the public domain. Leaks represent a prism through which one can explore journalistic practices and the quality of information.

Chapter 3 is specifically about the nature of political journalism and, in particular, the nature of British Parliamentary coverage. A number of different aspects of Parliamentary work are considered – select committees, reports, debates – in order to assess the overall 'adequacy' of that coverage. As this chapter also reports evidence relating to the coverage of political institutions in the USA and in Germany, it begins to address the much broader question of how such political institutions should be covered in a rapidly changing domestic and international political environment. It links up with issues found in Chapter 1, as well as with the whole question of the changing role of the media in contemporary democracies which is explored in Chapter 8.

Chapter 4 deals with information and its use by the media from a different perspective altogether. Here, the emphasis is on the ways in which different newspaper specialisms may have an impact on the nature of the content carried in the press. Rather than treat all reporters as interchangeable media professionals, this chapter suggests that some attention needs to be devoted to what the designation of 'specialist' actually entails as well as to the question of whether different specialisms or specialists bring something qualitatively different to their accounts of the world.

Chapter 5 looks at the ways in which the media and public opinion interact. By considering a particular government announcement and the ways in which a crisis in government came (almost) out of nowhere, this chapter seeks to develop a better way of understanding how the media work in relation to government, how they work in relation to the public and how they use, or reflect, the public's thoughts in their work. This chapter also suggests that one needs to have a proper understanding of the whole political context in order to have a good grasp of the nature, and impact, of political communication.

How much of an impact political communication may have is the main theme of Chapter 6. Whilst the other chapters explore media work, political contexts and such like, Chapter 6 turns the spotlight on the question of the way in which the public makes sense of the political content it confronts in the mass media. A prominent theme explored here is the 'construction' of politics, and it is pursued in relation to the ways in which young people, as well as adults, come to make sense of the political world. Particular attention is paid to some recent work in this field which seeks to delve deeply into the public's view of the political world.

Chapter 7 is devoted to elections, political marketing and political communication and the whole question of the significance of increasing similarities in practices across contemporary democracies. Although the focus is on British electoral communication, the context within which this discussion takes place is a much larger one, namely, whether the similarities between British and American practices, and the practices of other countries, are evidence of 'Americanization' or whether they point to some deeper process which could be termed 'modernization'. Once again, examples are drawn from many studies to support the main arguments.

Finally, Chapter 8 looks back to earlier chapters but also begins to identify some of the challenges which arise out of the 'globalization' of communications, and of political and economic activity. It also touches on topics such as the 'modern publicity process', the media and diplomacy, and media events and makes some tentative explorations into the ways in which the existence of international forms of communication alter perceptions of leaders, nations and national and international relationships.

Each one of the above chapters presents a collection of ideas which explore the ways in which the media operate in contemporary societies. And in each one of these chapters, it is possible to identify a whole range of questions which students of the mass media should be able to tackle. These include general questions, as well as specific ones. For example:

- are the mass media adequately resourced to survey the socio-political world? (Chapter 2);

- what are the implications of the growing similarity in communication practices during election campaigns? (Chapter 7);
- how should we approach the question of the public's understanding of politics and government? (Chapter 6);
- does the coverage of an event by different types of journalist produce different types of story? (Chapter 4);
- how do different media cover Parliamentary sittings or committee hearings? (Chapter 3).

Such questions are illustrative of the way this book opens up the field to a more informed and inquisitive exploration of the nature and content of political communication in contemporary societies. In doing so it also seeks to encourage the careful reader to use this material to contribute to, as well as confront, 'Grand Theories'.

1

The Communication of Political Information and the Creation of an Informed Citizenry

It is the broadcaster's role, as I see it, to win public interest in public issues . . . If broadcasting can arouse public interest, it can increase public understanding, and in this way make the organization of political consent to the actions of government more possible . . . it *is* their duty, for the sake of the successful government of society, to persuade their audiences to feel themselves involved in the issues which have to be debated . . . Broadcasters have a responsibility, therefore, to provide a rationally based and balanced service of news which will enable people to make basic judgements about public policy in their capacity as voting citizens of a democracy. (Curran, 1979: 114–15)

As we approach the end of this century, it is appropriate that we take a closer look at some of the ideas which have been the foundations of much contemporary writings on society, politics and communications. On the one hand, one can identify the long struggle for the adoption of democratic principles and democratic practices; on the other, one can point to the role of the media of communication in facilitating the adoption of democratic principles and practices. This is exemplified in Charles Curran's statement (above) taken from the account of his period as Director-General at the BBC during the 1970s.

But Curran's thinking reflects a specific moment in time and a particular understanding of the relationship between society, politics and communication. Broadcasting is accorded a key role in the process of creating public understanding, of engendering participation and involvement, of creating an informed citizenry. At the same time, however, broadcasting acts as an aid to government, perhaps even to aid the process of government and the maintenance of society.

Whilst Charles Curran's views are only those of one, of the many, individuals in charge of broadcasting in the post-war period, it may be possible to argue that they do emphasize the sense of mission which infected public service broadcasters at the dawn of broadcasting. A sense of mission which, in the days of commercialized media, may seem both outdated and even quaint. One can see this clearly in the very different perspectives adopted by the Pilkington Committee on Broadcasting of 1960 (1962) and the Peacock Committee on Financing the BBC in the mid-1980s (1986). Though separated by just over 20 years, the reports approach the subject of broadcasting from entirely different positions: the former arguing in favour of the continuation of a certain vision of broadcasting with identifiable 'purposes' (1962: 285–6); the latter prepared to re-evaluate 'existing attitudes to broadcasting' (1986: 2).

In many respects, then, the ways in which we conceptualize the purposes of 'the media' in the 1990s is qualitatively different from conceptualizations in earlier periods. To an earlier generation, the idea that television broadcasting systems could be organized around thematic or specialist channels with no attempt whatsoever to offer a balanced menu, with no attempt to play the part designated by Charles Curran, would seem to be no less than an abdication of the medium's potential and responsibilities. In fact, it is worth recalling that one reason that Independent Television was not awarded the third terrestrial channel in 1962 was due to the view, expressed by the Pilkington Committee, that ITV 'had not succeeded in realising' the purposes of broadcasting (1962: 245).

Lest one think that this sea change in attitudes towards broadcasting is something which is specific to that medium, it is useful to note that the current anxiety about the decline in Parliamentary reporting (see Chapter 3) can be read as no more than a similar concern about changes in media structures and the media's changing working relations with political institutions (and vice versa). The issue, in other words, is not so much about whether there is less or more coverage of Parliament than there used to be but how we can redefine the relationship between the media and politics so that Parliament does not find itself pushed more and more to the fringes of media activity. And, as with broadcasting, at the heart of this concern is the whole question of the duties and responsibilities of the print and broadcast media to Parliament and to the public as citizens. Looked at in this way, then, the concern about the decline in Parliamentary coverage reflects more than simply a degree of unease about the processes, and the outcomes, of change: change on the part of the media and change on the part of Parliament and its related bodies. It calls into question patterns of authority and relations between the public and government long taken for granted.

But does the fact of change – in society, in politics, in the economy, in technology, in media – necessarily lead to the conclusion that there can be no enduring template for the media and for their responsibilities? Does the fact of change mean that the 'purposes' of the media, to use the Pilkington Committee's phrase, and the duties and responsibilities of journalism can no longer be described in unchanging and 'traditional' ways? Does it mean that Charles Curran's views on the responsibilities of broadcasters should be consigned to the dustbin of history? That Delane's mid-nineteenth-century vision of the inquiring journalist seeking out truth (Steed, 1938) is no more than a romantic ideal? Or are there certain linking threads between these other traditions and the present which express older views not only in new ways but also in changing circumstances?

It is unlikely that there is a simple answer to these questions. According to Denis McQuail, 'we are at an uneasy juncture, when development of normative thinking about the press seems either ritualistic or simply "stuck" in a groove, while normative thinking about the new, and not so new, media is fragmentary or lacking legitimacy' (1992: 48). But one can still find strong arguments in favour of such notions as freedom of the press from controls, freedom to express a range of opinions, freedom to distribute opinions. There are, as McQuail notes, 'benefits' which accrue from such freedoms (1992: 70). Although McQuail lists these benefits as 'theoretical' ones since structures and practices limit them in one way or another, it would be relatively easy to point to instances when these benefits were far from 'theoretical'. Though the debates about 'freedoms' may have a sense of a ritual about them, of an incantation, to simply see them as such would be a mistake. What guides journalists in the late 1990s may be no different in intent and substance from that which guided them in previous centuries, albeit in very different circumstances. The connecting thread across centuries is then perhaps no more than a version of what James Curran proposes as a revised form of 'public sphere', that is, a structural organization of the media which is intended to 'facilitate' the provision, availability and circulation of 'relevant information affecting the public good' (1991: 83). After all, is this very different from Lowe's comments in 1852 that the press 'lives by disclosure . . . it is daily and forever appealing to the enlightened force of public opinion', and that for the press 'publicity and truth are the air and light of existence' (Steed, 1938: 76)?

The widely discussed topic of the 'public sphere' impinges on this in several ways. In brief, 'the liberal, constitutional "public sphere" is presented as permitting a rational, well-informed conversation between equals capable of resolving their differences by non-coercive means' (Schlesinger and Tumber, 1994: 9). Unfortunately, the many obstacles to the creation of such a 'public sphere' have also been well documented: they include the ownership and control of media, the rise of the 'public relations state' and the existence of social and economic inequalities (see Thompson, 1990) and this has raised significant doubts over just how far this idea can be taken. Can it ever identify anything more than an idealistic objective of communication processes and structures? How can it cope with the range of obstacles listed above or with the possibility that certain issues may not be open to resolution 'by non-coercive means'?

The obvious, and ready-made, answer is that it does not fit well. Nevertheless, it contains the seeds of an articulated vision of how citizens interact with each other and with the world of politics and this may be no different from those conceptions derided as 'ritualistic'. But what it does not do is touch on the fact of 'mediatization' (Thompson, 1990), the insertion of the media into most processes of communication and social organization so that the information about which much of the 'well-informed conversation' is meant to be conducted is itself the product of the media. After all, even the definition of the 'public sphere' is premised on the idea that 'relevant' information will be made available, that is, on the idea that a body or bodies will make decisions about what information is to be made available. We not only need to question the practices that filter information but we also need to confront the idea that information *per se* is unproblematic, that it has an obvious clarity which puts it beyond debate, that it is transparent. The latter problem has not always attracted sufficient interest but as the case study discussed later in this chapter illustrates, it has a bearing on our notions of what it is that citizens will discuss in the 'public sphere'. Before turning to these issues, it is necessary to explore the changing nature of government and government practices and the implications of both for the role of the mass media in creating an informed and active citizenry.

Old times, new times: the media in a changing world

It is often tempting to generalize and to discuss 'the media' as if one was discussing something unitary and unchanging. But the media have never been either: newspapers, for instance, have always displayed a rich variety of types and this continues to be the case today. The same is true of the broadcast media. Even in the early days of radio and television broadcasting, competing services developed to offer, albeit limited, choices to listeners and viewers. With the proliferation of systems of communication in the late twentieth century, it is tempting to say that it makes little sense to adopt Charles Curran's views on the role of the broadcasters: the era of plentiful communication is a far cry from that of scarcity and the broadcasters' moral and cultural leadership which may have been allowed to flourish in earlier periods can no longer be easily sustained. There are too many publications, too many radio services and too many television channels to permit the recreation of a hierarchy of tastes and authority.

But there is another sense in which Charles Curran's position can no longer hold and this has little to do with technological change and the ending of scarcity. The changes in British society taking place from the 1960s onwards began to undermine the sense of cohesion and stability which may have been a characteristic of earlier decades. Voting choices, for example, changed dramatically; attachment to the main political parties declined; the rise of other political groupings based around ethnicity and gender shattered the sense of consensus and continuity, and so on. Such accounts of change are part of a broader appreciation of social and political history.

It is much more difficult, however, to comment with any degree of confidence on changes that we are living through ourselves: not only is it too contemporary and, as it were, in process, but because we are part of it we are as much a cause as a product of it. Nevertheless, for many commentators, there is a strong sense that in the last 25 years we have lived through some fundamental changes in the way our societies are organized. As Hall and Jacques have argued, 'the world has changed not incrementally but qualitatively . . . Britain and other advanced capitalist societies are increasingly characterized by diversity, differentiation and fragmentation rather than homogeneity, standardization and the economies and organizations of scale which characterized modern mass society' (1989: 11). Consequently, the existence of individual citizens and citizen groups gives rise to a 'proliferation of sites of antagonisms and resistance' (1989: 17).

The significance of such 'new times' – if they are indeed 'new times' – for our understanding of past, present and future mass communication practices cannot be overlooked. Whilst the more traditional conceptions of representative democracies put the emphasis on the mass media as facilitating the democratic process by, for example, holding governors to account, providing a forum for debate and enabling the citizens to make rational decisions, proponents of the 'new times' also stress the many new forces that are currently in play and their demands for an active voice. If the 'old times' were characterized by a largely passive electorate exercising its democratic rights at infrequent intervals, the 'new times' represent a flowering of differences, diversity and activism. Similarly, if the battleground of the 'old times' was class politics and the politics of inequalities of power and economic resources, those of the 'new times' are of ethnicity, gender and 'postmaterial values' (Inglehart, 1977).

It follows that the means of *mass* communication are ill suited to the needs of the 'new times' and that as the old cleavages in society fragment into other associations of interest, ethnicity or whatever, those things which made the mass media what they were no longer offer adequate basis of support. Diversity in politics calls for diversity in its public representation; a diverse community can only be imagined in its diversity and not with a sense of unity. In this respect, the traditional mass media may have failed to make the systems of communication fully representative of the 'more variegated and heterogeneous society' (Hall and Jacques, 1989: 17) in which we are currently living. To quote Keane:

> A fundamentally revised public service model should aim to facilitate a genuine commonwealth of forms of life, tastes and opinions, to empower a plurality of citizens who are governed neither by despotic states nor by market systems. It should circulate to them a wide variety of opinions. It should enable them to live democratically within the framework of multilayered constitutional states which are held accountable to their citizens, who work and consume, live and love, quarrel and compromise within independent, self-organising civil societies which underpin and transcend the narrow boundaries of state institutions. (1991: 126)

The celebration of diversity and 'the proliferation of the sites of antagonism and resistance' (Hall and Jacques, 1989: 17) raises many issues for modern societies but it also confronts modern societies with the need to reassess the relationship between these diverse new movements and centres of association and identities with the centralized and bureaucratized institutions of government. And it goes without saying that the role of the media in these changing times also requires some thought. There is or can be a contradiction between a plurality of forms of life and the continuing centralization and supra-nationalization of political life and political power. But, as we shall see, although some thought has been given to the need to rethink the work of the media in the age of 'the public relations state', less attention has been paid to the changing nature of government and the ways in which this forces us to reconsider traditional concepts of 'communication and politics'.

The nature of modern government

The connecting threads between media and democracy are now so well established that their exposition does not usually meet any objections. For Schlesinger and Tumber,

> to the extent that given media systems in a variety of ways limit access to the production, distribution, and consumption of information they affect the capacity of the wider public to deliberate and determine decision-making processes in the state and in the wider society. (1994: 8)

And so the better the media systems are able to produce and distribute information, the better the other parts of the system work and the more likely that citizens can begin to make sense of their world and engage with it. Unfortunately, this particular formulation of the connecting link places responsibility on the media to ensure the successful workings of the democratic process. Little attention is paid to the wishes, desires or requirements of the citizens themselves. Moreover, little consideration is given to changes within the structures and processes of government which not only limit the effectiveness of the media but also raise important questions about the rationale for participation in the political system itself.

One way of exploring this issue is by tracing the evolution of modern representative democracy. In his account of modern democratic practice, Robert Dahl writes of 'the second democratic transformation' as the shift 'from the city-state to the national state'. But, he goes on to point out, 'beyond the national state now lies the possibility of even larger and more inclusive supranational political associations' (1989: 213). The second transformation, according to Dahl, changed the 'scale of the political order' (1989: 214); its 'consequences – representative government, greater diversity, the increase in cleavages and conflicts – helped to bring about the development of . . . modern representative democracy' (1989: 218). Dahl calls this 'polyarchy'.

Whilst 'polyarchy' aptly describes the formal process of government and the means by which governments come to power – free and fair elections, elected officials, freedom of expression, inclusive suffrage, etc. – it makes no reference to the nature of the political institutions themselves. As they change, the nature of modern democracies also changes. A good example of this can be found in Britain. According to the Labour MP Gerald Kaufman, a considerable amount of what was once done by government, or was the unquestioned responsibility of government, is now no longer. He points out that under the Conservative governments of the 1980s and

1990s, a large number of Next Steps agencies have mushroomed. These agencies, like the Child Support Agency, do work formerly done by government departments but they are separate from government and stand alone. He calculated that there were 104 such agencies in 1994–5 with about 50 more to be created in 1995–6. His main critique of such agencies is that they have taken on roles that were formerly those of government departments but that, unlike government departments, *they are not accountable to Parliament or to MPs* (1994: 20).

A similar point can be made about findings in the Nolan Committee's report on 'standards in public life' (1994). It identified 1,389 Non-Departmental Public Bodies (NDPBs) – not part of government or government departments – with a total expenditure of about £16 billion. It also noted that there were '600 National Health Service bodies, and perhaps 3,000 or more other bodies spending public funds. The NDPBs and NHS bodies alone involve over 42,000 appointments' (1994: 21). Though the committee acknowledged that there were 'clear lines of responsibility' between NDPBs through ministers to Parliament, it did identify the possibility that the processes of accountability were not what they could be (1994: 24). This point is taken up by Stuart Weir, Director of Democratic Audit, who is also critical of the way the 6,328 quangos (quasi non-governmental organizations) are largely unaccountable. For example, he notes that 'only 42% of all Quangos grant the public a right to inspect members' interests (1995). As with the Next Step agencies, the accountability of such bodies to the public is an issue that draws in the old 'watchdog': the media.

Paralleling this delegation of responsibility, there has also been a delegation of responsibility to Dahl's 'supranational political associations'. According to David Held, the rise of the international governmental and non-governmental organization has 'led to important changes in the decision making structure of world politics' (1989, 196). His data covering the period up to 1984 makes the point quite simply and effectively, though it should be noted that not all of these organizations are of a 'political' character (Table 1.1).

The outcome of these changes is partly the result of the 'downsizing' of government for ideological reasons and partly the result of greater technical specialization of knowledge. Increasingly such specialist bodies – and they may be concerned with nothing more serious than sporting or cultural activities – take over important tasks, and governments could not function without their help. But the processes of delegation impact on those areas which can be open to citizen influences. As the lines of responsibility get blurred, broken or elongated, as the chains of command shift away from arenas of political accountability, the realms of citizens' control via their political representatives and/or via the mass media as 'watchdog' shrink.

This poses some interesting problems. If I, as a citizen, can no longer affect how basic services such as transport, water, gas and electricity are delivered, the rates I am being charged or the pay structures of executives

Table 1.1   *Number of international intergovernmental*
*and non-governmental organizations**

Year	Intergovernmental organizations	International non-governmental organizations
1905	37	176
1951	123	832
1972	280	2173
1984	365	4615
1988		4518
1993		4830

* Figures for 1988 and 1993 are from Ray, 1995: 486

working within private enterprises; if the health services are being run by unelected and unaccountable trusts; and if local authorities are having their funding levels determined by central government, what level of decisions can I actually have an impact on? And what is the point of the media informing me of shortcomings at the financial institution of Baring Brothers, excessive pay increases in the now private British Gas, quangos that cannot control their expenditure plans, or disputes about the European Exchange Rate Mechanism? The institutions of government have become distanced from the reality of everyday life while continuing to have a great impact upon them. Thus, the possibility of exercising traditional forms of democratic pressure – media exposure, contacting MPs, letter writing – becomes more pointless as these bodies begin to move in a different orbit of power. In such circumstances, to be well informed may actually only increase the feeling of 'powerlessness'. This may explain in part why public participation in political activity is often limited to single-issue politics, be it road building or animal welfare: it addresses more immediate and more accessible locations of power.

Not that a wish to participate or to be well informed is necessarily uppermost in most people's minds! A recent report on the state of the American media revealed that half of the 18 to 24 age group never read a newspaper or watched the evening news. As the report notes, 'if "citizenship" is defined as active and informed participation in public affairs and the political process, they – the young in particular – have become non-citizens' (Harwood, 1994: 14). Kuhn reports that in France in 1988 'only one in four of the 15–24 age group regularly read a daily newspaper' (1994: 25). Lest this be thought a problem that does not afflict Britain, it is worth taking note of research published by Robert Worcester for the market research organization, MORI. Of his many observations, two stand out:

> Four out of five adults in Britain read at least one national newspaper daily, but fewer than two thirds in 1993 (63 per cent) read a national newspaper regularly, and of those who do, almost exactly half read either *The Sun* or *The Daily Mirror*. Only one person in six (15 per cent) in 1993 read a 'quality' national daily newspaper regularly. (1994: 5)

Worcester publicizes these findings in the context of a much broader examination of the state of the press in British society but their relevance for the present discussion cannot be emphasized too strongly. It suggests, as a minimum, that access to those media which would be deemed linchpins of the democratic process because of their information-carrying capacity is unequal, and that the vast proportion of the population are outside the sorts of debates and discussions which are the core of their activities.

Television, in this respect, may be a very poor substitute since the national main evening news programmes often provide little more than a headline service (see Chapter 3, below, for example) and so do not always aid the comprehension of news. With the ever increasing commercialization of the broadcast media, it is likely that the 'public service' element within broadcasting will be under greater pressure to change so as to cater for larger and larger audiences.

Two implications of these trends immediately stand out. The first is that the relationship between the citizen and those who govern can no longer be described in simple terms. With different bodies in charge of different parts of the whole, with supra-national bodies regulating domestic social and political activity and with the general dispersal of power the identification of authority becomes more difficult. Consequently, the role of the media becomes more difficult *and yet more crucial*: more crucial because it rests with them to highlight issues and concerns and to put pressure on governmental and non-governmental organizations. In these ways, the media take on a significant role to articulate, to organize, to voice the opinion of the public and to force others to act. Whereas the idea of the 'public sphere' is intended to create a forum for rational debate, the nature of modern governance may in fact require that the media articulate public concerns. Put differently, a rational conversation, as in the 'public sphere' disconnected from the location of power or from those forces that can bring pressure on those in power, remains no more than a self-serving conversation (see Chapter 5 for a discussion of this point).

The second point follows on from this. If the media now have to cast a much wider net and have to monitor things more carefully, do they have the capacity to adequately survey the ever-expanding political, economic and social terrain? Are journalists skilled enough to disentangle the latest financial collapse or the latest governmental scandal? Or to foresee them?

The point to emphasize here is that the changing make-up of contemporary societies forces us to reassess how the systems of communication which have traditionally been seen to connect the citizen to her government should also change. To take one example (discussed more fully in Chapter 3), it is now commonplace to argue that the coverage of Parliament in the press is not what it used to be and that this may have a detrimental effect on the public's understanding of government. This may be a valid argument but only if one assumes that Parliament today is no different from what it was yesteryear, that the nature of government and of opposition has similarly not altered, or that the role of the Civil Service has not changed. Yet all of these have changed in some way or other so that we should expect the media to refocus their attention on the parts of the political process which may be more important than in previous decades or to shift attention away from those that have declined in importance. It is this sort of re-evaluation of established institutions and practices that has to be carried out.

The 'public relations state': 'watchdogs' and experienced dog-handlers

If the onset of 'new times' calls for the development of a new form of media system, it also draws attention to the range of obstacles in its way. This explains, in part, some of the difficulties inherent in the creation or re-creation of a 'public sphere'. But the focus of attention should not be solely on the creation of a sound structure of ownership and regulation; it should also take in questions of journalistic practice and the ways in which governments use 'public relations' methods to release information to the public via the mass media. (See also the discussion of the 'modern publicity process' in Chapter 7.) As we shall see, the two themes are related.

The increasing use of carefully crafted communication strategies by governments to ensure that they get a 'good' press for their policies has often been referred to as the rise of 'the public relations state' (Deacon and Golding, 1994: 4–7). Simply put, governments have come to devote considerable energy *and* financial resources to ensure that the information they seek to impart to their citizens has an appropriate 'spin' on it. This, so the thinking goes, has the effect of promoting, and privileging, the views of governments rather than offering the media the opportunity to provide their own interpretation of the information. Whilst it is never possible to dictate the desired interpretation, governmental public relations strategies can usually facilitate the pursuit of some more than others.

It is not possible to date the rise of 'the public relations state' in Britain but there is some evidence that it became entrenched during the 1980s. One can point to the resources devoted to selling Conservative policies, as in the privatization programme. Deacon and Golding give some examples of such expenditure. These include: £2 million in 1994 on leaflets distributed to all homes outlining 'the government's views on morality, citizenship'; £4.5 million on promoting the 'right to buy' homes policy between 1980 and 1993; in 1992 the government spent £53 million on advertising; and so on (1994: 6–7). One can also begin to identify the reorganization of the government's information service in 1989 under Bernard Ingham, Prime Minister Thatcher's private press secretary. According to Harris, in one fell swoop, Ingham had acquired

> four separate functions. He was the Prime Minister's personal media adviser. He was the non-attributable spokesman for the entire government. He had responsibility for the 'recruitment, training and career development' of 1,200

information officers. He co-ordinated an advertising and publicity budget of some £168 million. (1991: 170)

The promotion or marketing of government has 'become a central activity of modern statecraft' (Deacon and Golding, 1994: 7) perhaps in the same way that all modern organizations have come to acquire publicity departments and public relations professionals. These activities form what Gandy has called 'information subsidies' and they do undoubtedly make it easier for journalists to collect and sift information (see also Chapter 2).[1]

But there is another dimension to this which often gets overlooked and this concerns the *performance* of the media and, in particular, the larger issue of journalistic activity and practice. If, for the sake of argument, one could assume that a 'fundamentally revised public service model' (Keane, 1991: 126) or that 'a model of a "public sphere" as a neutral zone where access to relevant information affecting the public good is widely available' (Curran, 1991: 83) could be constructed in contemporary societies, would this lead to a change in journalistic practices so that those things which stand in the way of 'good' journalistic activity – dependency on sources, news values, news genres, the rise of the 'public relations state', etc. – somehow disappear? Or would these continue to act as real obstacles to the production and distribution of relevant information?

By focusing more directly on journalistic practices – an issue almost totally ignored in discussions of the 'public sphere' – one can begin to identify a set of factors which may be more of an obstacle to the creation of a 'responsive and responsible' media system than is commonly acknowledged. As researchers such as Gandy (1982) and Sigal (1973) have long been at great pains to point out, media content (i.e. the news and information) which one presumes is designed 'to empower a plurality of citizens' is best conceived as the outcome of an unequal relationship between sources and journalists; a relationship which is often manipulated by those making the information available. Gandy's work is essentially about the means by which policy actors attempt to generate, 'beliefs about an uncertain world . . . [and] the methods and techniques utilised by interested parties in the policy process to influence decisions of others through systematic reduction of the costs of access to self-serving information' (1982: ix), and about sources and '*their* use of journalists and other gatekeepers to deliver information subsidies to participants in the policy process' (1982: 15; my italics).

In Sigal's earlier work, approvingly quoted by Gandy, the same themes surface in an equally stark fashion. His book, *Reporters and Officials*, is about the 'obvious, practical and theoretical ways in which *the press is (and can be) used by officials* to change relationships or to attempt to alter policy by handing or feeding information to those who make decisions so influencing the information on which decisions are premised' (1973: 133; my italics).

As both Gandy and Sigal argue, the press – and their books are about the mainstream elite press in the USA – may be no more than an instrument to be manipulated by competing powerful interest groups. Journalistic practices, and in particular the overriding need for news and for 'information as news', makes the press very much a ready and willing recipient of crumbs off the tables of the information rich and powerful. Whether the journalist is wholly or only partially dependent on powerful sources matters little (see also Gans, 1980; and Chapter 2). Similarly, the critical barrage directed at the 'primary–secondary definers' description of the source–journalist relationship – a relationship in which the journalist merely reproduces the definitions of the powerful – has left intact the notion that overall one is still dealing with

> broader questions about the nature of *information management* in society by a variety of groups in conditions of unequal power and therefore unequal access to systems of information production and distribution . . . the apparatuses of the state . . . enjoy privileged access to the media. (Schlesinger, 1990: 82; my italics)

The relationships portrayed in the above accounts draw our attention to specific problems in the conceptualization of the mass media as open vehicles for the dissemination of information. As Schlesinger and Tumber conclude from their study of the 'criminal justice arena', it

> strongly suggests that those with policy expertise have their own way of communicating with themselves. *The rest of us may listen in to the passing messages if we are so inclined.* For criminal justice professionals and pressure groups, the obvious interlocutors for their causes are the quality press and public service broadcasting . . . the rational public that counts, and the media that service it, are actually limited to the circles of the powerful and influential. (1994: 272; my italics)

A better description of the imbalances in the availability of information, power and even access to information would be hard to find. Yet what these accounts actually do is primarily address the organizational and structural analysis of the media and news production; they pay no attention to the nature and complexity of the *information* which is reproduced as news. The assumption here is that if we were to 'listen in' we too would be able to make sense of what is happening, but that can be far from the actuality. For, in addition to legal and other constraints which limit the supply of information, journalistic practices can also restrict the flow, and quality, of information. In his book on the press and local government, David Murphy explored some of this territory when he argued that

> 'council-minute language' and 'the journalist's "good story" [which] is typified by 'hard' facts or 'good talking point' controversy stand at opposite poles. The journalist as against the official is after a straightforward and brief summary of events. The official language is thus simplified. Alternatively, snippets of information are culled and reproduced. [This] is not . . . to be equated with investigating but with a process of finding suitable material for formulation in terms of the 'good story' construct. (1976: 145)

It is a pity that David Murphy did not follow through the logic of his analysis for it strikes at the heart of the problem of much modern journalism. The need to write a 'good story' is very often antithetical to writing a piece of investigative journalism. Where the former puts forward seeming certainties, the latter emphasizes the complexity of the social world; where the former goes for impact, the latter contributes to knowledge. Tom Bower, an experienced journalist, put it like this: '*The final product (of investigative journalism) is often complicated to read, unentertaining and inconclusive.* No major City Slicker has ever been brought down merely by newspaper articles . . . Financial journalists need the crash before they can detect and report upon real defects' (1991: 23; my italics).

Bower, like Murphy, points the finger at close links between press and ownership as restraining influences on journalists. Murphy also explains obvious omissions of pertinent details in a great many stories in local newspapers by referring to the panoply of legal controls which govern the local press, including the risk of litigation. (Coincidentally, Bower also pleads against the use of writs and injunctions by, amongst others, the late Robert Maxwell, to muzzle the press.) However, another plausible explanation could be that commercial media organizations (though public service broadcasting is not immune to this either) pursue the 'good story', an ephemeral, easily digested bite of information and discriminate against the carefully pieced, slow to chew, analytical meal. The distinction here is reminiscent of Golding and Middleton's comment to the effect that news about social security matters is 'news and not documentation'. Explaining this more fully, they contrast 'the policy process [which] grinds slowly, steadily and constantly, [with] the daily staccato of news bulletins or newspapers' (1982: 124).

The search for news appears, therefore, to be contrary to the search for information. Newspapers may be adequate for the first purpose – and their readers expect no more – but less so for the second. So that even when information which is 'non-promotional' or which has no political 'spin' on it is available, it is rarely taken on board. As Hugo Young recently wrote, in a slightly different context,

> the media are deplorably bad at using the cornucopia of official information which is already available . . . Newspapers and television often neglect, or never bother to find out about, the tedious details often tediously available in unglamorous government publications. (1992a: 18; see also Chapter 4 on this point)

It goes without saying that these 'tedious details' are, in fact, the foundations of critical debate.

Not surprisingly, such myopia has consequences, and not only for considerations of political accountability, decision-making and citizenship. As the Glasgow University Media Group (GUMG) pointed out many years ago, certain accounts or interpretations of events are downgraded or excluded altogether, so producing a significant impact on the public's perception of events. The picture of society constructed by television, they argued,

> at its most damaging includes . . . the laying of blame for society's industrial and economic problems at the door of the work force. This is done *in the face of contradictory evidence* which, when it appears is either ignored, smothered, or at

worst, is treated as if it supports the inferential frameworks utilized by the producers of news. (1976: 267–8; my italics)

They identify a number of occasions when accounts of *managerial* incompetence at the British Leyland car plant, rather than incompetence on the part of the shop-floor work force, were made public and were sometimes used by the media to counter the more widespread media interpretation of industrial problems. These accounts appeared, perhaps not surprisingly, in the journal *Management Today*, and in the daily broadsheet, the *Financial Times* (1976: 260). Furthermore, as the GUMG also points out, television news bulletins did not give any coverage to figures published in the broadsheet press which confirmed that management was in part to blame for the troubles of the car industry in the mid-1970s. One outcome of this absence of comment on contradictory perceptions of the causes, and effects, of the events taking place at British Leyland was that the overwhelming impression given to the public was of a strike-prone, work-shy labour force (1976: 264–7).

Though one may object to the suggestions that because such contradictory reports found space in some media they should have been given a higher profile, there is a significant point in here which must be addressed: the media in general should have treated all competing truth-claims – in this case about the British car industry – with equal seriousness. What the GUMG study does not suggest, though it is something which I shall address later on, is whether the media should simply make space for competing truth-claims as opposed to passing judgement on the validity of such claims.

Herein lies the problem: competing truth-claims are nothing more than competing statements about events and their causes. Presenting them as competing truth-claims does not, in itself, resolve the dilemma of which is, on balance, more likely to be truthful. To give a contemporary and random example: in 1994 allegations about Mark Thatcher and his dealings in the Middle East surfaced once more. Such allegations have been vigorously denied on many occasions by Mrs Thatcher, Prime Minister John Major and sundry other politicians. As we look back on these events, we are none the wiser about whether or not those allegations were founded or not.

These are not isolated examples and they alert us to the fact that information, and its uses, is itself a problem.

Information, news and truth-claims

The powerlessness of the reporter and the uncertainty that can infect the public mind in the face of competing truth-claims is also apparent in the following, more pitiful, example of recent years. Reporters covering the fighting in 'former Yugoslavia' – there is an almost identical series of events in the case of the fighting in Rwanda in 1993–4 – uncovered much evidence of atrocities. Eyewitnesses and victims of those atrocities have been ready to relate their experiences to reporters who have, in turn, confronted those accused of carrying out or ordering the very same atrocities. When questioned about their alleged involvement, the accused denied any knowledge of the atrocities.

But what is the television viewer to make of this? How does the reporting of competing truth-claims aid our understanding of what has actually taken place? Increasingly, it has become obvious that in spite of the advances in communications technologies and in the facilities television can bring to its coverage of events, the essential task of uncovering truths remains elusive. Reporters can now easily record experiences of atrocities and play them back to their alleged perpetrators but if the expectation is that the alleged perpetrators will break down in front of television cameras and admit the error of their ways, that expectation has not been fulfilled.

So the practice of giving space to competing truth-claims, though laudable, may produce confusion rather than certainties, sow doubts rather than shore up positions. This would also apply to the example of British Leyland discussed above: had the public been confronted by claims that management and labour were both at fault would it have helped the viewing and reading public make more sense of the causes and effects of industrial strife? At one level, the answer must undoubtedly be 'Yes', but even this answer works with a simplistic notion of information as neutral, transparent and unproblematic. We have recently seen how the Scott Inquiry into the sales of arms to Iraq (1994–5) has been weighed down by ministers and officials claiming that documents themselves do not tell the whole story and that there are other ways in which issues are discussed and decisions taken (Norton-Taylor, 1995).

One good example of the complexity of the issues discussed here can be found in another recent case of industrial affairs involving the British Aerospace (BAe) takeover of the Rover car group (ex-British Leyland) in 1988. This case study will feature at a different points throughout this book so it is worth becoming familiar with the broad outlines of the affair. In 1988 the British government decided to let a private company (BAe) buy the publicly owned Rover car group. At the time of the announcement of the proposed takeover, reporters found it difficult to pass judgement on the benefit of the deal. One dominant strain of thought was that the government was doing the right thing in getting rid of the troublesome and loss-making British Leyland heritage once and for all. But there was another, much less often discussed, option to float the Rover group on the stock market. This was clearly an alternative option but in the context of our present discussion it was never clear whether it was a *realistic* option. Again, as before, much information – and gossip and public relations material – is fed into the journalistic mill for regurgitation as news.

It may not be enough to balance accounts or alternatives as if one was weighing up different quantities of identical materials. Making information public is not the same as making a judgement about its truthfulness and its validity. To point to managerial incompetence as opposed to shop-floor difficulties is simply to add to the debate another contributory piece of information. For the media the real problem may lie in not being able to pass judgement on the quality and validity of the information presented to, and by, them. Does the media have the capacity to decide whether or not the problems of the car industry are due to shop-floor incompetence as opposed to managerial incompetence? Or whether a flotation is better than an outright sale? Putting both sides does not resolve the problem; it simply leaves the matter open to an inconclusive, and not always soundly informed, debate.

But the study of the takeover highlights other issues. It illustrates:

- the sheer problem of summarizing the volume of information available. Some means have to be developed in order to reduce the information;
- how the process of reduction is transformed into a process of filters, all of which eliminate the non-newsworthy, that is, making news as opposed to providing adequate explanatory frameworks;
- the media's inability, unwillingness or unpreparedness to confront and make sense of the complexity of causes and effects which surround events and happenings in the contemporary world;
- the problem of making sense of the available information. For the tabloid press, the affair was marked by a blip of attention; for the broadsheets by more continous, if at times confusing and inconclusive, accounts.

To highlight the need for 'factualness, accuracy and completeness', as Denis McQuail does in his discussion of media performance, is simply to alert us to the same sets of problems rather than to offer solutions (1992: Chapter 16). What does 'completeness' involve? What are the 'essential facts'? What can be considered to be 'sufficient' information? Indeed, these criteria suggest the need for an understanding of the purposes for which that information may need to be used. 'Sufficient' for what? For an historical account or for a news account, for an economic assessment or for informing the public?

All the examples used here turn on such difficult issues as a way of illustrating the very difficult task of making sense of complex events and of events which do not exist outside a politically mediated context.

How much is a company worth?

In discussing takeovers and mergers, financial journalists and City analysts circulate figures as a way of measuring the worth, wealth and performance of companies. In a world where small changes of fortune have a range of impacts on individual and corporate wealth, the value of information about companies is highly beneficial and can be a guide to would-be investors. At a more general level, such information can be seen as a barometer of economic activity in a particular sector of the economy or in the economy as a whole. All this activity, however, gives the appearance of accurate knowledge and precise calculations. Sometimes this is so but at other times there is so much uncertainty that it becomes difficult to answer fairly basic questions about the value of any particular company.

One often quoted criticism of the sale of the Rover car group in 1988 was that it was sold off too cheap, that it was 'the sale of the century' as the *Guardian* put it (see Negrine, 1992). The implication was that the government should have made a greater effort to extract more money out of British Aerospace which, after all, was getting the company, all its assets plus some important tax concessions and other aid for a mere £150 million (see also Chapter 2). But how much was the Rover group actually worth?

Rover was not a company which lived and operated in the open as other companies do and so it was difficult, according to journalists, to get hold of information on which to base any proper assessment of its worth. To provide a better understanding of a company's position one would have had to look at its corporate plan. In fact, 'a real appreciation of the company could only be obtained when journalists sat down with the Corporate Plan and worked out what the pattern of developments in the next three or four years were likely to be' (Rover executive, interview with author, 1990). This is not always easy to do and it depends, in part, on assessing or guessing a company's future performance. But the problems don't stop there, as some financial journalists explained:

> One problem is how do you go about valuing a company such as this? How do you go about making up your mind about what BAe paid for it? What do you decide today about it? We still don't know. There are still some things we don't know about. So £150 million is a bit of a nominal sum anyway. They paid £150 million but they got another £650 million back. (Interview with author, 1991)

> That's all hindsight and if you look at what has happened with the DAF [truck company which in 1988 was owned by Rover] share price, where 18 months ago it was possible to get a fantastic deal, today DAF is making losses. So BAe managed to strike a good deal at a very fortunate moment. (Interview with author, 1990)

> It was both the 'deal of the century' and an albatross. Certainly BAe was getting a hell of a lot of assets very cheaply. If those assets were loss making they were not much good to you; if those assets are going to make money then you've got a good deal. So you are taking a view on that. (Interview with author, 1991)

A different reporter, this time a business correspondent, observed that

> Valuations are very arbitrary. We do focus on the wrong things frequently. I think that the main weakness of journalism is that we are very dependent on picking up what other people are thinking about. We are not intellectually independent minded. You have quite a small amount of resources. And I think the fact that we did not start asking questions about what Rover was really worth was because no one else was saying that. What we would have needed to provoke us would have been a decent study by a merchant bank or whoever arguing that it was worth more or was worth less, because only then would you have the people within the merchant banks and the companies who had sat down and

> started to construct what something is worth. If professionals themselves are not looking at it you tend not to do so. (Interview with author, 1991)

At the same time, this journalist acknowledged that the questions of valuations were not easy to answer.

> What is a car factory worth? Is it worth its replacement cost or is it worth its value as agricultural land minus the cost of clearing the site? That sort of thing is crucial when trying to do a valuation of a company. Do you value it on the income flow it generates or on its break up value?
>
>   If you are making a takeover of a business, you are making a judgement about what, in the worst possible case, it is worth and that is what you bid for it. And then you hope that you will be wrong and that it will actually be worth double what you thought. In large takeovers, typically of £1 billion or £2 billion, the margins of error are well into millions.

Another financial journalist remarked that the land assets of Rover should have been taken into account, 'but that is quite difficult because by looking at accounts you really have no idea what the land is really worth on a development basis. So you need someone who knows the company fairly intimately to talk about it' (interview with author, 1991).

Concerning the DAF trucks company he admitted that

> if people had been able to spend long enough looking at the company and had been following the company for long enough then they should not have been so surprised [about its value]. But journalists on daily papers don't have that amount of time.
>
>   We rely quite a lot from a financial point of view on analysts to highlight things which are not obvious. And in the case of Rover, because it had not been a public company the emphasis on the coverage had always been political rather than financial. Even if it had been done by a financial journalist, it is essentially a political story. (Interview with author, 1991)

A different financial journalist also emphasized the political dimension:

> The whole focus [in 1988] was on 'here is the sale of the century, end of the Rover saga' but as far as the nitty-gritty was concerned, one should have said what do BAe see in it? We saw through things such as property but it couldn't be asset stripping because of the difficulties involved. But we also did not believe in this business of synergy and creating a British BMW. So what was really in it for them?

His answer had to do with 'the weakness of the BAe capital base. There was a £1 million capital supporting an £8 billion order book. Rover represented a quick injection and recapitalization' (interview with author, 1991).

This was a view not entirely shared by a colleague on another paper, who argued that it 'would be hard to find any straightforward financial rationale except the straightforward money one. Basically, BAe was paying nothing for it and getting a lot of cash out of it' (interview with author, 1991).

From these extracts from interviews with some of the broadsheet press's finest reporters one can see the danger of treating bits of information as unproblematic or of expecting simple answers to seemingly simple questions. The creation of a space for groups to talk to one another, to engage in debate, presupposes that the availability and the meaning of information is not a problem, that it will be readily understood and that some point of agreement can be arrived at which can be equated to 'how it really is'. Yet as this example shows, there is often no such agreement on fairly basic information. The problem becomes even more acute when one has to consider documentation or information which is derived from letters or papers. What becomes apparent here is the difficulty of inferring people's intentions.

An intent to deceive?

The deal that was struck between BAe and the Department of Trade and Industry (DTI) in July 1988 on behalf of the British government contained an agreement that BAe pay £150 million for the Rover car group. What was to emerge much later, in November 1989, and become a matter of public concern was that BAe had negotiated deferment of its payment of £150 million until March 1990, that is, nearly two years after it had gained control of the company. One outcome of this was that BAe had made a saving of about £22 million on its tax bill.

Why had this deferment been negotiated? Why had this been agreed to, and why had it been kept from public view? As the details of negotiations and the agreement began to emerge, it became clear that the whole affair was quite complex, with different participants making competing claims, or addressing aspects of the whole affair whilst leaving the matter of culpability off the agenda. Yet, in theory, apportioning responsibility, and blame, should have posed no problems. Why it did takes us back to the issue of competing 'truth-claims' and to the complexity of the socio-political world where in the profusion of information the citizen is left bemused about precisely 'where the buck stops' and 'who is to blame'?

Who asked for the payment to be deferred?

According to Roland Smith, BAe Chairman, the thought of deferring the payment of £150 million first occurred to him 'in the early part of June' (Trade and Industry Select Committee [TIC], 1990: 3). Smith then negotiated with Lord Young at the DTI who, in turn, discussed the question of deferment in a letter to Smith dated 12 July (although Smith has suggested that the first correspondence on this matter may have been a little earlier than this date). The letter of 12 July is perhaps the key to the affair. In it Lord Young discusses the question of the deferment of payment. The relevant section of the letter reads as follows:

(iii) On deferment of payment of the £150 million consideration, I can offer three possibilities, in ascending order of risk that the deferment will be picked up by the European Commission, in which case they might require repayment of the notional interest saved. The possibilities are:

(a) *Payment on 31 December 1988.* The payment would appear in your accounts, and in the Government accounts for 1988/9, just as if they had been made in August.

(b) *Payment on 31 March 1989.* The payment would still appear in the Government's accounts for 1988/9, but would appear in your 1989 accounts.

(c) *Payment on 31 August 1989.* The deferment would be apparent from both the Government's accounts and your own. In addition, *in order to avoid seriously misleading Parliament when we table the revised Estimate for the cash injection on the day of the Statement,* we cannot include the £150 million as a receipt due this year. The omission is likely to be spotted by at least some Members. (TIC, 1990: 44; my italics)

Lord Young concludes 'I am content to take whichever of these options you [Smith] prefer' (TIC, 1990: 44).

There was some further correspondence on this matter and, in a side letter to the agreement, dated 14 July, a representative of the Department of Trade and Industry noted that the

Secretary of State hereby irrevocably instructs and agrees that the date upon which the Share consideration is to be paid is whichever is the earlier of:

(a) [a response from the Inland Revenue]
(b) 30 March 1990 . . . (TIC, 1990: 50–1)

As the letter makes clear, Lord Young appeared to be agreeing with one set of actions in respect of Roland Smith and a set of actions which may have been contradictory to his actions in respect of the European Commission. For, as far as the European Commission was concerned, the payment for the Rover car group was due immediately (EC, 1988). In effect then, as Roland Smith later admitted, 'the principle certainly is that on the same day that the Commission was making that judgement [about immediate payment] we were also negotiating with the DTI to delay the payment' (TIC, 1990: 28).

All this appears to be consistent with Lord Young's statement in the House of Lords on the deal on 14 July 1988 to the effect that 'BAe will still pay £150 million for the Government's shareholding in Rover Group. The precise timing of the payment will follow the clarification of certain tax matters arising out of the change of ownership of the company.' Under questioning, Lord Young merely repeated his statements and he revealed nothing directly about the timing of the payment. One has to assume that those reading Lord Young's statement, or listening to it, would be alerted to some delays in the full payment of £150 million – perhaps not unreasonably so since tax matters would need to be sorted out – but not a deferment of 18 months!

Roland Smith's own account of negotiations over the deferment tend to support a sympathetic interpretation of Lord Young's correspondence. In answer to questioning by members of the Trade and Industry Select Committee, Smith made the point that although 'we [BAe] do not think in actual fact that the tax difficulties will be finalized by 30th March [1990] . . . we will be paying the £150 million on that date' (TIC, 1990: 3). For its part, the DTI was also at pains to explain the deferment as an unexceptional matter, and nothing like the 'sweetener' label which the *Guardian* had put on it.

In such circumstances, how does one unravel the 'truth' or simply decide what 'really happened'? The media themselves were unable to sort the matter out to everyone's satisfaction. Neither did the select committee (Negrine, 1992).

Summary and conclusion

The significance of this lengthy exposition of a specific case study can be seen when considered alongside the discussion of the transparency (or not) of information and journalistic practices. In the first instance, journalists were unable to provide a coherent account of the value of a large car manufacturer; in the second instance there were, and continue to be, doubts as to whether there was any attempt to deceive. This raises a key problem for advocates of a 'public sphere', advocates who have tended to focus on the structural dimension of the debate and not so much on the availability and processing of information. But as we have seen even from this case study,

- there is an enormous amount of information that requires careful study. The account offered here is drawn from a larger study and is the product of careful reading of numerous documents covering many pages. Should this be *de rigueur* in the 'public sphere'?
- while it is easy to report certain news, it is not so easy to make sense of events and issues. The task of interpretation cannot be abdicated by journalists though it may be one that they cannot sometimes undertake, perhaps for professional reasons or reasons of competence;
- much of the information which helps the process of interpretation is often not easily available, sometimes it is confidential, and sometimes it is just ambiguous.

None of these points should be seen as explanations for the shortcomings of the press and television in a competitive environment but they do draw our attention to a dimension of a problem in mass communication which is often overlooked. Addressing the structural side of the equation may indeed be a good starting point but there is more to creating an informed and debating citizenry than providing an arena for debate; the content of the debate and how it is conducted and by whom are equally critical issues.

A final consideration is that the creation of a 'public sphere' presupposes that the debate connects with decision-making structures. This too needs careful attention and some clear thinking about the mechanisms in question. Similarly, we need to think much more about the changing balance of forces as between citizens, the media and government/governmental organizations.

Up to the recent past, the media's role was seen as either equal to ('watch-dog', 'holding governments to account') or dependent upon that of governments. Certain trends in modern media are tending to place the journalist and the media in a position above that of government and of politicians. For example the idea of 'neutral' journalism, the practice of probing politicians, of treating them with 'disdain', of almost disbelieving whatever they advocate (Blumler, 1990) puts the media in a superior and judgmental position. Yet we tend to forget that the private media are, in the final instance, only accountable to their proprietors for their actions, so that their increased (self) importance and enhanced role within the political process may be taking the place of, or become a replacement for, public participation in political debate and for the processes by which governments are called to account by the wider citizenry. Rather than see the media and their insertion in the 'public sphere' as a solution to contemporary ills, they may in fact be part of the problem.

In the end, one returns to the sorts of concern outlined in the introduction to this book: how should those who exercise power be made more accountable and what roles should the mass media play in that process? Can the public 'monitor the exercise of power' without the existence of a strong and inquisitive media? Can the public come to define the 'general interest' without engaging in a conversation with, and through, the means of mass communication? Such questions are not easy to answer, yet as this chapter has explicitly and implicitly suggested, the mass media continue to be important, if often very imperfect, sources of information and so continue to feature prominently in enabling others to make sense of the world. The overriding task may be to improve on these features of their work and alter them in ways which will make them reflect more fully the shifting alliances of these postmodern times.

Note

1. There is a separate issue here which is rarely addressed. Governments do not have an independent mechanism for informing the citizenry of their intentions, policies, and so on. Nearly all information about government is mediated. Should there be such a mechanism, e.g. a government paper, or should all governmental information be received through the broadcast media and a (politically) partisan press?

2

'Public Information', Leaks and the Production of News

Studies of news and the production of news rarely pay much attention to 'leaks' and the 'leaking' of information on the grounds that they are exceptional situations in the more routinized process of news production. Yet it is possible to argue that no study of the production of news is complete unless it pays some attention to 'leaks' and acts of 'leaking' since they actually throw into stark relief the extent to which the production of news has become routinized. A 'leak' may illustrate no more than a departure from the more usual methods of collecting and processing information employed by reporters. It need not necessarily involve the disclosure of confidential, i.e. 'secret', information.

Similarly, whilst studies of the production of news correctly emphasize the many factors which play a part in transforming available information into news, they pay little attention to the pool of information from which reporters can draw. Studies of the production of news tend to focus on a small part of a much larger whole, a whole in which a mass of information exists. As we shall see in Chapter 3, even those who comment on Parliamentary work draw on a fraction of the available information. What they focus on will, by and large, be deemed 'newsworthy' but this neither negates the value of the material which is ignored nor does it deny its ready availability. It merely highlights both the very limited amount of information that is often used and the consequences of keeping much information out of the public domain.

There is *in the public domain* a considerable amount of information which is rarely explored by reporters. Butcher, for example, estimates that there are some 9,000 HMSO titles, that is, 'official' publications, as well as between 11,000 and 20,000 non-HMSO publications a year (1991: Chapter 1). Such publicly available information differs in kind from the information which is in restricted hands and which only becomes available when an 'insider' decides, for whatever reason, to release it. Yet the work practices of reporters, including those of news-conscious news editors, keep much of that sort of material out of public sight. One implication here is that the public is perhaps less well informed than it could be; another, that media coverage often lags behind what others have been fully aware of for a considerable time. This point will be examined in more depth when the case of the BAe–Rover 'sweeteners' is discussed below.

To make sense of this larger whole, and the place of both news production and leaks within it, it is first necessary to explore in fairly general terms the nature and availability of information in most liberal democratic political systems. One of the reasons for this exploration is to focus attention on the much rawer product that makes the news; another is to move from the interaction of reporters and sources and towards some analysis of information *per se*. That is, to begin to ask questions about its nature, its availability, who controls it, how it is released and, finally, whether introducing legislative change in the form, say, of a Freedom of Information Act will make it any easier to get information into the public domain via the mass media.

A brief exploration of information

Reporters work with a sense of what is 'newsworthy' and this directs their attention towards some issues and away from others. But an account of why certain issues are covered and others not does not fully explain why the coverage given to issues is often so very similar. Part of the reason is undoubtedly that reporters adopt a common approach to their subject matter. This is because when they work alongside other reporters, a common set of perceptions of events often develops. Nicholas Jones, one of the BBC's crop of political correspondents, recently reflected on how he and other reporters 'found themselves carried along on a roller-coaster of news stories [about abuses of trade union power]' during the last few days of the Labour government in the late 1970s. As he put it, 'there was something infectious about those days' (1994: 27). Such infections in journalism are not uncommon and they spread through packs of reporters like chickenpox in a nursery school. But there is another reason why the coverage is often so similar and this directs our attention to the ways in which reporters work.

In reality, there is a limited number of ways in which information for news stories can be collected and/or shared. These include press conferences, handouts, personal interviews/contacts, sifting through documents, and talking to other reporters. Some of these activities are collective, others are more individual. (The 'making up' of stories is not considered here.)

In his 1971 study of journalism in the UK, Tunstall gives a breakdown of the amounts of time reporters spent on each of these newsgathering activities (Tables 2.1 and 2.2). His data show that a considerable amount of time is spent 'talking to sources – over the telephone or face to face – and to journalists' (1971: 150). Other evidence collected by Tunstall emphasizes the significant amounts of time spent attending press conferences (1971: 82) or sifting through public relations material (1971: 177).

Stephen Hess' study of Washington reporters confirms the basic pattern but he also throws some light on why the major activity of specialists revolves around 'talking to sources'. Indeed, he suggests that a beat is more desirable if *no documents research* is required. When reporters are asked why they do not want to cover the regulatory agencies they cite the reliance on documents, which in their minds means endless hours in musty archives, while reporting is supposed to be a constant interchange with colorful, unusual, important people. (1981: 52)

Table 2.1   *Time spent on newsgathering activities**

	Political	Mixed	Audience	Advertising	All
Face-to-face interviews	59 (87)	20 (59)	39 (64)	13 (48)	25 (58)
Telephoning sources	19 (41)	52 (86)	61 (91)	30 (70)	39 (72)
Communal meetings, e.g. press conferences	9 (44)	7 (43)	3 (12)	4 (48)	5 (34)
Talking to other journalists	50 (81)	9 (34)	6 (30)	4 (22)	15 (38)
Dealing with documents	34 (94)	43 (82)	12 (42)	26 (78)	33 (75)
Dealing with letters	0 (3)	5 (11)	0 (0)	4 (35)	3 (11)
Writing and sending stories	75 (97)	52 (86)	58 (85)	61 (87)	69 (91)
Other	9 (9)	5 (14)	12 (21)	4 (13)	9 (16)
N	32	44	33	23	186

* Percentage of specialists spending 10 hours or more in an average week on specific activity (with percentage spending 5 hours or more a week in brackets).

Source: adapted from Tunstall, 1971: 151

Table 2.2   *'On an average weekday how many separate PR letters have you got?**

	PR letters per day
Foreign correspondents in Washington	21
Foreign correspondents in Bonn/Rome	22
Political lobby	7
Labour correspondents	20
Education correspondents	15
Aviation correspondents	20
Football correspondents	6
Motoring correspondents	27
Fashion correspondents	25

* Including invitations, tickets, handouts, etc. but excluding material on general sale.

Source: adapted from Tunstall, 1971: 177

One television network diplomatic correspondent cited by Hess is reported to have done 'hardly any documents research' during one week in which he did 21 stories (1981: 56–7).

The reluctance to use documents – a significant point, to which I return – and the other newsgathering practices identified are only part of a complex equation which helps us understand how information collected by reporters becomes transformed into news. The other parts of the equation take in explanations of what is/is not considered newsworthy and, most importantly in our present context, the relationship between sources and reporters which has a bearing on what information is made available and how it is made available.

Sources and reporters, private and public information, front and back spaces

In the study of news and the production of news, the source–reporter relationship has often been identified as a means whereby sources may be able to dominate the supply of news. In this way, it is argued, sources can ensure that their perspectives frame the reports of events. One much used description of the source–reporter relationship is provided by Herbert Gans (1980). For him, that relationship is 'a dance, for sources seek access to journalists, and journalists seek access to sources . . . either sources or journalists can lead, but more often than not, sources do the leading' (1980: 116). Recent research has suggested, however, that the source–reporter relationship is much more complex than at first appears and that the nature of that interaction needs more careful study. One attempt to do just that can be found in Schlesinger's critique of 'primary' definers (sources of information) and 'secondary' definers (the media) as used by Stuart Hall et al. (1978) to explain how the media elaborated on the comments of the police and the judiciary. According to Schlesinger, one has to take into account the strong possibility that there may be more than one primary definer and that, consequently, the primary definer/secondary definer relationship need not necessarily imply a degree of dominance on the part of any one source of information. Furthermore, over time the fortunes of different sources of information ebb and flow so that a static view of the primary and secondary definers relationship is bound to be rather restrictive (see Schlesinger, 1990).

Although this critique points to the fact that different sources of information have different degrees of access to, and control of, resources and that there is no 'level playing field' when it comes to gaining media attention (see Deacon and Golding, 1994: 12–13), it does alert us to the possibility that non-governmental sources of information can often contribute to the work of the reporter (Schlesinger and Tumber, 1994: 33). The complexity of the relationship emerges quite clearly in the proposed amendment to Gans' description (above) offered by Deacon and Golding, namely that 'although the dance steps may be well defined and broadly rehearsed, not all journalists pursue (or are pursued by) the same partners, and not all news organizations can afford (or want) to enter the same ballroom' (1994: 150).

If one accepts that the nature of the source–reporter relationship is a complex one and that sources compete unequally for media attention, does this mean that reporters *actively* seek out different sources of information and that they are continuously on the lookout for those other official and non-governmental sources of information that would complete their stories? Do they, following the analogy proposed above, go to other ballrooms and engage in other dances?

The evidence for this is not strong. In their study Deacon and Golding stress the dominance of the major political parties in the coverage of the poll tax and the extent to which a rather narrow group of actors was constantly referred to (1994: 160–1). Other studies confirm a similar pattern. In their study of science coverage in the British press, Hansen and Dickinson observe that 39 per cent of all stories are media initiated, that is, 'these are stories in which a journalist uses his or her own established scientist contacts (the "known experts" in a particular field)'. By contrast, less than a fifth of all stories (18 per cent) emerge from the 'science forum – in publications in learned journals and conference presentations'. Source-initiated stories accounted for 23 per cent of all stories or items (1992: 371–2).

Hansen and Dickinson's findings suggest that reporters have a search process for information which is fairly restricted: it relies on being contacted and on contacting people who are already well known for being sources in the field. Only a small part of a reporter's output (18 per cent) is the product of active research activities. It is possible that studies of other fields of journalism would give rise to different conclusions but one suspects that those conclusions would not be significantly different. Reporters are, in the main, made aware of events, issues and the like; they are often 'driven' by events and they rarely have the time or work within a structure which would permit them to adopt an indeterminate and pro-active search strategy. (This statement applies differently to different media with, for example, the broadsheets giving their reporters more autonomy than the tabloids.)

If one of our preliminary conclusions is that reporters rely on a narrow range of sources for their information, it partly follows that those sources on whom they rely – and those sources who initiate stories – may have refined their methods of communication with reporters so as to facilitate the latter's collection of information. Sources of information may have developed a sense of what reporters and editors consider newsworthy and have come to 'subsidize' the costs for reporters of collecting information. By making it easier for reporters to collect information, sources may be better able to ensure that their versions of events come to the fore. As Gandy describes it, 'often the value of an information subsidy for any source is increased to the extent that the source can disguise the promotional, partisan, self-interested quality of the information. This is often accomplished when news stories convey the desired information without identifying its source' (1982: 14).

Although information subsidies are often considered to be physical resources, such as handouts or press releases, they can have other properties. An interviewee who appreciates the needs of reporters can make life easier by giving an appropriate 'sound-bite'. This not only increases the chances of the 'bite' being used but lessens the need for reporters to go elsewhere for a quote. Overall, then, an information subsidy, apart from making life easier for reporters, reinforces a pattern of work which already places a great deal of emphasis on the collection of information from authoritative or regular sources. According to Graber, one reason for this reliance, and for reliance on press releases and handouts, could be that 'reporters find it difficult to penetrate the walls of silence erected by publicity-shy agencies' (1984: 120). It is certainly true that publicity-shy agencies will not make it easy for reporters to gather information about them, but Graber may be overstating the case when she implies that reporters actively seek 'to penetrate the walls of silence'. If one looks at journalistic routines and practices, one observes just how unchallenging reporters can be and how reliant they are on publicly available information, on 'subsidized' information. *Paradoxically, it is only when information is leaked to them that one begins to become aware of either just how much information remains hidden from reporters or is simply untouched by reporters.* What Graber does introduce to the discussion is a sense that not all sources are ready, willing or able to divulge information to reporters; or, to put it in Gandy's terms, sources will be happy to subsidize only the information they seek to release.

There are many reasons why sources may wish to retain control over information. One reason could be that sources feel that they would lose control over the manner of its presentation once that information is handed out to reporters and enters the public domain. According to Ericson, Baranek and Chan (1989), although sources may wish to exercise control over reporters by controlling the access to, and flow and content of, information, the power of the controller of the information is matched by the power of the reporters to define what is news and to give that information whatever spin they wish. 'Thus, the source is very likely to have her own understandings and meanings escape her as they become translated and objectified in the news' (1989: 14). So the 'information subsidy' lubricates the supply of, and demand for, information but it cannot guarantee that the information will be processed as desired by the source.

Ericson et al. make an implicit distinction here between information – those bits of evidence, data or whatever – handed out to reporters, and what becomes of that information, namely, news. Clearly, the more the source comes to understand the needs of the reporter the greater the source's ability to ensure that what becomes news is close to the original information released. 'Sources wishing to communicate in the news media must share values with journalists, including core values of the dominant culture,' according to Ericson, Baranek and Chan (1989: 14). This point is pertinent to the developing field of public relations and it hints at one reason why reporters often take on jobs in public relations.

In general terms, sources might only wish to release information in their own way and on their own terms in order to ensure favourable coverage. Sources are less willing to release information which is likely to be

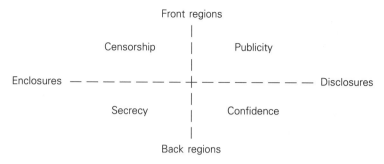

Figure 2.1   *Regions and closures (Ericson et al., 1989: 9)*

problematic for them or their organization. Here the concern is 'with how sources work to protect their organization against intrusion by journalists, while concomitantly achieving favourable publicity, which is seen as an important means of maintaining control over the organizational environment' (Ericson et al., 1989: 8). In order to explain this concern further, Ericson et al. make a distinction between what sources are willing to release for public consumption and what they wish to retain, if only to ensure some privacy for their work. The distinction here is between the 'front regions' or 'those areas where the public business of the organization is transacted' and the 'back regions' which are open 'only to the purview of those who are officially authorized to be there' (Figure 2.1). In this representation of the source–media relationship, there are instances when secrecy is the order of the day ('enclosure') and instances when efforts are made to communicate to the public ('disclosure'). Significantly, 'disclosure in the front regions is the normal condition of publicity' (1989: 9–10). As Ericson et al. go on to show, there are variations across organizations, with different organizations pursuing different strategies to legitimize themselves in public and in private.

This conceptualization of the sources–reporter relationship is extremely useful. However, its main emphasis is on the 'negotiation of control' rather than on the object of control, namely, on information itself. In order to pursue this related area of study, I wish to overlay the 'front' and 'back' region distinction with one which equates the 'front region' with information that is public and the 'back region' with information that is private. One reason for doing so is to enable us to explore the work of the reporter in the context of the ranges of information available to him/her.

As with the back/front region distinction, the distinction between public and private information is not a fixed one. We are operating with a continuum along which information may shift. In fact it is possible for 'private information' – confidence, secrecy and acts of censorship, in Ericson et al.'s figure – to become transformed into 'public information' usually via the mass media. (The term 'public information' is preferred to 'publicity' since the latter implies an element of promotional activity, whereas the former describes the almost physical location of information and makes no reference to its content or to the intentions of its 'manipulators'.) On the other hand, it is conceptually impossible for 'public information' to become 'private information'. In this respect, once it is in the public domain private information ceases to be private. So, although a transformation of information from one level to another can take place it is almost always a one-way movement from the private to the public domain. A leak of information is a good example of this.

Another way of looking at this distinction is to conceive of it as being made up of two layers of information: the 'private' layer of information is once removed from the public domain, it is 'beneath' the layer of information deemed to be in the public domain. But there are other properties of 'private' information which deserve some attention. First amongst these is that 'private' information need not necessarily be 'secret' information in the sense that it is completely hidden from view. All of us are, in our various roles, as employees or employers, participants in organizations, etc., 'privy' to some information which, in appropriate circumstances, may be problematic for particular organizations or groups. Second, there is a considerable amount of information about events and their causes and effects available within any political system. On occasions, information which is not retrieved or used is alleged to be hidden from view but is, in fact, in the public domain. Third, private information may be qualitatively different from public information in both its wealth and its depth. These may either get lost or remain unused once the private information becomes public. When 'private information' surfaces, usually in the form of news and comments, it loses its private character, and may lose the attendant wealth of detail.

Examples of these two layers are easily found. Whether one is describing the generation of policy within the executive ('private information') and its discussion in public and in the press ('public information'), or policy decisions being taken by private organizations ('private information') and the announcement of such policies in public ('public information'), the conceptual distinctions between the two terms revolve around the notion of a bundle of information to which only some are 'privy' and many are not. Those who are 'privy' to it, are 'privy' to it for a variety of reasons: they may be working in fairly closed environments such as public or private enterprises and have access to information because of their locations, e.g. heads of departments, business leaders, ministers; they may have access to information because it enhances their status; or because of its classification as secret, and so on. The reasons for information being private may thus have nothing to do with an intent to keep information private although such circumstances do often occur, as the following excerpt from the Scott Inquiry into arms sales to Iraq shows.

'Did a decision [to change the guidelines dealing with arms sales] depend on the public not being told?' asked Scott.

Blackley replied, 'If there had been an outcry, I am not sure it would necessarily have reflected the view of the country, only of people prepared to comment.'

Scott, at one point, suggested to [Geoffrey] Howe that the former foreign secretary was adopting 'a sort of "government-knows-best" approach'.

Howe replied, 'It is partly that. But it is partly, if we were to lay specifically our thought processes before you, they are laid before a world-wide range of uncomprehending or malicious commentators. This is the point. You cannot choose a well-balanced presentation to an élite parliamentary audience.'

Scott: 'You can, can you not, expose your hand to people of this country?'

Howe: 'There are reasons for caution. Justice is exposed to emotional misunderstandings in this country.' (Norton-Taylor, 1995: 96)

Apart from such instances and the more usual cases of extreme secrecy, or extreme confidentiality, there is a whole swath of information which is not made public in the mass media simply because it is deemed not of sufficient interest to the mass public. It may, nevertheless, reside in the public domain, as the 'arms to Iraq' affair also demonstrates.

In the long history of conflict in the Middle East, Britain's attempt to steer a middle course between Iran and Iraq was born out of both pragmatic and political considerations. The 1985 guidelines on the sale of arms were designed in such a way as to ensure that both sides were treated in roughly the same way and that no arms which would give either side an advantage would be sold. This policy remained in place until the cessation of hostilities between Iran and Iraq in 1988, at which point, it is now claimed, the British government and Whitehall began to tilt away from Iran and towards Iraq. In other words, from some time in December 1988 – and as a result of changing circumstances in the Middle East – the government and Whitehall began to adopt a more flexible approach towards the arms trade with Iraq.

As the Scott Inquiry was to hear in 1993 and 1994, the evidence of a tilt towards Iraq was not something to which ministers and civil servants readily admitted. Different interpretations of statements and different interpretations of words and clauses made it difficult to pin down shifts in policies. Furthermore, with ministers and civil servants denying responsibility for much of what went on, it became difficult to pin responsibility on any particular individual or group of individuals.

What was clearer, though, was that the government and the Civil Service had accepted that their public position on the sale of arms to Iraq would continue to be one that denied the existence of such a trade. Throughout 1989, 1990, 1991 and 1992, successive ministers repeated the claim that the 1985 guidelines remained in force and that 'there were certainly no arms sales to Iraq' (Archie Hamilton, July 1991, quoted in Norton-Taylor, 1995: 84). Yet, as the Scott Inquiry in 1993–4 found out, arms had been sold to Iraq, either directly or indirectly via third countries. In effect, from 1988 onwards the trade with Iraq was anything but dead.

One important strand of this affair is that the government had consistently misled Parliament and that it had taken every possible effort to conceal the tradein arms. Furthermore, when prosecutions for selling arms to Iraq were being considered – the production and sale of the 'supergun' in 1989–90 and against the directors of Matrix Churchill in 1992 – the government continued to deny knowledge of arms sales. An admission would have destroyed the cases against both the manufacturers of the 'supergun' and the directors of the Matrix Churchill engineering company.

Whilst it is true that ministers persisted in denying that arms were being sold to Iraq throughout 1989–92, it is not the case that there was no public knowledge of the arms trade. From 1989 onwards, one can find newspaper accounts which hint, and sometimes more than hint, at the continuing links between Britain and Iraq. Significantly though, the information does not create the sort of circumstances which provided the conditions for an inquiry on the scale, or of the sort, of the Scott Inquiry. In a recent letter to the *Guardian*, Dr Alan George argued that 'with one or two exceptions – notably the BBC's *Panorama* programme (whose report was extensively based on material provided by me) and the *Financial Times* – the mainstream media did not see Iraq's clandestine military-procurement activities in Britain as a story worth reporting'. As George concludes in his letter, the rejection of his story by most of the British media leads him to the conclusion that 'the media was as culpable as Whitehall in keeping the facts from the public' (1995: 14).

As some journalists have suggested, the subject of arms sales was not of 'interest' to the media (Young, 1992b: 18), whilst others have suggested that the media rely heavily on 'whistle blowers' in the arms trade to make sense of what is going on. In the absence of these, the media 'need far greater resources and motivation if they are to provide their own oversight of the arms trade' (Sampson, 1991: 23). Although those comments may have some truth in them, it is less than obvious that newspapers had little interest in arms sales. Here we need to identify three periods in which the significance of information about the arms trade is treated very differently. The first is the period of conflict between Iran and Iraq. This covers the years up to 1988 and includes the years in the mid-1980s, 1984 and 1985, in which the Howe guidelines on arms sales were formulated and published. The second period is immediately after the cessation of hostilities and before Iraq's invasion of Kuwait in August 1990. The third, and final, period is that after 1990 when Iraq became *persona non grata* on the international scene. Once Iraq became a public enemy, Britain's relationship with it was transformed into a problematic one.

What is the evidence for this interpretation? There are several such pieces. The first is that the announcement of the guidelines in a Parliamentary answer brought no publicity whatsoever. The guidelines were not mentioned in either *The Times* or the *Financial Times*. Had the arms trade been treated as a significant issue, one presumes that the publication of the guidelines would have occasioned some media interest. The second piece of evidence again relates to press coverage. In 1989, a year in which Norton-Taylor identifies at least seven occasions when members of the government denied the existence of the arms trade to Iraq (1995: 84), none of these occasions is referred to in either *The Times* or the *Financial Times*. There are occasions when the arms trade is mentioned as part of a debate about Britain's relationship to Iraq but this is in the context of more general Parliamentary debates, of the 'to and fro' of politics.

The third piece of evidence relates to the manufacture of the 'supergun' by British manufacturers for Iraq. According to Christopher Cowley, a metallurgist who worked for Walter Somers the manufacturer of the supergun, '69 British companies set out their stalls at the post-war Baghdad Military Fair in 1989, with the deliberate intention of selling battlefield kit' (Cowley, 1992: 113). The fair occasioned little dramatic response. *The Times*, for example, saw fit to mention this fair in the context of good Iraqi–British relations and Britain's award of 'an "exceptional" gold medal for its display' at [the] Fair'. Furthermore, Cowley claims that a 'table-top model of it [the supergun]' was 'openly on display' (Cowley, 1992: 3) at the fair. Nevertheless, it was not until April 1990 that it became an issue, and that was because the Customs and Excise decided to prosecute the makers of the 'supergun'.

What is also interesting in relation to the 'supergun' is that much of the comment surrounding the seizure of the gun by Customs and Excise in 1990 already refers to past sales of arms to Iraq. In other words, it was not a 'secret', although it was something that was clearly not publicized. From April 1990, the Labour Party is already asking for an inquiry into the sale of the 'supergun' on the grounds that a 'cover-up' is taking place (Sharrock, 1990), and by July 1990 David Pallister is able to comment on the means by which Iraq was able to build its arsenal; means which included arms sales from Britain. As he wrote – in the context of comments on the previous year's International Arms Fair – 'although Britain has a policy of not providing material that would enhance the lethal capacity of the Iraqi armed forces, *its stance has been eroded by commercial pressures that allow dual-use items to escape embargo*' (1990: 3; my italics). Henceforth, the pressures on the government begin to build up.

From this example, one can argue that the search process does not always work to highlight major issues that are of concern yet are not considered 'newsworthy'. And so a combination of a reactive search process on the part of reporters, a competitive media system hell-bent on covering only the 'newsworthy', and a growingly sophisticated management of information must inevitably lead to a rather myopic world view. One could clearly imagine a situation where it could be otherwise – a reformed 'public sphere', perhaps – but that would be a system of communication very alien to that which currently operates in most Western liberal democratic countries.

If this analysis is correct, or even partially so, it shows why the notion that opening up currently closed institutions, with 'freedom of information' provisions for example, may actually have a very limited impact on media coverage of events. It is not that there is not enough information available – more can always be made available, including previously classified material

– but that the willingness to sift through it and to get it published is often not present. This is why May and Rowan may be overstating their case when they suggest that it is governments which 'close their doors and . . . secure them with an impressive battery of legislative locks and bolts' and so stifle public debate (1982: 11). Governments undoubtedly do that but this does not deny the fact that the media could do much better at getting hold of, *and publishing*, the sorts of information which could engender public debate. As the BAe–Rover case study amply demonstrates, much of the information that would have enabled the public to make 'sense' of the affair was always in the public domain. Much more information could have been obtained with the greatest of ease, though a significant proportion could not. That the press and television did not make much of this information 'public' had more to do with their perception of its newsworthiness than with the question of availability. In other words, the absence of much widespread comment on the affair, or on other affairs, cannot be explained away by pointing to the non-availability of information.

Governments (and other sources) certainly do restrict the flow of information but this should not be taken to mean that all information is beyond the reach of the media. Much 'private information' is available – if only the media sought it and attempted to make use of it. The failure of the media to use information is not only an indication of their passivity as information processors – transmitters, passive observers, conveyor belts – but also of their organizational priorities, which turn them towards the newsworthy and the immediate. In fact, it is possible that reporters could aid the process of opening doors if they changed the pattern of their newsgathering activities and their news priorities. Reporters can transform what May and Rowan call 'inside information' into what I have described as public information (or information on the 'outside').

So we need to have a better appreciation of the content and the nature of information within the political system rather than simply work with a crude distinction between information that is available and information that is not. The major distinction is that between information which is public – in the front region, publicity – and that which is private – unexplored, 'inside information', including levels of secret information. Information can seep upwards from the private to the public levels. Some of that seepage takes place as part of a determined effort by sources to release information (an information 'subsidy') but it can also take place when reporters uncover snippets of 'hidden' information or when information is leaked. To these two levels of information one can perhaps add a third level, which could be described as the news level of information. This refers to the mass media version of public information: it is organized around considerations of newsworthiness and the needs of the news organization. It is thus a summary and a mediated form of public information which may, or may not, be co-extensive with public information. More than that, the 'public story' takes in the most public dimensions of 'public information', and of 'publicity'. This is represented in Table 2.3.

Table 2.3   *Levels of information*

Levels	Actors
The public story/news level	Mass media, public relations professionals, political actors, decision-makers, City analysts, civil servants, etc., in their public roles
Public information	Mass media, public relations professionals, political actors, decision-makers, City analysts, civil servants etc. in their public roles, but also in their private roles as sources of information
Private information	Public relations professionals, political actors, decision-makers, City analysts, civil servants, etc., in their private roles as insiders as well as inside sources of information
Secret or 'inside' information	Information which is restricted for reasons of security or for other operational or organizational reasons

With respect to our analysis, the 'public story' is essentially the surface information that finds its way into the public domain sometimes, but not often, supported by other 'public information'. The ideal piece of journalism is almost by definition journalism which immerses the public story in both public and private information. After all, the classic investigative piece works at all levels, unearthing information which is not to be found lying easily on the surface like some autumnal windfall of fruit. A direct contrast to investigative journalism – although often acting as a spur to investigations – is the story built around a 'leak' of information. Whereas the former suggests an active reporter, the latter finds the reporter as a recipient of information; whereas the former implies a process of unearthing, of piecing together bits of information, the latter short-circuits all this and catapults the information into the public domain. In so doing, it also highlights the shortcomings of day-to-day journalism.

Leaks and the leaking of information

There is, as yet, no extensive in-depth study of leaks. Part of the reason for this may be a general belief that leaks are no more than variations on the more common pattern of the release of information by unattributable powerful sources. For example, in the case of political reporting it is often noted that politicians brief reporters in a way which would advantage them (and disadvantage others). This is a common point made in the context of the study of British lobby journalists where the information is given to the reporters on an unattributable basis, that is, on lobby terms. That information, once released into the public domain, gains a life of its own and can cause havoc.

The 'I brief, you leak' frame of mind which is common amongst politicians is clearly of significance for our understanding of the source–reporter interaction described above, and the use to which such a

relationship can be put. In fact, according to Stephen Hess, it is at that
level of political life that 'leaks' of information are most likely to occur. His
study of press–government relations in the USA led him to conclude that
the leak 'is rarely a tool of press offices, whose domain is the formal
channels of information . . . Nor is "leaking" often practised in the lower
civil service.' It is, he concludes, the executive which leaks the most (Hess,
1984: 74–6). As Douglas Cater put it, the leak is 'symptomatic of rivalry in
the higher echelons of government itself' (1965: 135). Indeed, a quick
reading of any books on political reporting in Britain or in the USA will
confirm the plethora of examples of the media being leaked information by
political actors for personal or political advantage. Robert Harris, the
unauthorized biographer of Bernard Ingham, Thatcher's private press
secretary would probably claim that he, Ingham, perfected this particular
art form. The existence of such leaks within the body politic makes it
difficult to adopt a censorious view of other forms of leaking. As the
Committee of Privileges noted in 1990 during its own investigations into
the leaking of a memo to the *Guardian* (on pp. 39–43), it was difficult to
define secrecy in government when those in government so consistently
abused the rules. In a section headed *Whitehall and Westminster – the truth
about 'secrecy'*, it summarized some of its concerns:

> Your committee believes that the House should look at what actually happens to
> information supposed to be kept secret, and the way in which such information is
> actually received, transmitted and used by ministers, civil servants, members and
> others in and around Whitehall and the Palace of Westminster.
>
> For, despite may attempts that have been made to preserve secrecy and
> confidentiality, it is well understood that the rules are widely and generally
> disregarded by those who know how the system works.
>
> There are hundreds of information officers, press officers, lobbyists, journalists
> and specialist correspondents who live in and around Government and Parlia-
> ment, and who are paid to release and receive information, by official and
> unofficial briefings, by 'leaking', and in many other less formal ways, over
> lunches and diners and in the tea room and smoking room and corridors of
> Whitehall and Westminster . . .
>
> *In the opinion of Your Committee the pretence of maintaining secrecy and
> confidentiality, when everybody knows it is so widely disregarded, represents a real
> threat to parliamentary democracy because it goes on on such a scale as almost to
> amount to a 'conspiracy by the governors against the governed'.* (Committee of
> Privileges, 1990: ix–x; my italics)

Nevertheless, it should be borne in mind that not all 'leaks' of information
consist of political actors talking off the record and for the purpose of
gaining some personal, political or other advantage. Although such reasons
feature prominently in Hess' typology of leaks as 'viewed from inside
government' (1984: 77), he does include in it one category 'the whistle-
blower' leak which differs from the others in part because it is exercised by
career personnel rather than political actors, and in part because it is often
designed to right a wrong. ('Whistle blowing,' though, 'is not synonymous
with "leaking"; some whistle blowers are willing to state their case in
public' (1984: 78).) Like others who leak information, whistle blowers are

involved in the *unauthorized* release of information. By revealing what is taking place beyond the public gaze and away from the sight and hearing of reporters, whistle blowers seek to draw attention to certain information which has been overlooked or kept hidden from view. Two classic British cases of 'whistle blowing' are those of Sarah Tisdall and Clive Ponting. Both cases took place in the 1980s and involved civil servants who felt that they were being asked 'to behave improperly at ministerial behest' (Linklater and Leigh, 1986: 137) and in ways contrary to Civil Service traditions.

But studies of leaks need to go beyond this definition in order to explore who 'authorizes' the release of information in any single organization. Where information is classified, the 'rules of the game' are fairly straight-forward, but in most organizations information is not usually classified yet there may be a sense amongst employees about what sort of information, if released, is likely to be beneficial to the organization and which is likely to be harmful. The distinction between the 'front and back region' or between 'public and private information' often leaves room for a flexible interpretation of what can/cannot be released, although it is abundantly clear that those who release information *without being authorized to do so* seek unattributability because of a sense of 'wrongdoing' or of breaking informal rules of operation. Anonymity allows the source a line of defence and a means of airing a grievance without necessarily putting the whole organization at risk.

Given the fact that governments are themselves major leakers, and that the motivations of leakers are many and various, it is difficult to adopt a dogmatic position on what should be judged a harmful leak and on what sorts of penalty should be attached to leaks. From the point of view of a government department, all information classified in one way or another may be said to cause some harm if released. Otherwise, so the argument runs, it would not be classified. But from the reporter's point of view, the classification of documents is merely a device for maintaining unnecessary secrecy about information which should be of public interest, and 'in the public interest'.

The belief that government departments over-classify information adds to these criticisms, since information which is of an innocuous character is often treated very confidentially. As Clive Ponting has written,

> Whitehall has its own elaborate system for classifying pieces of paper on their alleged sensitivity. The official definitions about their release are:
>
> Restricted: undesirable in the interests of the nation
> Confidential: prejudicial in the interests of the nation
> Secret: serious injury to the interests of the nation
> Top Secret: exceptionally grave damage to the nation. (1986: 137)

With other classification also in the system, Ponting goes on to observe that 'nobody in Whitehall knows what these definitions really mean', and that 'inevitably, the system is regularly abused' (1986: 137). More critically, 'most of the information given by Whitehall is really designed to back up decisions already taken in secrecy within the bureaucracy. On every occasion . . . Whitehall has repeated the view that information is what Whitehall chooses to release to the public and not what the public may want to know' (Ponting, 1986: 203).

Lest one believe that Ponting was describing a bygone era, answers to questions tabled in Parliament in 1994 revealed that over 1,500 files were being withheld from the National Audit Office. The Department of Transport, for example, 'withheld the most files, with 684 marked Not for the Eyes of the NAO' (Hencke, 1994: 5).

Just as the motivations behind 'leaks' of information will vary quite considerably, so too will the effects of leaked information. Leaks 'may destroy the timing of political negotiations, alienate the parties . . . cause substantial political harm by disclosing politically sensitive matters . . . bring important suppressed issues to needed public attention' and so on (Graber, 1984: 237), but only in certain circumstances. The more newsworthy, the more likely it is that the effects Graber describes will take place, but often leaks will not scale those heights of destructiveness. If considered newsworthy enough to merit a place in a newspaper – which newspaper? and why that particular paper? – a story based on a leak may survive only one edition before it disappears from public view (though the effects of the leak on the object of the leak may continue for some time).

One can demonstrate some of these points by identifying cases of leaks reported in the press in any particular year. This is easier to do nowadays given the introduction of newspapers on CD-ROM but even an electronic search has its problems: 'leaks' can be identified in various ways such as 'leaked information', 'leaked documents', 'leaked memo/s', 'leaks to the press', and so on. Despite these difficulties, a search of the *Guardian* for 1994 identified between 70 and 80 stories which featured 'leaks' of information of one kind or another. A similar exercise for *The Times* and the *Sunday Times* identified between 20 and 30 stories which featured leaks of one sort or another. Admittedly, this is a very small fraction of all stories in a year's worth of publication but perhaps a larger number than a 'guesstimate' would suggest.

Not only do we have a different news agenda in these newspapers when it comes to leaks – thus confirming the point that not all leaks are regarded as of importance – but we also have a vast range of stories. It includes stories which involve life insurance companies, job losses at the Post Office, court papers, airline companies, student loans, dirty tricks campaigns, as well as a fair number of leaks involving government and government departments. Phrases such as 'a confidential Whitehall memorandum', 'we learn via a leaked memo', 'Whitehall leakers', etc. are fairly common in press reports. Leaks lubricate journalistic work and push stories in directions in which they would otherwise not go. Had it not been for the leak itself, the routinized nature of newsgathering would have continued uninterrupted. Whether or not they are, can be or should be, a substitute for more active investigative work or not is a point to which we return in the next section.

Case studies

We can see many of the themes developed above in three very different examples of leaks which created waves in their wake. The first concerns information about the privatization of the British coal industry; the second, the leaking of the joint Anglo-Irish framework document on the future of the relationship between the Republic of Ireland and Northern Ireland. These examples were chosen at random. The third case is a more detailed study of the leaking of the Comptroller and Auditor-General's Confidential Memo about the sale of the Rover car group addressed to the Committee of Public Accounts to the *Guardian* in 1989.

British Coal's profits

Many leaks cause few waves. One such concerns British Coal and the fact that in mid-1995 it was due to announce 'a record profit of more than £500 million for its last year of mining operations because of the government's £1.6 billion debt write-off sweetener to the new private pit owners, a leaked Department of Trade and Industry memorandum has revealed' (Milne, 1995: 2).

The story goes on to contextualize the leaked memorandum and to place it alongside the government's privatization of the coal industry aided by huge handouts of public money. It also uses the leaked memorandum as a way of introducing much more information about British Coal's accounts.

For the reporter, the leak of information becomes a way of breathing life into a story and hoping that it can then develop in some way and run for several more days. If the story is given front-page treatment one can assume that there is a high chance of that happening: prominent actors would be asked to comment, a controversy will ensue as different statements are issued and dissected, and so on. But on many occasions a leaked story does not get such treatment. The above example was given three columns of about 10 centimetres at the bottom of page 2: itself an indication of its importance and the likelihood that other media would run with it.

As for the reader, this story adds one other bit of evidence concerning the government's privatization programme and its treatment of the coal industry: issues on which the *Guardian* has very strong views, and views to which the story itself lends further support. Other papers – with other agendas – would presumably treat this leak differently, either giving it the same sort of (low-ish) prominence, or completely ignoring it. A leak does not automatically have explosive effects.

The Anglo-Irish framework document

After 25 years of 'the troubles', the many parties to the continuing political turmoil in Northern Ireland began to edge forward to a solution of their problems in 1994. From that point onwards, a so-called 'peace process' was put in motion. This involved, amongst other things, the production on behalf of both the British and Irish governments of a discussion document which would establish a 'lasting' peace. That peace would inevitably impact on the existing relationships between Britain, Northern Ireland and the Republic of Ireland. Whereas Sinn Fein and the nationalists generally favoured a 'united Ireland', Unionists in Northern Ireland favoured the continuation of 'the Union' with the United Kingdom. Consequently, any document which explored possible ways forward would need to tread a careful path between these two extremes, but at the same time ensure that the momentum of the 'peace process' would not be halted, so opening up the possibility of a return to military confrontation.

With so much at stake, including the political reputation of the Prime Minister, John Major, any disruption to the delicate negotiations was bound to be viewed with great suspicion. And the leaking of the joint Anglo-Irish framework document on 1 February 1995 in *The Times* was just such an unwelcome disruption. Just how unwelcome became clear when John Major decided to broadcast to the nation the day after the framework document had been leaked. One aim of the broadcast was obvious: to stem the tide of speculation about what the final document would contain in the form of proposals and so to allay fears that one, or other, parties to the conflict in Northern Ireland was somehow being sold short or abandoned.

The other measure of the significance of this particular leak is the interest and coverage which it occasioned in other newspapers. Some of that coverage was critical of *The Times* for putting at risk the whole peace process; other papers criticized the paper on the grounds that the reporter who wrote the story, Matthew D'Ancona, was sympathetic to the retention of the Union and was thus using the leak to further a specific position. But such criticisms apart, all the national media acknowledged the significance of the document by simply, perhaps grudgingly, devoting space to it. And over the next few days, and well into the next month, what the framework document would and would not contain became a significant debating point.

What the leak did, then, was to put the government on the defensive because it made information public at a time which was not of the government's choosing. The leak was inconvenient because it revealed the hidden process of discussion and decision-making. By contrast, when the British and Irish governments did release the full document in March 1995, not only did they court publicity but they made copies of that document freely available over all post office counters in Northern Ireland.

The 'sweeteners' memo

Controversy surrounded the sale of the Rover car group to British Aerospace from the moment the proposed sale was announced in March 1988. The affair went through many stages, including a period of relative calm, when suddenly it burst on to the scene once more in November 1989 with the publication of a confidential memo from Mr John Bourne, the government's Comptroller and Auditor General, in the *Guardian*.

In the memo, classified 'confidential', John Bourne outlined certain details of the agreement which BAe had struck with the Department of Trade and Industry with regard to the sale of the Rover group. This included deferment of payment for the car group, and some reimbursement of costs (see Chapter 1, pp. 15–21 for more details). For the *Guardian*, this memo provided something other than mere details of negotiations. The article written by David Hencke and Andrew Cornelius was headlined '£38m sweetened Rover deal' and began, 'The Department of Trade and Industry has hidden from the European Commission details of £38 million in "sweeteners" given secretly to British Aerospace to buy Rover, according to a confidential memorandum' (1989: 1). The largest 'sweetener' involved permitting BAe to defer paying the government for the purchase of the Rover group until the end of March 1990. This deferral effectively saved BAe £22 million on its tax bills.

The 'spin' put on this may, or may not, have been justified. The rancorous sessions of evidence-taking at subsequent Trade and Industry Committee sessions did not fully clarify whether or not there was any intention to deceive. Nevertheless, every subsequent turn of this affair was carefully watched by newly attentive reporters. However, and in spite of the increased interest in the matter which the leak provided, parliamentarians viewed the whole affair of the leak itself with some unease. For many of them the question was whether or not it was advisable and proper to publish the memorandum when it reached the reporters. This was the task which faced the Privileges Committee when it was set up to investigate the 'premature disclosure' of the memorandum.

The case against disclosure was made by Mr Robert Sheldon, Chair of the Public Accounts Committee, amongst others, and it turned around a number of key arguments:

- the memorandum was classified 'confidential', that is, it was considered by the DTI that its publication would be 'prejudicial to the national interest';
- the committee 'would have considered later whether or not' it should be published, with it being likely that it would be published;
- the leak constituted 'a substantial interference, or the likelihood of such, with the work of the committee';
- publication 'could seriously undermine the competitive position of Rover group and British Aerospace in international markets' or reveal 'commercially confidential information';
- publication might be 'prejudicial to future relations with private sector bodies if such bodies were to believe that confidential approaches might subsequently be disclosed without their consent'. (Committee of Public Accounts, 1989: v–vii)

In all these arguments we can see parallels with the previous example: there is the concern that established relationships and routines of work will be disrupted by publication; that matters classified confidential should always remain confidential because their classification must never be queried; that what goes on behind closed doors is in the interest of the state and again should not be questioned, and that since publication would take place anyway at a later time, premature publication is unnecessary and unhelpful.

The *Guardian*'s reply indicated that none of these arguments was sufficiently strong to make a case against publication. The then editor, Peter Preston, argued that:

- the memo put 'into the public domain an account of affairs correcting official but inaccurate reports presented to Parliament on the real cost of the Rover sale' (Committee of Privileges, 1990: 11);
- of four memos classed as confidential by the National Audit Office, only one (the Rover sweeteners memo) was ever published and then only as a result of the leak in the *Guardian*;
- there was no evidence to demonstrate how publication would influence the nature of Parliamentary or other deliberations;
- there was no evidence that this matter would damage national security. Indeed, as the radical left-wing MP Tony Benn pointed out during the session, the concept of the national interest is itself suspect given that Britain should be abiding by European laws and interests, rather than strictly and arcanely British domestic ones.

Once again, we can see the way the debate divides into those who seek to retain control of information, for whatever reason, and those who question that control in circumstances which they judge to be controversial: particularly if, as Preston indicated, the leak placed in the public domain information that would correct hitherto 'official but inaccurate reports'.

But what is really interesting about this 'leak' is not so much the furore it caused but the way it breathed life into information which, it could also be argued, was actually and already *in* the public domain. To understand the implications of this point, one has to return to the issue of whether or not there was any attempt to deceive Parliament by not giving full publicity to the fact of deferment.

As far as the Department of Trade and Industry was concerned the deferment was not an exceptional matter, and nothing like the 'sweetener' label which had been put on it. But at the same time the DTI was careful to point out that information about the deferment had in fact *not* been kept secret. This being the case, the DTI, and others, could hardly be accused of hiding the information from anyone who wished to use it. The evidence of Peter Gregson, Permanent Secretary at the DTI, is therefore especially interesting:

> When the revised supplementary estimates were produced in July of 1988 they made it clear that the consideration of £150 million would not be received in the financial year 1988–89, and the estimates for 1989–90, which were published on budget day (March 1989), do show that the consideration of £150 million is expected to be received within this (1989–90) financial year. (Committee of Public Accounts, 1989: 7)

When asked specifically about certain other payments totalling £38 million which were to be made to BAe, Gregson once again referred to a series of governmental publications where these had been identified. Payments 'were reported to Parliament in estimates in the normal way. The . . . £9.5 million . . . is specifically referred to in the annual report on expenditure . . . published on 21 September [1989]. The . . . £1.5 million . . . was included in the revised supplementary estimate' (Committee of Public Accounts, 1989: 13).

All told, then, specific detailed information about the BAe–Rover deal was contained in *four separate documents published between July 1988 and September 1989*. These were: the revised supplementary estimates produced in July 1988, the estimates for 1989–90 which were published on budget day (March 1989), the annual report on expenditure published in September 1989, and the revised supplementary estimate. *How* this information was presented can be seen in Plates 2.1 and 2.2, where the relevant sections from the 1989–90 estimates are reproduced.

As the *Investors Chronicle* observed when the leaked documents revealed that there had been a deferment in the payment for the car group, the

> revelation came as a bit of a bombshell to analysts who thought Rover was safely out of the way. Ahem, says an embarrassed BAe: it didn't actually lie to anyone, just failed to prevent them leaping to false conclusions. It had promised the government that it wouldn't let on to anyone what was going on, presumably as a quid pro quo for Lord Young's munificence.
>   The eagle eyed could have deduced there was something amiss from BAe's last annual report. In the column for application of funds there is a £165 million item for acquisitions which clearly includes the payout for Rover, which is fair enough. But tucked away in Note 22 to the balance sheet is a figure for 'other creditors falling due after one year', which jumps mysteriously from £51 million in 1987 to £208 million in 1988. A stray £150 million owed to the Government for March 1990 ought to do the trick. Had analysts done their homework properly they might have noticed it, but they didn't. (1989: 65)

A harsh comment on analysts perhaps, but is this too harsh a comment on journalists? The short answer would be most definitely 'Yes.' Journalists work to a cycle which requires them to turn round material at a fairly rapid pace. The use of handouts and press releases ('subsidies') are of great benefit to them because they enable them to get stories with no great effort being put on the 'discovery' of material. Such practices undoubtedly make journalists dependent on their sources and they can have the added effect of directing the work of the journalist towards certain conclusions and away from others.

The actions of the various departmental bodies producing the estimates re the deferment of the £150 million payment could be no further away from being an 'information subsidy'. As can be seen from the plates, the relevant information is obscured rather than immediately visible. It was not highlighted in such a way as to alert readers to its significance. By contrast, one can argue, when government departments *do* want to alert journalists to material deemed relevant they go out of their way to ensure that such

Class V, Vote 1
Regional and selective assistance, support for aerospace, shipbuilding, steel and vehicle manufacture

Introduction 1. Expenditure borne on this Vote is not subject to a cash limit.

2. This Vote contains a large part of the Department of Trade and Industry's support for private industry. It includes provision for regional development grants (RDG) and regional selective assistance (RSA), which is aimed at encouraging investment and employment in industry in assisted areas. As announced to Parliament on 12 January 1988, RDG closed to new applications from 31 March 1988. This Vote makes provision for expenditure arising from existing commitments under the original and revised RDG schemes. Provision for the business development initiative including regional enterprise grants appears on Class V, Vote 2 at section B. Selective financial assistance concerning certain sectoral schemes and support for major projects closed to new applications during 1988 being replaced by a scheme to assist exceptional projects. This Vote makes provision for the new scheme and for expenditure arising from existing commitments under the closed schemes. This Vote also covers support for aerospace (including development of the EH101 helicopter and the A330/340 airliners as well as Airbus sales support payments), assistance to shipbuilding (including interest support costs under the Shipbuilding Credit Guarantee Scheme, merchant shipbuilding subsidies for the private sector and residual payments under the Shipbuilding Redundancy Payments Scheme) and benefit payments to redundant steel workers. Administrative costs associated with this Vote are borne on Class V, Vote 3.

3. The forecast outturn for this Vote in 1988–89 is expected to be £976 million compared with the provision of £1,036.9 million. Supplementaries of £558.3 million were taken principally to reflect the arrangements for the sale of Rover Group plc to British Aerospace plc and to cover the overall increase in demand for RDG, selective financial assistance to industry and grants from the shipbuilding intervention fund.

4. The provision for 1989–90 shows a reduction of £573 million compared with the total provision for 1988–89. This reflects the substantial provision of some £549 million required in 1988–89 only for the sale of Rover Group plc together with the remaining £24 million reduction comprising lower demand for regional and selective industrial assistance partially offset by increased provision for support for aerospace, shipbuilding and steel manufacture.

5. In addition to contingent liabilities arising from statutory and non-statutory commitments which are reported separately to Parliament on an annual basis, there currently exist non-statutory contingent liabilities for which this Department takes administrative responsibility. The most significant of these contingent liabilities relate to assurances given on behalf of the Government whereby it agrees to support fully British Aerospace plc's participation in Airbus Industrie and, to this end, to stand behind the discharge by British Aerospace plc of its financial obligations to Airbus Industrie.

6. Symbols are explained in the introduction to this booklet.

Plate 2.1 *Supply estimates 1989–90*

Class V Department of Trade and Industry and export Credits Guarantee Department.
Class V, Vote 1 Regional and selective assistance, support for aerospace, shipbuilding, steel and vehicle manufacture.
H.M. Treasury, March 1989, Session 1989–89, HCP 231-V, pp. 6, 11.

Regional and selective assistance, support for aerospace, shipbuilding, steel and vehicle manufacture

Part I

£463,527,000

Amount required in the year ending 31 March 1990 for expenditure by the Department of Trade and Industry on regional development grants, regional selective assistance, selective assistance to individual industries, certain other services including UK contributions arising from its commitments under international commodity agreements, a strategic mineral stockpile, and the film industry and support for the aerospace, shipbuilding, steel and vehicle industries including loans, grants and the purchase of assets and assistance to redundant steel workers, and other payments.

The **Department of Trade and Industry** will account for this Vote.

	£
Net total	463,527,000
Allocated in the Vote on Account (HC 691)	215,365,000
Balance to complete	248,162,000

continued overleaf

Plate 2.2 *Supply estimates 1989–90*

Plate 2.2 (*continued*)

Part II Summary and subhead detail

	1987–88	1988–89	Summary	1989–90		
	Net outturn £'000	Total net provision £'000		Gross provision £'000	Appropria-tions in aid £'000	Net provision £'000
Regional and general industrial support (Sections A to C)	249,723	346,809		308,837	35,384	273,453
of which: net contributions to the EC (In addition expenditure estimated at £860,000 is offset by receipts from the EC, borne on a net token subhead)	(–17,652)	(–24,100)		—	19,685	–19,685
Support for aerospace, shipbuilding and steel manufacture (Sections D to F)	76,117	140,839		229,317	39,283	190,034
of which: net contributions to the EC	(–5,797)	(–4,000)		—	1,800	–1,800
Other (non-public) expenditure (Section G) (In addition expenditure estimated at £4,050,000 is offset by receipts from the EC, borne on a net token subhead)	679	501		40	—	40
Assistance to the vehicle industry	—	*548,800*		—	—	—
Total	326,519	1,036,949		538,194	74,667	463,527
		Forecast outturn £'000 976,325				

1987-88 Outturn £'000	1988-89 Total provision £'000	Subhead detail (contd)	1989-90 Provision £'000
		Section G: Other (non-public) expenditure	
679	500	**G1 Transfer payments of regional development grants ●**	39
		Transfer payments of regional development grant under the original and revised schemes to local authorities and newtown corporations	
—	1	**G2 Agency payments on behalf of EC Commission (net) ●**	1
		Payment of £4.05m to local authorities for support of small firms offset by receipts from the European Regional Development Fund. The Department makes payments acting solely as agents for the EC Commission.	
679	501	**Net total**	40
		Assistance to the vehicle industry	
—	547,000	*Support for Rover Group*	—
—	1,800	*Privatisation expenses*	—
—	548,800	*Total*	—

continued overleaf

Plate 2.2 *(continued)*

Part III   Extra receipts payable to the Consolidated Fund

	1987–88	1988–89	1989–90
	£'000	£'000	£'000
In addition to appropriations in aid there are the following estimated receipts:			
(1) Receipts from the sale of Government shares in Rover Group Plc	—	—	150,000
(2) Interest on loans and investments	3,977	6,919	3,834
Miscellaneous receipts	285	—	—
Excess appropriations in aid	3,233		
Total	**7,495**	**6,919**	**153,834**

Table 1 Long term projects – Details of projects costing over £25 million and reconciliation with the Estimates

Project	Year of start: Original estimate of year of completion	Current estimate of year of completion	Original estimate of cost £000	Current estimate of cost £000	Probable expenditure to 31 March 1989 £000	Estimates provision for 1989–90 £000	Estimated expenditure after 31 March 1990 £000
Development of the Westland 30 helicopter	1982–83/1986–87	Not known	41,000	41,000	39,317	—	1,683
Development of the Westland EH101 helicopter	1984–85/1990–91	1991–92	60,000	60,000	31,326	12,010	16,664
Development of the A330/340 airliners	1987–88/1990–91	1990–91	450,000	450,000	116,000	154,000	180,000
Total projects costing over £25 million						166,010	
Other projects						—	
Total subheads D1 and D2						166,010	

1. Expenditure occurs on subheads D1–D2.
2. Provision of launch aid to Westland Helicopters Plc as a contribution towards development of improved versions of the Westland 30. All payments have now been completed except for £1.6 million in respect of learning costs which could become payable in the event that the aircraft went into production.
3. Provision of launch aid to Westland Helicopters Plc as a contribution towards development costs of a civil version of the EH101. Contributions will be paid over seven years from 1984–85 and are repayable by means of a levy on future sales.
4. Provision of launch aid to British Aerospace as a contribution towards development costs of the A330/340 airliners. Contributions will be paid over 4 years from 1987–88 and are repayable by means of levies on future sales.
5. Reflecting the nature of the contracts all costs are expressed in cash, not 1989–90 prices, and the current estimate of cost equates to the original estimate of cost.

material is brought to their attention. From this, it would be quite plausible to conclude that the departments concerned were not particularly interested in drawing journalists' attention to the figures.

It may be that these departments did not feel that the matter deserved any special treatment or that it was part of the detailed negotiations they are routinely involved in. This is a perfectly understandable position to take but it does lose some of its credibility if one remembers that the takeover was a controversial affair and produced many a front-page headline. In this case it is difficult to believe that at some level of departmental responsibility, whoever was in charge of setting out the figures – as opposed to simply typing them in – would not have been aware of their significance.

One cannot do more than speculate about the series of events which led to the figures being included in the relevant tables in the way they were. But it is obvious that the manner of their inclusion and the nature of the documents in which they were included made it highly unlikely that the data would be picked up, and for three reasons. First, who would be likely to pick them up? Political correspondents are, by and large, generalists and would in all probability merely skim – if that – documents such as these. Unless they were alerted to the figures, it is improbable that they would spend time and effort combing through them to find a news story. Second, journalists are supplied with considerable amounts of information and these documents would be part of a much larger bundle. Third, statements concerning the payment did not make any reference to the possibility that a deferment of 18 months would take place, and so journalists' (unfounded) expectations were that the matter would be concluded speedily.

It may only be the financial/City analysts with an interest in the car industry – and one must remember that Rover had been a public company and so had few documents in the public domain – or a journalist with (a) an interest in *the details of* the Rover deal, (b) access to the estimates, and (c) a knowledge of accounting practices, who would have had a chance of picking them up. So, at the end of the day, because the journalists were not alerted, the figures could be published in the sure knowledge that they would be overlooked.

In spite of the grave differences of attitudes over the disclosure of this piece of information – and particularly the broader context within which such processing of information takes place – the Committee of Privileges' report was highly critical of the *Guardian*. It did not accept the case made for disclosure and preferred instead to support the argument that premature disclosure could have detrimental effects on relationships, on the giving of evidence to committees and on the work of committees.

Finally, it may be useful to illustrate how the Committee of Public Accounts, and by extension other committees, would seek out the leakers. Following the leak of the Comptroller and Auditor General's memo, the Chair of the committee wrote to all those who had access to the memo in order to determine the source of the leak. There were only two questions in his letter:

1. Do you know how this 'leak' came about?
2. Do you have any information as to the source of the 'leak'? (Committee of Public Accounts, 1990: x)

Needless to say, the source of the 'leak' was never discovered.

Conclusion

Although this chapter began with a discussion on the nature and content of information within the political system, the examples of leaks given immediately above lend support to some of the points developed in earlier sections. We can see from these examples how certain information is kept from public view and how even reporters are often unaware of the importance of bits of information which they come across. They work with material in the 'front region', with public information, and much less, if at all, with material in the 'back region'.

Leaks tend to disrupt this routine. They sometimes confirm suspicions, suspicions that cannot be justified in any way except by the existence of the documentation passed on to the reporter. Had the reporter not had the document to hand, would the nature of the BAe–Rover coverage, of the coal industry, of the Anglo-Irish framework have been anything other than that desired by the acknowledged and authorized sources of information? It is in this way that leaks highlight the sense of disruption of routines and established practices: they reveal what reporters should have been looking at, but were not.

Admittedly, the secret nature of the transaction of information – so different from public relations activity which courts the public eye – tends to add spice to the story, to confirm suspicions, to give an air of mystery. It offers an insider's view, a view rarely articulated because those working in particular organizations are often unaware of the value of the information which is within their world. Clearly, little of that information connects with the sorts of worlds inhabited by journalists or political actors or others who are powerful enough to be troubled by irksome 'secrets' revealed by individuals. Do reporters care enough about the irregularities in universities, in local councils, in local firms, in news organizations, to accord them space in public? It is only when such instances connect with other events and news agendas that those snippets of information suddenly become valuable.

Would any of this change if 'freedom of information' legislation was passed to sweep away the sorts of classification of information described above? If the above analysis is correct, then the answer can only be a guarded 'Yes.' Certainly, information would become more openly and easily available but not all information is valued in the same way. It is the magical combination of newsworthiness, timeliness and particular news agendas which seems to make the significant difference, not the intrinsic importance of the information.

3

Reporting Parliament, Reporting Politics

In October 1993, the British MP Jack Straw published a paper in which he argued, quite simply, that there had been a decline in the newspaper reporting of Parliamentary debates between the late 1980s and the early 1990s. Coming across some newspapers from 1979 – his first year in Parliament – he was reminded 'of the extensive coverage then given to Parliamentary debates, and of the relative frequency with which the contributions of back-benchers to debate were carried in the press gallery reports of the broadsheet newspapers' (1993: 1). His sense of loss could not be disguised and even though his paper was designed to draw attention to a specific trend, the media coverage it generated was placed within a broader context: a context which sought to address the continually changing role of the British Parliament in the modern democratic process. In other words, the journalists accused of neglecting Parliamentary debate sought to cast their defence in ways which highlighted the changing pattern of Parliamentary work, the changing working routines of MPs as well as the changing practices of the media themselves.

Whilst it is important to acknowledge these changes, it is also crucial that the main features of Jack Straw's argument are not ignored. Although Straw is critical of the decline in the coverage of Parliamentary debates, his reasons for this have more to do with the place of argument and debate in society than with a simple desire to go back in time. As Straw notes right at the beginning of his paper, conflict resolution must be achieved 'through the political process' if peace and harmony in any society is a goal. 'At the heart of that process', he continues, 'is argument.' This suggests not only the right to ask questions and to debate, but also the need for a forum in which those questions are asked and answered, and seen to be asked and answered. If 'people are to have confidence in the political system, then they must be able to see it working, as a process, and not as a spectacle' (1993: 3).

Few have the opportunity, as Straw admits, to see the arguments in Parliament at first hand, so they rely on journalists to 'distil the argument, and highlight the strong and weak' elements in various cases. They rely on journalists to relay the warp and woof of debate, of *argument*. Unfortunately, according to Straw, over the last few decades, less and less newspaper space has been devoted to just such a relaying of argument. There has been

- a decline in the 'systematic daily reporting of Parliamentary debates in the broadsheet press', and in some cases a decline to a quarter of what it was only some five years ago in 1988–9;

- a decline in the overall coverage of Parliamentary proceedings. 'In 1988, readers would have received substantial information about what went on, as well as a flavour of the debate' (1993: 4). Not so in 1992, with coverage substantially reduced. Though political stories continue to feature on front and other pages of newspapers, there is 'no evidence that the decline in Parliamentary coverage on designated (Parliamentary or Politics) pages identified by the study has been offset by an increase in coverage on other pages' (1993: 8);
- a change in the *nature* of Parliamentary coverage with lobby correspondents becoming more adept at retailing gossip rather than the substance of argument.

Though there are some obvious limitations to the Straw study – it only considered broadsheet front pages, for example – it has nonetheless re-kindled interest in the question of reporting Parliament and the coverage of politics more generally. Unfortunately, that interest has focused perhaps too much on the 'debate in Parliament' issue rather than the broader question of the reporting of politics in, and out, of Parliament. The two are not the same: debates in Parliament are, as all MPs who are rarely seen in the Chamber always insist, a small part of its work. MPs sit on committees, for example, and they often attend meetings with groups of representatives and constituents. This too is part of their work, and the work of Parliament. It follows that to report Parliament requires much more than simply reporting debates.

But how valid are Straw's allegations and what do they reveal about the interaction of journalists and politicians which, in spite of Straw's report, still features so prominently in much of our national mass media? What do these allegations lead us to conclude about *how* Parliament ought to be reported? What are the implications of these findings for the coverage of politics and political matters more generally?

After reviewing some recent research on the coverage of Parliament, this chapter will seek to explore these larger questions. The first part will focus primarily on the evidence for a decline in Parliamentary coverage. This will be followed by an analysis of two different examples of coverage which, in their own way, throw some light both on the contemporary nature of political coverage and on the changing place of Parliament in the daily news agenda. These Parliamentary 'set pieces' involve the coverage given to Parliamentary select committees and given to reports published by the Parliamentary Public Accounts Committee. The final part of this chapter will return to the larger questions posed above.

Reporting Parliament: the evidence of decline

It is perhaps useful to note that Straw's concern about a decline in Parliamentary coverage of debates parallels similar concerns about the declining coverage of political institutions which have been voiced for some time in the USA. Stephen Hess, for instance, notes that a comparison of Congressional coverage during one week across four decades showed that 'there is a pattern of decline of government/politics stories as a percentage of the front page: 1965 – government/politics stories, 84 per cent; 1975 – 73 per cent; 1985 – 63 per cent; 1992 – 55 per cent' (1993: 14). Other evidence cited by Hess merely confirms the trend. According to Professor Kimball, the 'three [networks] now make no serious attempt to cover Congress' (quoted in Hess, 1993: 13). It is important to note, however, that a considerable amount of the American literature has gone beyond this basic form of analysis and towards charting in great detail the developing relationship between the media and law-makers, and the consequences of this relationship for legislative bodies, legislators and law-making (see Hess, 1986; Cook, 1989). Whether coverage of political institutions has, or has not, declined is thus only part of a much broader issue of the interaction of the media and political institutions, and the question of the adequacy of that coverage for the attainment of something akin to representative democracy.

Studies from outside the USA hint at some similarities. Evidence from a study of the coverage of the German Bundestag suggests that although the German broadcast media give coverage to the 'all important plenary sessions' their coverage of other sessions is more erratic (Schatz, 1992: 238). Unlike the American experience, however, Schatz goes on to suggest that the television coverage 'is merely part of the coverage of politics and consequently is subject to similar expectation by the political parties' of 'objective' and 'balanced' coverage (Schatz, 1992: 242); the contrast here is with evidence of, for example, an imbalance of coverage between the major American political parties in the Senate as reported by Stephen Hess (1986: 55–8). But perhaps like the American experience, Schatz reports that 'the bulk of media attention' is given to 'no more than 10 per cent of the House membership' (Schatz, 1992: 248). Hess suggests that the 'top third' of the senators 'represent 80 per cent of the entire Senate's media score' (Hess, 1986: 57). A study of the American Congress also points to the concentration of coverage on a quarter, or just over, of all representatives (Cook, 1989: 60). Whether this reflects simply a 'publicity hierarchy', as Schatz suggests, rather than being an acknowledgement of different amounts of power exercised by different politicians, e.g. the front bench as against backbenchers, party in power as against party in opposition, is clearly an important consideration when making such comparisons.

Unfortunately, it is difficult to go much beyond these simple comparisons without having to offer major qualifications to each and every statement and without embarking on a complex study of the insertion of the media into very different legislative bodies. Nevertheless, the comparisons offered above are indicative of trends which may be common, given the media's own commercial and other requirements and the 'problem' of how to cover political institutions which have many members working together in groups (i.e. as parties, or more loosely) and competing against one another, and

Table 3.1   *Average percentage news composition for three groups of newspapers, 1975*

Mean % of news space given to	'Quality' group: Guardian, Times, Daily Telegraph	'Middle' group: Daily Express, Daily Mail	'Popular' group: Sun, Daily Mirror
Home political, social and economic	19	16	15
External political, social and economic	17	7	4
Sport	18	33	47
Sex-related content	–	2	4
Parliamentary debates	3	–	–
Finance/business	18	9	–
All external	24	17	10

Source: McQuail, 1977: 29

which legislate across an enormous range of ('newsworthy' and non-'newsworthy') issues.

How far are these findings reflected in studies of the British case? In general, the British case is much less well documented than the American one, so it is necessary to collect material from a range of sources in order to comment on the alleged decline in Parliamentary coverage. There are three main sources of evidence which illustrate the pattern of decline *in general* and the particular form that that coverage currently takes.

The first is Denis McQuail's *Analysis of Newspaper Content*, produced for the 1977 McGregor Royal Commission on the Press. This contains a series of tables which quantify the percentage share of a number of different news, and other, categories in a range of print media. One table gives a breakdown of the 'average percentage composition for three groups of newspapers' in 1975 (McQuail, 1977: 29; Table 3.1).

The most important point to note here is that by the mid-1970s only the qualities were giving space to Parliamentary debates. At 3 per cent of total news space it was not a great deal but by the 1990s even this practice had stopped for the broadsheet or quality press. As for the coverage of 'political' news more generally, the precise figures are more difficult to calculate since the table lumps together 'political, social and economic' news. In contrast, Seymour-Ure's analysis of newspaper content in 1965 puts the percentage of editorial space given to 'politics' – defined as 'any story that relates to Parliament, the political parties or the institutions and processes of government, with appropriate adjustments for "overseas politics"' (1968: 61) – at 26 per cent, at the top end of the quality press (1968: 65; Table 3.2).

One common way of interpreting these figures is to argue that the space given over to 'politics' is considerable, especially at the quality end of the press, and that it diminishes as one goes to the tabloids. Whilst these figures are unfortunately not directly comparable to McQuail's they do confirm the prominence of 'political' news across a section of the national press.

Table 3.2   *Percentage of politics space given to news, special articles, etc.*

	% editorial space given to:		% politics space given to:					
	Politics	Other	Home news	Overseas news	Total news	Special articles	Leading articles	Other
Daily Telegraph	26	74	46	25	70	8	6	16
Guardian	32	68	45	29	74	9	9	9
Express	15	85	43	25	68	10	7	15
Mail	19	81	39	29	68	12	3	17
Mirror	12	88	46	22	68	8	5	20
Sun	16	84	42	24	66	13	6	15

Source: adapted from Seymour-Ure, 1968: 65

Table 3.3   *Coverage of Parliament in three regional dailies, 1900–72**

	Yorkshire Post		Manchester Guardian/ Guardian		The Scotsman	
	Coverage as % of		Coverage as % of		Coverage as % of	
	Total space	Total editorial	Total space	Total editorial	Total space	Total editorial
1900	–	–	7.6	11.4	6.3	9.6
1912	5.3	6.9	8.4	12.0	6.7	10.2
1924	5.5	7.6	5.8	8.0	5.9	9.8
1936	3.8	4.7	4.1	5.2	6.2	8.0
1948	1.7	2.1	8.3	12.0	6.7	10.6
1960	2.0	3.4	3.3	5.3	3.6	5.8
1972	1.6	2.9	3.0	4.3	3.9	4.8

* Sample: ten days in each Parliamentary session.

Source: Seymour-Ure, 1977a: 113

The more interesting and unanswerable questions relate to whether the proportion of space given over to political news in general has declined and whether the nature of that coverage has changed (see pp. 58–61 below).

The second source of evidence, Seymour-Ure's work for the McGregor Royal Commission, points to a decline in Parliamentary coverage (1977a: 113, Table 3.3) although he does not supply any other figures which would permit a comparison with his own work a decade before. So, once more, we have some information on the decline of Parliamentary coverage – not clearly defined here – but nothing more specific on Parliamentary debates or on political coverage more generally.

Despite the impossibility of comparing, and contrasting, the findings of these studies – are the categories sufficiently watertight, are they quantifying the same things, and so on – they do appear to lend some support to Straw's analysis: the days of reporting Parliamentary debates are long gone. This is also confirmed in recent analysis by Franklin on the reporting of

Parliament (Franklin, 1995b). (Incidentally, and perhaps as part of a response to Straw's comments, in 1995 the *Guardian* introduced a weekly half-page of extracts from Parliamentary debates.) But the disappearance of coverage of debates does not mean that press coverage of 'politics' in general, itself a much broader category, has declined. There is a sound argument in favour of incorporating coverage of Parliament (with or without extracts from debates) *into* political coverage rather than simply giving over space to debates themselves.

Have the broadcast media treated Parliamentary coverage any differently? Here the evidence is just as difficult to interpret, as very often no distinctions are made between political coverage (however defined), Parliamentary coverage in general and coverage of Parliamentary debates. Part of the reason for this is that television and radio coverage of Parliament did not begin until the 1980s and so neither broadcast medium had access to Parliamentary debates. Coverage of Parliament was then no more than political coverage, broadly defined, with no actual extracts from inside the Palace of Westminster. Nevertheless, data drawn from the Glasgow University Media Group's analysis of television in the 1970s can be used to show just how prominent coverage of politics is in the broadcast media. This study reported that on the BBC1 *Nine O'Clock News* 21.6 per cent of (826) items were in the 'politics' category; the figure for *News at Ten* was 21.1 per cent (GUMG, 1976: 98). There are no specific findings relating to either Parliamentary coverage in general or Parliamentary debates in particular and it is clear from the Group's content analysis schedule that the 'politics' category is narrower than the 'political, social and economic affairs' category used for newspaper analysis (GUMG, 1976: Appendix 1). Thus the category of 'politics', as defined by the Glasgow University Media Group, dominates broadcast news to a far larger extent than it features in the national press.

The third study which merits close attention is Blumler et al.'s study of Parliamentary coverage on television *after the introduction of television into the House of Commons* in 1989. According to the research findings, BBC1's *Nine O'Clock News* carried, on average, 3.4 Parliamentary stories per day and led with a Parliamentary story on 8 of the 15 days sampled. *News at Ten*'s figures were similar: 2.9 stories and the same number of days led with a Parliamentary story (Blumler et al., 1990b: 10). If we assume that these flagship news programmes carry on average 11 or 12 stories (GUMG, 1976: 87) we can estimate that about 25 per cent of all bulletins are made up of Parliamentary stories. What is more difficult to assess is whether the introduction of television cameras into the House of Commons has increased the number of Parliamentary stories. Common sense would suggest that the availability of television pictures makes it more likely that broadcasters will use them, although it is possible that this would be at the cost of other sorts of coverage. Again, only more rigorous and longer-term research would throw light on the changing contours of Parliamentary and political coverage.

Two findings from the Blumler et al. study also show that there are broad similarities with the German and American studies. In general, 'Conservatives (who were in power at the time of the study) attracted more coverage than Labour speakers' but broadcasters nevertheless made great efforts to achieve political balance (1990b: 14). Second, although there was emphasis on the political leaders ranging from 2 per cent in regional weekly programmes to 28 per cent in ITN's *News at Ten*, other Parliamentary actors also achieved some prominence (1990b: 14). However, since the study does not give a breakdown of which individual MPs were given coverage, it is difficult to offer any conclusions as to the range of actors covered by the broadcast media. Nonetheless, the study strongly suggests a concentration on those who, for want of a more appropriate phrase, wield power.

The absence of longer-term, quantitative social scientific research, particularly with regard to the British (and perhaps European) scene more generally, has not prevented Straw's allegations from coming to the surface, and it is very proper that they should encourage a debate about the reporting of such a significant political institution. Yet the allegations – and the other studies quoted above – cannot properly be understood unless they are placed within a broader conception of Parliamentary and Congressional coverage, the continually changing nature of representative democracy and of government itself. This is perhaps the greatest weakness in any allegation which claims that coverage of Parliament has declined since it assumes that there have been no significant changes in the last century which have had a bearing on current media practices.

Yet these changes, one can argue, permit us to understand better why coverage of Parliament or of Congress has evolved into its present state. In describing the evolution of political journalism in the USA, for example, Timothy Cook points out that the focus of journalists shifted away from the House of Representatives as legislative power moved elsewhere and also in response to other emerging requirements of newsmaking and newsworthiness.

> The diminution of newsmaking on the House floor revealed and reinforced new political priorities. The earlier preference for debates, recorded with little interpretation or comment, had been founded on an egalitarianism that opened up the process of the people's branch to all for scrutiny. By the end of the century the correspondent had emerged as one who would make sense of the goings-on of Capitol Hill for a mass audience that was perceived to demand colour and excitement more than details of policy disputes. (1989: 22)

Subsequent changes in the balance of power within Congress, and the emergence of a more visible and active presidency further diminished the attention that was once paid to the House of Representatives. The intrusion of the broadcast media merely reinforced this trend by concentrating on leaders and on conflict even further, at the expense of attention to debate and discussion (Cook, 1989: Chs 1–3). The changing nature of the social and political system in tandem with changing requirements of news organizations – for instance, the development of the 'New Journalism' which shunned verbatim reportage and the development of the interview as a form of journalistic activity – thus brought about a change in the relationship between the press and the major political institutions in the USA.

Just as in the USA, the impact of the 'New Journalism', the commercialization of the print media, and the beginnings of the telegraph changed the style and requirements of most British national and regional newspapers. Verbatim accounts gave way to shorter, more interpretive pieces and the straight reporting of Parliamentary speeches declined in importance (Lee, 1976: 120–5). Just as significant may have been changes in news gathering and processing activities. In 1938, Wickham Steed was already bemoaning the fact that newspapers were no longer put together in a leisurely pace and well into the night with proper care and attention to detail.

> Morning papers [now] have to be planned, at latest, in the early afternoon of the day before they appear. Those with large circulations are obliged to print a first edition for the provinces by nine or ten p.m., and those with smaller circulations not later than midnight. (1938: 31)

Such changes undoubtedly had an impact on how institutions like Parliament, which held debates well into the night and into the following morning, were to be covered. At other times, news organizations could decide to change the nature of their coverage of certain areas, including Parliament. While one might regret the decline of the Parliamentary coverage in the *Financial Times*, it is worth recalling that 'the start of daily reports of Parliamentary proceedings' did not begin until the late 1960s (Kynaston, 1988: 353).

These changes are suggestive of processes of evolution, of relationships being reassessed and of new forces coming into play rather than a once-and-for-all template of reporting practices. Another example of these sorts of evolutionary change would be the changing nature of the political (lobby) reporter. In the period up to 1914, political correspondents were relatively few and far between and so there was a considerable amount of individual newsgathering activity. Moreover, these correspondents were often elite newspaper editors (Tunstall, 1970: 9) mixing with political actors in a fairly restricted political world. After 1945, and as their numbers grew, it was more proper to describe the lobby as being involved in 'collective newsgathering' (Seymour-Ure, 1977a: 114). Today, there are nearly 200 correspondents working in a fairly small space, and mixing freely, sometimes with friction, with MPs (Ingham, 1994).

Just as their organization changed, so too did their 'job descriptions'. They were no longer simply there to report the visible dimension of Parliament, that is, the speeches; they sought to penetrate behind the scenes, believing that the set pieces of Parliamentary debate were of less significance than back-room manoeuvres. And, as

> the interest . . . in public affairs grew, it became necessary to explain and expound official policies in popular terms as they arose. So another task was

added to those borne by Lobby journalists. They had to find out and then explain what all these documents meant, what would be their effect on the ordinary person, what was likely to happen when they came before Parliament and generally to build up into a news story easily understood by the casual reader. (quoted in Ingham, 1994: 551)

Similarly, as pressure on lobby correspondents built up, they ceased to be seekers of 'quality' stories only (Ingham, 1994: 552). The measure of their output mattered. They became, in the words of one such correspondent, 'sausage machines' turning out three, four, five stories per day (interview with author, 1994).

Important changes were also taking place in Parliament, and in the practice of government. Parliament's work was becoming more diversified, government's responsibilities extended into most areas of public life, non-governmental bodies mushroomed, Parliamentary committees raised their profile, political parties increased their control over individual MPs, and so on. And the press to some extent may have responded to this by reassessing the contents of its Parliamentary coverage. With broadcasting also imposing its own requirements, the scene must surely have been set for some rethinking of what had gone on before. To note two contemporary examples, the usefulness of the unattributable source may be in decline if one can find a (usually maverick) MP to voice the same opinion to camera, and the briefings, and speeches, in Westminster may become less important as prime ministers choose to publicly address political correspondents in other settings. The current Prime Minister, John Major, for example, has held a number of press conferences in the garden of his Downing Street home in front of both journalists and cameras. In this way, he has altered his relationship not only to the media but also to his colleagues in Parliament itself.

We can see in these sketches of change a process which can neither be halted – assuming, that is, that one could even identify all the contributory forces that brought that change about – nor reversed. And it is this more than anything which undermines the case of those who, like Jack Straw, look back to a golden age which in practice was always more tarnished than an earlier one. After all, it is only 20 years since Michael Foot – curiously, another Labour politician – was voicing concern that Parliamentary news is 'at risk'. But as Seymour-Ure noted presciently then, although the criticisms were understandable, 'How could it be otherwise in a modern newspaper?' He continued:

To deplore such tendencies, it can be argued, is to misunderstand the nature of politics . . . Politics has no existence apart from the communications media prevalent in society. . . . With mass politics and modern technology, forms of political communication have necessarily changed. TV is the prevalent medium and inevitably tends to impose its own manners on its subjects. This is not to 'distort' politics, for there have never been politics that were not conditioned by the dominant media of the day. What Michael Foot regrets . . . is not just the passing of a type of Parliamentary reporting (which in principle might be re-introduced) but the passing of a type of newspaper – which could not. (1977a: 114–15)

With these echoes of past concerns and debates reverberating around us, are Straw's allegations merely repetitions of past concerns? Is he, like Michael Foot before him, calling for a return to an age long gone? In one sense, the answer is in the affirmative.

Undoubtedly, debates are part of the process of *argument* so dearly beloved by Straw, but these are often very lengthy affairs. Providing snippets, or highlights, from debates may be as unsatisfactory a way of reporting them as not reporting them at all if, that is, the purpose of the report is to give publicity to an argument. But there are other reasons why privileging debates may be misplacing one's concern: it could be argued that committee inquiries are fundamental to the process of accountability and that these too merit substantive coverage. Indeed, the more debates become set pieces with party allegiances determining the outcome of discussion, the less important they become and the weaker the case for their coverage. So there is no rational case for according debates a privileged place in the press or on television; moreover, as the nature of Parliamentary institutions changes so too must their place in any ranking of priorities.

It is obvious that what lies at the heart of this discussion is the issue of the supremacy of the Parliamentary system, and particularly of the Chamber of the House of Commons itself. To take one simple illustration of this, one notes that Straw's research compared newspaper content 'with the subject of debates and questions in the House of Commons for the day . . . as indicated on the title page of Commons Hansard for that day' (1993: 7). But there is nothing in Hansard, for example, which lists committees, the reports of committees, or the discussions which take place in committees. These are to be found in other documents, but are they less important than the debates – all debates? – in Parliament? There are then some important questions which the allegations made by Straw should address and these revolve, very loosely, around the much broader issue of how politics in the late twentieth century should be reported in the mass media. And one of the considerations which must be taken into account when looking at this issue is the changing nature of government itself. With so many Non-Departmental Public Bodies (NDPBs) in existence, is a debate in Parliament more worthy than an investigation into a Regional Health Authority?

But there is an even more serious objection to the main thread running through Straw's report concerning the declining coverage of Parliament: the trend he has identified can be traced back not only to the 1980s but to the 1880s! One of the characteristics of the birth of a more commercialized press in the 1870s, and of a press influenced by the New Journalism, was precisely the reduction of space devoted to the verbatim reporting of political speeches. Even Seymour-Ure's analysis (see Table 3.3) dates the decline to the period just after the Second World War.

Only an exceptionally detailed study could throw light on the nature of change in Parliamentary coverage since the 1880s. Moreover, such a study would have to include a sensitive appreciation of the changing local,

national *and* international social and political milieux within which the
media operate. Would a trend downwards (or upwards) necessarily lead us
to conclude that we know less (or more) today about how we are governed?
So, whilst there is certainly a case for saying that our media and Parliament
have changed, such arguments make no sense without an appreciation of
the larger context. To return to the example of quangos (above), the
location of power over everyday life may have shifted away from
Westminster and this is in itself a good reason to refocus the media's work.

Admittedly, this does raise questions about the adequacy of the media in
dealing with a much broadened agenda of issues but it may be that the
discussion then dissolves into one of exploring individual cases of coverage
rather than politics or Parliament itself. Was the poll tax adequately
covered? Was the pit closures announcement in 1992 adequately covered? Is
the environment discussed adequately? Such specific investigations may be
preferable to a blanket request for more Parliamentary coverage. With
these particular objectives in mind, the next two sections examine specific
cases where one can pass judgement on how well the media coped with
Parliamentary activity.

From 'Question Time' to select committees

One of the more commonly covered parts of the Parliamentary process is
Question Time. One study has suggested that the introduction of television
into the House of Commons has given Question Time a much higher
profile and has made the setting a familiar one for most of the television
audience (see Franklin, 1992). Certainly, television has focused on this
occasion for much of its news coverage, and for much of its weekly live
coverage, and for good reasons. Question Time offers dramatic confrontation between party leaders, between ministers and between MPs. The
visual quality of such dramatic political confrontations makes them
supremely important for television producers, so it is no coincidence that
they regularly feature in television news bulletins.

On the surface, then, any coverage of Question Time and of Prime
Minister's Question Time is beneficial, and the more the coverage the
better. It offers a window on to Parliament and its work and it gives a
sense of political and ideological divisions. It also offers, in the words of
Jack Straw, a forum for argument and for the visibility of argument. But
such an interpretation does not do justice to the real place of Question
Time in the Parliamentary process. First, Question Time lasts no more than
30 or so minutes on four days of the week. It is therefore a small window.
That it has gained such prominence may be a direct result of its importance
as a dramatic event for the television cameras; that it ever came to occupy
the afternoon slot in the Parliamentary timetable is a result of parliamentarians' desire to take into account the convenience of newspapers. This
demonstrates, once more, the changing relationship of politics and systems

of communications, and the adaptation of the one to the other (Seymour-Ure, 1977a: 90; see also Seymour-Ure, 1979, and Barnett and Gaber, 1992).

Second, the nature of the confrontation is anything but spontaneous. As Borthwick and others have noted, ministers come to Question Time fully briefed and are thus unlikely to be tripped up by 'surprise' supplementary questions. Question Time has become no more than 'an attempt to *secure favourable recognition* for each party's point of view and . . . favourable recognition for individuals, both frontbenchers and backbenchers' (Borthwick, 1993: 78).

Notwithstanding the significance of favourable recognition, and the impact of a good Parliamentary performance on a political party, the substance of Question Time is quite different from its external appearance. It is a show with all the trappings of professionalized politics at its most extreme (and most visible). So for journalists the dilemma must surely be whether to treat Question Time as a showpiece or whether to treat it as a serious political confrontation. Should they report the content or should they merely report the surface appearance by concentrating on the *performances* of individuals, and on their abilities at the dispatch box?

Covering Parliamentary select committees[1]

In 1979, a new set of Parliamentary select committees was created. The powerful Public Accounts Committee was retained and 14 new departmental select committees were established to shadow departments of state. Each committee is made up of a cross-section of MPs from the House, so giving it an implicit political divide. Such committees, like their predecessors, 'are essentially instruments of accountability' and they play 'no direct part in the processing of government business, either legislative or financial, but they have the procedural freedom to choose their own subjects of inquiry' (Rush, 1990: 139) and to call for papers and witnesses.

In recent years, select committees have attracted a considerable amount of media attention. The sometimes dramatic confrontations which take place in committee sessions are a natural attraction. Yet despite their higher profile, select committees remain, in the eyes of seasoned commentators, bodies of inquiry with little real power to effect change. According to Peter Hennessy they merely open 'up the occasional crevasse from which the sounds of creaking and groaning would emerge' (1990: 333).

Such views are based on some fairly commonplace criticisms of a process of inquiry which seriously circumscribes the effectiveness of committees. Committees were created to scrutinize rather than to effect change, and their pattern of work reinforces that limited role. Committees usually open their investigations after the event and this makes it difficult for them to intervene in the policy process itself. It also makes it very difficult to redress wrongs. Another weakness is that civil servants do not divulge information about the advice which they have given to ministers and so committees are unable to indicate where, or why, ministers did or did not take up departmental advice.

Nevertheless, it is commonly believed that the select committee system has benefited from its heightened profile. As John Wheeler, Chairman of the Employment Committee, observed, 'I am sure that the coverage on television of committee proceedings has made the public more aware of the existence and work of select committees' (Select Committee on Procedure, 1990: 147). But there is a downside to media attention: 'editorial decisions on which committee to televise encourage piecemeal and selective coverage (e.g. if a Minister is present, the cameras are; if officials attend, the cameras are absent). The picture of select committee work which results is therefore inaccurate' (Select Committee on Procedure, 1990: 148).

Before turning to the coverage of committees, it is important to describe very briefly their basic pattern of work. A committee will 'shadow' a department by looking at certain aspects of the department's work, though it may also raise issues which have become relevant to that specific department. Once an inquiry is established, MPs will spend one or more sessions taking evidence from witnesses. These are (usually) held in public. Such sessions may last several hours. The verbatim transcripts or Minutes of Evidence of these sessions are subsequently made publicly available, usually within a short time of the actual session. At some point after the conclusion of the inquiry, the committee will publish a report of its findings. Sometimes these are 'controversial' – perhaps because the subject matter is deemed 'newsworthy' – but, more often than not, the reports are published with varying degrees of media attention being paid to them.

The reports may or may not be raised in the House of Commons, and may or may not elicit a response from government. According to Judge, in the roughly 10-year period up to June 1990, committees published '591 reports and 231 special reports' at great expense (1992: 95). More detailed analysis quoted by Judge suggests that of the 25 per cent which had been the subject of debate in two sampled years, 'only 13 (out of 116) had been the subject of a substantive motion or an adjournment motion' (1992: 96). The Trade and Industry Select Committee report on Rover (Trade and Industry Committee, 1991) was rewarded with a governmental written reply consisting of only eight short paragraphs (see Negrine, 1992).

The pattern of work described above does makes it possible for both the press and television to have access to an enormous amount of information from a very broad range of committees. In the course of the Trade and Industry Select Committee inquiry into the sale of Rover, for instance, there were well over 160 pages (two columns to a page) of verbatim evidence in addition to numerous appendices and two reports; the same committee's inquiry into the sale of arms and military technology to Iraq resulted in over 500 pages of evidence (Trade and Industry Committee, 1992). Other committees, investigating other issues, would similarly generate enormous quantities of material.

How much of all this information ever surfaces? How much coverage do committees actually get, and what sort of coverage is it? What is included in that coverage, and conversely, what is excluded? Do the media, in the words of John Wheeler (quoted on p. 64) provide an 'inaccurate' picture of the work of select committees?

Television coverage of select committees

The most recent detailed study of the television coverage of Parliament was carried out by Jay Blumler and colleagues (1990b) in the period November 1989 to March 1990. In spite of the fact that the period of study covered the actual public *experiment* in the televising of Parliament, its findings echo some of the hopes and fears of John Wheeler (quoted on p. 64).

According to the research findings, the 'three main national news programmes paid 8–12 per cent attention to the work of committees (expressed as a proportion of all Commons events presented)' (Blumler et al., 1990b: 13). On the main BBC1 evening news programme, select *and* standing committees made up 8 per cent of *all* Parliamentary coverage; on Channel Four's 50-minute-long evening news programme, the figure was 12 per cent. In real terms, BBC1 carries an average of 3.4 Parliamentary stories per day in contrast to ITV's main evening news programme average of 2.9 (Blumler et al., 1990b: 10). So committees represent a very small part of the Parliamentary whole. More generally, the researchers found – perhaps not surprisingly – that the longer the news programme and the more dedicated the programme to Parliamentary affairs (and consequently the smaller the audience), the greater the proportion of time devoted to committees.

There is no objective measure by which to judge the significance or value of this coverage. On the positive side, one can say that such coverage – complemented by actuality content – is likely to raise the profile of committees. Furthermore, it may be coverage where none existed before. On the negative side, 8 per cent of all Parliamentary coverage is probably not enough air-time to do justice to any committee inquiry. Moreover, such coverage is itself highly problematic: the bare figures quoted above offer no real insight into an enormously more complicated problem. We can see this in the case of the coverage of the takeover of the publicly owned Rover car group by British Aerospace (BAe) in 1988 (see Chapters 1 and 2 above, and also Negrine, 1992).

In the period between the announcement of the takeover in March 1988 and the final report by the Trade and Industry Select Committee in 1991, there were 12 Parliamentary committee sessions devoted to this controversial affair: 10 were held by the Trade and Industry Committee and were devoted to matters relating to the sale itself; one was held by the Public Accounts Committee as a response to the National Audit Office (NAO) report; and one was held by the Privileges Committee to look into the matter of the leaked memorandum. The first three Trade and Industry Committee sessions were held in 1988 and prior to the emergence of this affair as a 'controversy'; all other sessions were held after December 1989 and mainly in response to the leaked documentation and the revelations they contained.

How then did television cope with this overabundance of events and information? The sessions held in 1988 were not covered on BBC1's *Nine O'Clock News*, though they were given some coverage in the press. By contrast, once the affair had become controversial, coverage was much more consistent. Given that a government minister was deeply implicated, this was hardly surprising. But what this pattern of coverage also suggests is that unless committees are deemed to be dealing with 'controversial' issues, they are often overlooked. Paradoxically, it may be the media who help define what is a controversy, as they did in 1989 and in response to the NAO report and the leaked documents.

Even when attention was paid to select committee sessions of evidence, the nature of that attention was highly problematic. In January 1990 Lord Young, the Secretary for Trade and Industry, made his second appearance in front of the Trade and Industry Select Committee. This particular session lasted some two hours; about one hour, the first hour, of the session was televised live in the early afternoon on BBC2's *Westminster Live*. But assuming that a viewer had stayed to watch all the live coverage, what would he/she have made of it? The question and answer format, the bickering over words and phrases, the continual references to different characters, events and dates spanning nearly two years would have probably puzzled most viewers. Open access on television to such sessions, although laudable, may be of limited value unless it is sustained and put into a broader context, usually by reporters. But there is one other concern. The verbatim transcript of this particular session runs to some 24 pages, with two columns to the page (excluding appendices). The *Westminster Live* programme carried the equivalent of 13 pages. The main BBC1 *Nine O'Clock News* used verbatim just 19 lines drawn from one column of the Minutes of Evidence; this amounted to 44 seconds of a 150-second item (a further 15 seconds of committee visuals were used as background for the correspondent's voice-over).

On occasions such as this – and this example is probably not unique – the actuality is interspersed with commentary from political correspondents who, in their own way, set the scene as well as summarize some of the content of the committee session. Nevertheless, it is valid to ask whether it is ever possible to do justice to such extensive evidence-taking sessions in such short news clips. As the research into the televising of Parliament found, the average length of a Parliamentary item was 164.5 seconds on BBC1 and 160.8 seconds on ITV's *News at Ten*. Where actuality material was used, this amounted to some 41.7 seconds on BBC1 and 43.7 seconds on ITV (Blumler et al., 1990b: 10) – hardly enough time to make sense of complex issues and processes.

What also emerges quite clearly from even a superficial inquiry into this topic is that television's coverage is episodic. As with the press, television

Table 3.4 *Coverage of Trade and Industry Select Committee sessions on the BAe–Rover takeover**

Session dates	*The Times*	*Guardian*	*The Financial Times*	BBC *Nine O'Clock News*
11 May 1988	Yes	Yes	Yes	No
18 May 1988	No	Yes	Yes	No
26 May 1988	No	No	No	No
2 November 1988	Yes	Yes	Yes	No
17 January 1990 (a.m.)	Yes	Yes	Yes	No
17 January 1990 (p.m.)	Yes	Yes	Yes	Yes
28 February 1990	No	Yes	Yes	No
7 March 1990	No	Yes	Yes	Yes
14 November 1990	Yes	Yes	Yes	No
18 December 1990	No	Yes	Yes	No

* Coverage is taken to mean a reference, however brief, to proceedings in any session.

news workers make judgements about the newsworthiness of events, including select committee sessions. The danger here, as elsewhere, is that the end product of these decisions may be a very eclectic ('inaccurate') view of the work of committees. Again, the research into the televising of Parliament throws some light on this. The researchers identified 93 select committee sessions as having been televised in the period from 21 November 1989 to 23 May 1990 (although they do not specify the extent of the coverage nor on which types of programme these committees were televised) (Blumler et al., 1990b: 68). This represents 37 per cent of *all* select committee sessions held during that period. More interestingly, there appears to have been no systematic pattern to that coverage – there were omissions, such that an inquiry on a particular subject would be covered one day but not on a different day. Even the Trade and Industry Committee's sessions held in 1990 on the BAe–Rover affair did not receive constant coverage on BBC1's *Nine O'Clock News* (Table 3.4). Overall, the proportion of committee sessions covered on television across all channels and programmes varied from a low 17 per cent of total sessions held by the Select Committee on Procedure to 57 per cent for Social Services. The exception was the Committee on European Legislation, which was covered on both occasions on which it met during the sample period.

More detailed secondary analysis shows that coverage of committees is almost non-existent *on the main news bulletins*. Furthermore, only one of 15 separate committee sessions held on the 15 days which made up the broadcast news sample in the Blumler et al. study featured on the BBC1 *Nine O'Clock News*. This was the Trade and Industry Committee session on the afternoon of 17 January 1990 with Lord Young as a witness (see above). It is also curious to note here that the morning session on the same topic but with different witnesses did not feature in the news. One other committee session was used as a backdrop to a political story. This data suggests that general news values determine whether or not material from committee sessions is used: actuality from committee sessions will be used to complement stories already in the news, rather than evidence from committee sessions driving the news.

To summarize, then, television's news coverage of select committees is limited not only in the amount of time devoted to them on the main bulletins but also with respect to the eclectic nature of that coverage. More generally, and as with other media, there is a very real problem of how to transmit such considerable amounts of information to a wider public.

Press coverage of committees

Press coverage is, almost by definition, more difficult to assess. There is no comparable, recent or systematic study of the reporting of Parliament to guide the interested researcher and there are many more national daily and Sunday newspapers than national television channels, although the tabloids, by and large, ignore all but the most 'controversial' or 'news-worthy' aspects of any political story.

The three newspapers selected for this particular study – the *Financial Times*, *The Times* and the *Guardian* – gave the BAe–Rover deal an enormous amount of coverage, and that coverage was much more extensive than could be found in either television or in the tabloid press. Thus, whilst BBC1's *Nine O'Clock News* featured the BAe–Rover affair under a dozen times in 1988, each of the three broadsheets gave the matter considerably more coverage. *The Times* carried 67 stories which dealt primarily with this takeover, the *Guardian* 63 and the *Financial Times* 77 stories; almost half of that press coverage – 29 stories, 25 stories and 29 stories respectively – was during the month of March 1988, the month in which the deal was announced and a conditional agreement struck. The *Sun*, by comparison, carried only five stories in March 1988.

The relationship between the broadsheet press and select committees is, in many respects, unlike the relationship between broadcasting and select committees. Press coverage can afford a more systematic overview of select committees by following through the inquiry from beginning to end. The press is also not dependent on visuals in order to grant coverage to events.

As the above figures suggest, press coverage of the takeover deal could be examined from many angles. However, the press–committee relationship is particularly complex: are committees able to bring to light issues which have not already been discussed in the press, and would such issues be sufficiently newsworthy to attract the attention of the press? Do they have to deliver 'new' and 'controversial' material for them to be given coverage? Conversely, if reporters are only on the lookout for 'controversial' material, is it possible for them to overlook details of evidence which in retrospect become not only significant but also 'controversial'?

Analysis of the coverage of the first four select committee sessions in 1988 (Trade and Industry Committee, 1988a–d) throws some light on these questions. Three of these four sessions were held in May 1988 in the period after the deal had been agreed but before it was concluded in July 1988. The fourth was held in November 1988 as a direct result of public announcements made by the Chairman of the Rover car group in July 1988 regarding future closures of several Rover car plants; closures which came as a surprise to the committee and others because they were not mentioned, or even hinted at, during an earlier committee session in which the Chairman himself appeared as a witness. Had he, therefore, misled the committee? This fact alone made the fourth session both 'controversial' and newsworthy, and guaranteed it press coverage.

But we need to turn to the first three sessions in order to better appreciate the media–select committee relationship. There are two reasons for this: first, during these sessions the Trade and Industry Select Committee attempted to make sense of the BAe–Rover deal and, second, in these sessions there were already indications that the deal had some unusual features. If the committee was ever likely to fulfil its promise as a forum for investigative work – and the media to carry out their role as channels of communication – it would be in this period that one would need to look for the appropriate evidence. To that extent, the 1990 and 1991 sessions are less important since much of the significant information about the sale had already been made public through the publication of the National Audit Office report and the leaked memorandum (and other leaked documents!) in 1989 and after.

The analysis of the press coverage of the first three sessions leads to two major conclusions: (1) that the broadsheets tend to be extremely selective in which issues they cover, although they appear to cover broadly the same ones; and (2) that their selectivity and focus do occasionally produce significant blind spots. The first of these two conclusions should come as no surprise. Committee sessions last several hours and produce Minutes of Evidence which run into many pages and it is the reporter's duty to condense that information into short, and interesting, newspaper stories. Inevitably, the processes of selection and reproduction raise questions about the press's ability to produce an accurate account of committee sessions.

In the case of the first session, for example, the *Guardian*, the *Financial Times* and *The Times* all led their reports with the question of investment in the Rover company. Each report gave a slightly different version of how that investment would be generated, so painting a slightly different picture of the Rover car group's strengths and profitability at the time of the takeover discussions. This, one can argue, had a significant bearing on how positively or negatively one assessed the *value* of the company being sold.

Despite the brevity of these reports – from 525 words in the *Financial Times* to 312 words in *The Times* – all three newspapers also managed to mention a few of the other issues that had been discussed in the first session. Clearly, it is not always easy to make a judgement about which issues should have been selected and reported and which deserved no mention whatsoever. Journalists – individually and collectively – establish

JOHN MOORES UNIVERSITY
AVRIL ROBARTS LRC
TITHEBARN STREET
LIVERPOOL L2 2ER

their own priorities and ideally these should correspond not only to the newsworthiness of the subject matter but also to the general overall importance of the information at hand. Sometimes, as in the case discussed above, there is a fairly loose correspondence between the session and the, albeit brief, press reports. At other times, the behaviour of the press is more problematic. Thus, the second committee session was ignored by *The Times* and merited 80 words in the *Guardian*, though it did get some coverage in the *Financial Times* (548 words). The third committee session fared worse. It was completely ignored by all three broadsheets.

It would be difficult to argue that little of importance was said in these last two sessions and that this was the reason for the lack of coverage. Whilst it may be true that the evidence of the trade union witnesses in the third session could not materially affect the course of events, their contribution was an important piece of the whole jigsaw puzzle and so deserved some mention. Similarly, the evidence of Lord Young, the Trade and Industry Secretary, in the second session deserved much greater coverage than it obtained, and not only because he had made the crucial decisions about the sale of Rover. In his evidence one can find some significant pieces of information which ought to have set off alarm bells, but nothing was even considered important enough to merit mention in *The Times* or the *Guardian*.

Nineteen months later, however, and triggered off by the publication of the National Audit Office (NAO) report and the leaked memorandum, the press 'rediscovered' Lord Young's evidence. In this different context, the fact that he 'had not placed any value on Rover's sites, machinery and assets' and that he had given 'British Aerospace a "blank cheque" to sell off Rover's surplus land without even valuing it' (Hencke, 1989) was enough to send the *Guardian* into a rage.

Yet that information was never confidential. It was in Lord Young's evidence to the committee in May 1988. The real problem here is that the value of any piece of information can never be judged in isolation; the overall context alters its significance. Ideally, reporters who had carefully followed the Rover affair in 1988 ought to have been aware of the importance of Lord Young's statements at the time that the evidence was being given, and so too should have committee members. Neither, however, appeared to give that particular piece of evidence a second thought. The publication of both the NAO report which suggested that the Rover group had been undervalued and, soon after, of the leaked memorandum triggered off the whole process of rediscovery.

But the press is not always, and only, reactive. When it performs more positively as an investigative agency it can also be of immense help to committees. The most obvious example is the publication of the leaked memorandum in December 1989. The publication of a leaked confidential letter from the Auditor and Comptroller General to the Public Accounts Committee galvanized the press and politicians. The letter revealed that in July 1988 Lord Young had agreed to certain concessions being made to

BAe as part of the overall deal to buy the Rover group. These concessions included deferring payment for the Rover group until March 1990 and were worth some £38 million. Significantly, they were never made public or given in evidence to the select committee, nor were they included in the NAO report.

On one occasion, the press alerted the Trade and Industry Committee to events which, though germane to its inquiries, remained hidden from view. When the Chairman of the Rover group was asked, in May 1988, about the possible disposal of Rover assets, he replied that there were 'no assets which we have not publicly identified which I am presently aware may become available within the time horizon specifically to generate cash' (Day, 1988). And as the committee appeared to have no other information, it presumably took his comments on trust. Yet by September 1988, just over three months after he had made this statement, a report was published in the *Guardian* outlining how BAe was aiming 'to recoup the £150 million it is paying for . . . Rover from the near £400 million stock market flotation of the Leyland/DAF trucks business (a subsidiary company)' (Cornelius, 1988). In the event, the sale in May 1989 of 60 per cent of Rover's share in DAF realized £87 million – more than half of what BAe had (as it later transpired, still not yet) paid for the whole Rover group!

The report in the *Guardian* thus alerted the committee and, in due course, questions were raised about the DAF sale and its value to BAe. But, as with other examples, there was little the committee could do to change the course of events. More worrying, the committee did not seem to have sufficient relevant information about DAF and its value to Rover/ British Aerospace to be able to quiz the Chairman of the car group more effectively.

The above analysis of the coverage of the first four sessions raises many questions about the overall representation of select committees in the press as well as the efficacy and thoroughness of committees. What is clear, however, from this case study is that once a story acquires political over-tones, and more particularly party political overtones, coverage becomes more consistent simply because of its newly found status. In other words, once the leaked memorandum began to prise open the 'crevasse', the press gleefully reported the emerging 'sounds of creaking and groaning'. In this respect, not only were the post-1989 committee sessions on Rover more likely to be reported but they were also used as a means of weaving together a narrative about the affair. Thus, one would find reports about forthcoming hearings, reports about the likely outcome of those hearings, reports about why those hearings were being held, and so on. The broad sweep of committee work was both a crucial part of the ongoing debate and a source of information for *generating* debate. To take but one example, whilst both the Trade and Industry Committee and the Public Accounts Committee were mentioned in only 10 per cent of all BAe–Rover stories in the *Financial Times* in 1988, in 1989 they were mentioned in 34 per cent of all stories, and in 1990 in 82 per cent of all stories. These figures

– and figures for the other two papers point to a similar pattern – suggest that in this case study select committees became central to the continued newsworthiness of the story.

These comments, conclusions and patterns may be a feature of this case study. Other committees, looking at other topics, might feature very differently in the media. They may also play a different role *vis-à-vis* the development or unravelling of any particular series of events. More comparative work is needed before arriving at any firm conclusions. Nevertheless, the case study examined here does highlight certain features of the media/select committee relationship which need to be taken into account when exploring this topic.

Covering Parliamentary reports: the case of the Public Accounts Committee (PAC)

The allegations that the coverage of Parliament has declined should also apply to the coverage of committee reports. Whilst the discussion above has focused on a specific topic, this section will concentrate on the work of the PAC in the period October 1993 to October 1994.

The PAC is a standing committee of the House of Commons and it investigates the use and expenditure of public moneys. Like all committees of the House, the PAC is an all-party committee which reflects the divisions in the House. It works closely with the National Audit Office, a professional body of civil servants charged with investigating the expenditure of public funds.

Introducing a debate on the PAC reports in 1994, the Chair of the PAC, the MP Robert Sheldon, stated that the task of the committee was 'to ensure economy, efficiency and effectiveness' in the use of public money. Later in the debate, he restated a continuing concern of the committee: that 'any failure to respect and care for public money would be a most important cause of a decline in the efficiency of public business' (Hansard, 26 October 1994, cols 901–2).

In order to supervise the conduct of public business, the PAC selects specific areas for investigation and after an appropriate period – in which evidence might be taken from witnesses – it publishes a report on the subject. Once a year, the House is offered the opportunity to debate the work and findings of the committee. In 1994 that debate took place on 26 October; in 1993, the debate took place on 19 October. It is this period which will form the basis of the present discussion and if, as Straw alleges, there has been a decline in the coverage of Parliament and politics generally, one would expect to find this reflected in some way in the coverage of the work of the PAC.

In the 1994 debate, Robert Sheldon asked the House to take note of 49 reports included in the debating motion. (In the 1993 debate, 42 reports were tabled.) Only the most dramatic cases (and hence reports) of financial wrongdoings were referred to in the debate itself, but these reflected the tone of much of the committee's work over the previous year. The 63rd report was perhaps the most extreme case of public waste identified by the committee. It revealed how the Wessex regional health authority 'wasted' more than £20 million on computer projects by failing to keep control of expenditure. It was, by all accounts, an example of mismanagement and of lack of control by a public body. Other reports from the committee high-lighted shortcomings involving waste of public funds in a great many other bodies. All in all, the 49 PAC reports in the 1993–4 Parliamentary session contain numerous examples of mismanagement.

If Parliament was not being adequately reported would one expect these reports to be given any coverage? Would they be totally ignored (in preference to other content)?

Table 3.5 identifies both the individual PAC reports and their coverage in the media. It shows, not surprisingly, that the press gave coverage to many more reports than did either the BBC's *Nine O'Clock News* or Channel Four's evening news. The *Guardian* covered 23 reports, the *Financial Times* covered 19, and *The Times* 17 reports.

The nature of that coverage varied enormously and though the nature of the variations are not directly related to the present discussion, they have an important bearing upon it. The variations included:

- disagreements over the newsworthiness of individual reports, as in the case of the 62nd report;
- different amounts of coverage; the report on the Overseas Development Administration in the *Guardian* read, 'Delays by the ODA in handling disaster relief were criticised by the all-party Public Accounts Com-mittee in a report published yesterday. The report attacks the Ministry for "significant delays" in handling humanitarian crisis in Uganda, Eritrea and Angola' (28 July 1994);
- whether the source and name of the report was given or not. In some cases, a title was given, but not in other cases. Even within newspapers, there was a lack of consistency with regard to attribution;
- different emphasis being placed on different aspects of the reports.

Summary

The above discussion points to a continually changing relationship between the media and Parliament. That relationship has been influenced by new forms of communication, by changing priorities within the media, by changes in government and by changes in the role of MPs. Unlike American politicians in office, most British MPs do not yet have full-time press officers to 'facilitate' their relationship with the media and to ensure that they get maximum publicity (Cook, 1989). When British MPs do get similar help, we are likely to see some other changes in the relationship between the media and politicians as politicians no longer simply set about 'making laws' but henceforth devote energy also to 'making news'.

Table 3.5   *Public Accounts Committee reports and their coverage in broadsheets, BBC1's 'Nine O'Clock News' and C4, 1993–4*

No.	Subject*	released[†]	FT	Gdn	Times	BBC1	C4
		1993					
55	MoD/Gulf War	1 Dec	–	–	–	–	–
56	Forestry Commission	1 Dec	–	–	–	–	–
57	West Midlands regional health authority	26 Nov	yes*	yes*	yes	–	yes
58	DSS: Combating organized fraud	25 Nov	yes*	–	yes	–	–
59	MoD: use of training simulators	1 Dec	–	–	–	–	–
60	Inland Revenue: inheritance tax	15 Dec	yes	yes*	–	–	–
61	Health services for disabled people	16 Dec	–	–	–	–	–
62	The administration of student loans	9 Dec	yes*	yes	–	–	–
63	Wessex Regional Health Authority	10 Dec	yes	yes*	yes		
		1994					
1	Dept. of Agriculture: N. Ireland	12 Jan	–	–	–	–	–
2	Training and employment of disabled persons	12 Jan	–	–	–	–	–
3	Centre for Applied Microbiology & Research	13 Jan	–	–	–	–	–
4	MAFF	19 Jan	–	–	–	–	–
5	Export Credits Guarantee Dept.	21 Jan	–	yes*	–	–	–
6	OFTEL	27 Jan	yes*	–	–	–	–
7	Dept. of Employment computer systems	10 Feb	yes?	yes	–	–	–
8	Proper conduct of public business	28 Jan	yes	yes	yes	yes	yes
9	Grant-maintained schools	3 Feb	–	yes	yes	–	–
10	Cost of decommissioning nuclear facilities	4 Feb	yes	yes	yes	–	–
11	Excess votes	23 Feb	–	–	–	–	–
12	DHSS & acute hospital services in N. Ireland	2 Mar	–	–	–	–	–
13	Dept. of Environment: N. Ireland	3 Mar	–	–	–	–	–
14	N. Ireland Audit Office estimates	17 Mar	–	–	–	–	–
15	University purchasing in England	24 Mar	yes	–	–	–	–
16	British Council account	1 Apr	yes	yes*	–	–	yes
17	Pergau Dam	31 Mar	yes	yes*	yes	–	yes
18	Company directors disqualifications	28 Apr	–	yes	–	–	–
19	HM Customs and Excise: account matters	29 Mar	–	–	yes	–	–
20	Housing Corporation: financial management	5 May	–	–	yes	–	–
21	Sale of Scottish Bus Group	5 May	–	–	–	–	–
22	English estates: disposal of property	11 May	–	–	–	–	–
23	Development Board of Rural Wales	13 May	yes	yes	yes	–	–
24	Welsh Office accounts	19 May	yes	yes	–	–	–
25	Financial reporting to Parliament	19 May	–	–	–	–	–
26	MoD: movement of personnel, etc.	26 May	–	–	yes	–	–
27	Disposal by sale of defence equipment	26 May	–	–	–	–	–
28	Inland Revenue: account matters	29 June	–	–	–	–	–

Table 3.5   *(continued)*

No.	Subject*	released†	FT	Gdn	Times	BBC1	C4
		1994					
29	Data protection controls and safeguards	1 July	–	yes	–	–	–
30	MoD: contract for helicopter platforms	7 July	–	yes*	–	–	–
31	Dept. of Transport: sale of trust ports	8 July	yes*	yes*	yes	–	yes
32	Sale of the British Technology Group	13 July	–	–	–	–	–
33	DSS: Social Fund account	14 July	–	–	–	–	–
34	Driver and Vehicle Licensing Agency	20 July	–	–	–	–	–
35	Health & Safety Executive	21 July	–	–	–	–	–
36	Advances to health authorities: Birmingham HA	28 July	yes	yes	yes	–	–
37	Overseas Development Admin.: emergency relief	28 July	–	yes	–	–	–
38	National Audit Office estimate	19 July	–	–	–	–	–
39	The financial affairs of people with mental illness	4 Aug	–	yes*	yes	–	–
40‡	Property Services in royal palaces	8 Sept	yes*	yes*	yes	–	yes
41	Business and VAT compliance	5 Aug	–	yes*	yes*	–	–
42‡	Renewable energy research	9 Sept	yes	yes*	yes	–	–
43‡	Industrial injuries scheme	22 Sept	yes?	–	–	–	–

* The report is covered in the press but the story does not always accurately reproduce the actual title of report.

† The date in this column is the date on which the press coverage on these reports appears. Television news coverage would be on the previous day. Where there was no press coverage of a report, the date of publication was obtained from the House of Commons weekly information bulletin.

‡ These reports were not included in the 1994 debate. See *Hansard*, 26 October 1994, p. 899, col. 1.

? = half a reference, e.g. 'PAC. HMSO. £8.10'

These aside, four other points emerge from this chapter:

• Despite a lack of systematic evidence the available data do suggest that there has been a decline in Parliamentary coverage, particularly of debates (Franklin, 1995a).

• The nature of Parliamentary coverage has also changed alongside, or because of, changes in the duties and roles of lobby correspondents.

• Select committees and Public Accounts Committee reports, like other reports, have to fight their way on to the news agenda.

• Journalistic judgements on these set pieces of Parliamentary life dictate whether or not they make it on to the agenda. The more 'newsworthy', the more likely is the Parliamentary item to feature in the media. There is, however, one qualification to this which may be significant. The *Guardian*'s coverage of PAC reports is dominated by David Hencke, a

Westminster correspondent. Hencke pursues specific types of Parliamentary stories and consequently generates many more such stories for a media organization which grants them space. Without that sort of reporter, it might be that the more usual lobby material would be featured in media.

There may be other factors which have to be taken into account in order to explain the changing nature of Parliamentary coverage and some of these may apply both in the USA and in Britain. Stephen Hess identified four such factors (1993). These were:

- a shift of power away from political reporters to executives and editors located outside Washington. For his part, Straw suggests that there has been 'a generational change among political editors of broadsheet press' (1993: 5) which has brought about a vigorous questioning of the prominence of Parliament in news coverage. One other consequence of this, according to Straw, is that it has forced MPs to resort to the press release in the 'near absence' of coverage of their speeches;
- changes in technology which have allowed news from Washington to be easily replaced with news from other sources and locations;
- low consumer interest in news about Congress in an increasingly competitive media environment; and
- changes in the definitions of news, with a shift away from Congress towards other stories.

These, in general, also emphasize the dominant role of news judgements in determining coverage of certain types of political discussion, debate and communication. But they also highlight the power of commercial forces and competition in the media in bringing about a reassessment of the place of politics in the media. Herein lies the danger of commercialization and perhaps the main concern of those who see, or fear, a decline in Parliamentary and Congressional coverage. Whilst Seymour-Ure may be right in claiming that one can regret the passing away of a certain type of reporting (which could, in principle, be reintroduced) but not the passing of a type of newspaper (which could not), it is perhaps too sanguine a position. The issue is not simply the passing away of a type of newspaper but of one central feature *in* the definition of a national newspaper of importance. Furthermore, the changing content of the newspaper has not been improved by its coverage of other areas of political importance. Where other Parliamentary set pieces are reported, these are treated in a variety of ways and not always fully adequately.

These issues may be the ones which need to be addressed, because they do not simply explore the specific topic of the coverage of an institution but the more general one of communicating politics and creating the infrastructure for representative democracy. We do need to consider how governments can communicate with their citizens. What mechanisms can be created to permit a pattern of communication which offers the citizen the opportunity to become fully informed? How can the focus of attention be on all issues rather than on those which are deemed controversial? As Timothy Cook concluded from his study:

> If representative democracy is to work well, there must be more participation not merely by news organizations on behalf of the people but by the people themselves in shaping the options and decisions of government. Bringing the public back into politics, of course, entails many possible steps not connected with either Congress or the media. (1989: 177)

Yet it may be that the construction of the political process by the media has played a part in creating the public's perception of that process, and contributed to their degree of willingness to participate in it. Has it, for instance, impacted on public confidence and trust in government generally, and, if so, in what way? What the media do is crucial: different forms of coverage, such as dedicated channels for political institutions, may provide more direct access, better insights into the process, and may even galvanize some to act (see, for example, Lamb, 1992). But if we depend on commercial media, then it is clear that commercial criteria will intrude; if political actors rely on journalists as mediators, that too will influence how and what they attempt to communicate. Although this may not be the only problem of communicating politics, it certainly needs to be addressed as part of the solution.

Note

1. This section is derived in part from Negrine, 1995.

4

Specialization in News Organizations: Producing Better News?

There has long been a concern about the changing nature of the mass media and, in consequence, the changing nature of media content. One way in which this concern has been expressed is through accusations that the media have become more 'tabloid' and that public affairs content has suffered as entertainment news and features have increased in prominence (Negrine, 1994: 71–5). However, it is often difficult to justify such accusations since they are often premised on an assumption about what the content of the mass media should be like: as we have seen in the context of the concern over the decline in Parliamentary reporting (Chapter 3), there has never been a 'golden age' which can be taken to represent some sort of ideal of Parliamentary reporting. Nevertheless, what these accusations do is to highlight the need to view mass media organizations as complex and constantly changing, and the need to explore them in those terms.

The reasons, and causes, of change are too complex to explore here and they must include changing perceptions of the role and importance of different institutions in society, changing media priorities not only in terms of media perceptions of what is newsworthy but also in their targeting of different audiences and revenue streams, and general social and political change of the sort which marks off one time period from another. Often the change is imperceptible but over a longer time-span it becomes apparent that change has taken place and that the mass media have reflected it in their own way. A good example of this can be found in the (declining) fortunes of the labour correspondent in the British media: 'Traditionally, the Labour Correspondent focused on trade unions and their activities. This was at a time when the trade unions were very powerful. Now the media have switched to the opposite extreme and rarely cover trade unions' (Labour Correspondent, national broadsheet, 1994).[1]

The changing fortunes of the labour correspondent illustrate the changing priorities of the media and their perceptions of change in society. As many a labour correspondent has discovered in the last decade, external socio-political change impacts on the internal make-up of any news organization. News organizations are continually rearranging their newsgathering activities to meet changing circumstances or, perhaps more accurately, their perceptions of changing circumstances. Old specialisms (labour, aviation) decline in importance and new ones (media, law, environment) come to the fore. Moreover, the focus of these specialisms may also change with time just as the focus of the specialism may vary from one paper to the next: one media correspondent may concentrate on the 'showbiz-entertainment' side of the media, whilst another may concentrate much more on the business dimension. In other words, there is often no single newsgathering pattern which can be said to apply to 'the media'. There are significant differences between different media (broadcasting, print), and within each medium (private and public broadcasting, tabloid and broadsheet news-papers) which make definitive statements about newsgathering activities difficult to justify (see Tunstall, 1971).

One way of exploring differences between media organizations is by looking at the organization of their newsgathering activities, yet it is surprising how few such studies exist. Jeremy Tunstall's study of British specialist journalists, *Journalists at Work* (1971), still features quite prominently in discussions about the organization, and work, of journalists in the British media even though it is based on research conducted in the mid-1960s. A study of American journalists by Stephen Hess, *The Washington Reporters* (1981), offers some interesting comparative material. Other, or more recent, contributions to the study of journalism have been much narrower in their conception and operations and have illuminated only parts of the whole. We still have an inadequate grasp of the ways in which the organization of journalism relates to the production of news and newspapers. This is echoed in Kepplinger and Köcher's review of pro-fessionalism of journalists[2] across Europe where they comment that 'the structure of editorial work has *presumably* considerable consequences for journalistic activities, although this aspect has not yet been systematically investigated' (1990: 292; my italics). This is even more true of the analysis of specialist correspondents: though some work on the meaning of special-ization in journalism exists, there is usually less interest in the relationship between the organization of specialisms and the nature and quality of the news output (see, for example, Ericson et al., 1989).

Yet the specialization and personalization of newsgathering activities is a common feature of most news organizations even though it might not have reached the level found in the British and American media. Paolo Mancini's work on Italian 'political journalists' and their routines and patterns of newsgathering, for example, is suggestive of the sorts of separation of responsibilities which are part and parcel of different 'news beats' (in America) or 'specialisms' (in Britain) (1993).

That such divisions of responsibility should have evolved is perhaps not surprising since it enables the process of newsgathering to be organized on more regular and routine lines. It also ensures that individual, identifiable, journalists are located at those points where news is likely to be made (Tuchman, 1978). Sometimes, though, the reasons for the introduction of specialization and the personalization of news do not simply relate to the need to create a core of experienced staff. David Kynaston has suggested that one of the reasons behind the 'increasing number of articles being accorded bylines' on the *Financial Times* in the mid-1960s was the need to retain the loyalty of the staff at a time when poaching from other news organizations was rife (1988: 348). Nevertheless, and in addition to personalizing journalism, the use of specialists undoubtedly aided the process of creating an efficient newsgathering organization: reporters could become knowledgeable about specific areas of work and generate and process news more quickly and more regularly. In this way, both the designation (media correspondent, social services correspondent, political correspondent) and the personality (Raymond Snoddy, Media Correspondent, *Financial Times*) are deemed to add something special to the news story beneath their names. In such circumstances, a specialist journalist is someone who is known both to the public *and* to his/her sources and whose judgement is based on his/her 'expertise'.

But the increased use of specialists can also have a knock-on effect on other reporters in a news organization. According to a news executive with experience of working on several broadsheet national dailies, 'newspapers are veering far more towards specialists and away from generalists partly because the wire services are so good and the technology allows us to get wire copy so quickly that we can get most of our general news stories that way' (news executive, national broadsheet, 1994). So, the creation of specialists and the development of sophisticated information technologies can minimize the need for general reporters on the pay-roll of a national broadsheet. By contrast, a tabloid paper may rely less on specialisms because of the nature of the content which such papers seek to carry: with few designated environmental, science, medical, etc. correspondents those types of story are less likely to appear and the less likely they are to appear, the less need for such correspondents.

The proliferation of specialists can also have a knock-on effect on the way a news organization organizes its newsgathering activities and on the way that events are (or are not) covered. An experienced journalist who does not carry a specific specialist designation explained this problem in the course of a discussion as to why the media were so slow to report the implications of the 'supergun' built by British companies for the Iraqi military in 1989–90:

> There was no immediate specialist who would pick it up. The initial specialist would be the defence specialist but they get too close to the Ministry of Defence (MoD). The MoD had an interest in smothering this sort of thing. That was a problem. So you had to go to almost free-wheeling people. People had to be put on to that sort of story; it would involve a conscious decision by an editor to say to a reporter to keep an open brief on it or to take time off to do that and only that. But that does not happen very often in British journalism. We have too many specialists, we are too heavy on titles and too compartmentalized. (Broadsheet journalist, 1994)

While more and more reporters are finding their names under headlines and above stories, it is less obvious whether or not that degree of specialization has had any perceptible impact on the quality or the content of the news stories they write and whether or not it makes for better media. In fact, there has been a noticeable absence of academic interest in the whole question of what specialist correspondents bring to news stories. One obvious illustration of this can be found in Schlesinger and Tumber's (1994) book on 'the treatment of crime and criminal justice' in the media. Though they acknowledge that this category of news was covered by 'crime', 'home affairs' and 'legal affairs' correspondents – once again different media cover the same sort of terrain in different ways – there is no exploration of either the rationale for such a division of labour or the differences in content that may subsequently arise. This is somewhat surprising since these sorts of issues impinge directly on the whole question of media performance. Thus, if newsgathering activities are too compartmentalized, reporters are not specialists or have little knowledge about specific areas then obvious gaps will appear in the coverage. Conversely, if reporters are specialists and get too close to their sources, it may act as a restraint on how they cover issues: 'you get to know the people too well and you are building relationships with people which may colour the way you approach a story' (section editor, national broadsheet).

The aim of this chapter is to contribute to our understanding of specialisms in journalism and the implications of specialization for news coverage. Rather than concentrate on one group of specialists ('media') or on reporters who cover one area (e.g. 'crime and criminal justice') this chapter will examine specialization as it relates to the development of one particular news story. In this way, it will become possible to look at the way different news organizations organize their newsgathering activities and the possible relationship between that organizational pattern and the news output. The three key questions which will interest us here are:

- Which specialisms cover particular stories and why?
- Does the content of the news stories differ according to which specialist reporter is involved?
- Does specialization in journalism lead to 'better' media?

Specialist correspondents: what's in a name?

Specialist correspondents are of relatively recent origin and their proliferation is partly related to the increasing involvement of the state in many features of contemporary life as well as to the growth in the number of governmental departments. In general terms, new government responsibilities, and departments, spawn new journalistic specialisms to cope with them or, alternatively, lead to a widening of certain journalistic responsibilities (Seymour-Ure, 1968: 251–63).

Such statements have to be qualified, since news organizations have long had structures which reflect a division of labour in journalism. Whilst bylines and designations were rare before the Second World War, even a cursory glance at the make-up of *The Times* leads one to conclude that responsibilities were designated to different groups of journalists. In the

1920s, for example, *The Times* included articles by a 'Medical Correspondent', 'a Labour Correspondent' and 'an Agricultural Correspondent'. In the same period, the *Daily Express* had a plethora of 'critics' in the arts – cinema, art, music, dramatic – and it also had an 'Air Correspondent' and a Parliamentary representative. Both newspapers also had, needless to say, City pages with City editors. These arrangements are well reflected in Wickham Steed's account of a newspaper office in 1938:

> The monarch or, at least, the prime minister, is the editor. A foreign editor and a number of assistant editors are his colleagues and advisers. Other colleagues are the home and foreign news editors, the chief sub-editors, the City editor and the heads of various departments. Lesser folk . . . are sub-editors, home and foreign, and the reporters. Special places are held by the Parliamentary reporting staffs, the lobby correspondents and the expert [*sic*] writers on innumerable subjects. (1938: 228)

It remains unclear from Steed's account who these 'experts' were and what the nature of their expertise was. Were they like the defence correspondents who became specialists on account of 'the staggering technical cold war complexities of the subject' or were they like the 'Home Department Reporter' who brought 'specialist knowledge to Home Office subjects . . . like prison reform or immigration' (Seymour-Ure, 1968: 251). Or were they specialists by the nature of their location (e.g. Parliament, Paris) rather than by the nature of the subject matter? Moreover, how do these divisions of responsibility sit alongside the more usual division of specialist reporters into those who 'specialize in gallery, court, or grandstand reporting' and those who 'specialize in the behind-the-scenes of politics, crime or whatever the topic may be' (Tunstall, 1971: 74)?

The very different ways in which one can describe specialists and their areas of responsibility suggests that many factors account for the mosaic of journalism. On the one hand, news organizations seek to create specialisms in order to divide up responsibilities and so ensure a supply of news from a multiplicity of sources; on the other hand, they seek to ensure that those who supply that news have a degree of familiarity with the areas they cover. So specialization is something which is to the advantage both of a news organization and of the readership. It is also to the advantage of reporters who may have a desire or wish to specialize in specific areas (for whatever reason).

Tunstall has suggested that the designation of a journalist as a specialist has more to do with an editor's decision, and thus organizational needs, than with special competence in a specific field. As he puts it, when 'he is designated as a specialist by his Editor the journalist becomes if not an instant expert, at least an instant specialist' (1971: 76). Nevertheless, and with time,

> specialists inevitably acquire a good deal of tactical autonomy, based on their knowledge, their reputation and by-line, their specialized sources of information, their personal choice (in most cases) of which stories to cover, and their

membership of an informal group of 'competitor-colleagues' who in practice define the specialist field's current story agenda. (Tunstall, 1983: 188)

But even a 'specialist' area can be a fairly broad one and though there may be sub-specialisms there are also some obvious groupings of interests. As Seymour-Ure noted, science correspondents were expected to cover a diverse area. As he explains, the range of topics covered 'plus the movement of particular developments in and out of the field, is reflected in the variety of papers' arrangements for science writing. The commonest connection . . . is between *science and medicine.* Other common connections are with *technology, defence* (decreasingly) and *aviation*' (1977b: 61).

Hansen's recent research confirmed the existence of this general pattern. He noted that

> while individual newspapers have varying degrees of sub-specialisms under the general areas of science, technology, medicine, health and environment (e.g. consumer affairs, transport, computing) the journalists interviewed . . . represented three primary specialisms: science/technology/computers . . . environment/agriculture, and health/medicine/social affairs. (1994: 113)

Schlesinger et al. also identified broad, and co-existing, categories of specialism in their study of media coverage of 'crime and criminal justice':

> Journalists covering crime and criminal justice fall under the rubrics of 'Crime', 'Home Affairs' and 'Legal Affairs'. Although these categories encompass the whole field, not all national newspapers have separate correspondents covering each area as there are variations in the designations of personnel (Schlesinger et al., 1991: 406)

Thus, although the home affairs correspondent's area of coverage is 'shaped mainly by the remits of the Home Office' (Schlesinger et al., 1991: 407), they also point out that the 'scope of Home Affairs varies across the press and can at times depend on the news editor's definition of the story, with the previous experience and contacts of the individual correspondent also playing a part in defining the brief' (Schlesinger et al., 1991: 407).

Another factor which may account for variations is the changing nature of, and in, the area of interest over time. Changes in the nature of crime, e.g. an increased interest in financial and institutional crimes and a general downgrading of crime news in the press, tend to impact on what a crime reporter can cover. Such shifts of interest and responsibility are not new and allow for the growth of new specialist areas (media, computing/technology) but also lead to the demise of older ones. The classic example of this is the demise of the labour correspondent. According to Tunstall, 'Labour correspondents . . . have long been called "Industrial" correspondents . . . but by the 1960s there was an increasing tendency for the field to split into Industrial (Labour) and Industrial (Industry)' (1971: 20). As the nature of the industrial landscape changed and the fortunes of the labour movement dramatically declined, the need for a labour correspondent has all but disappeared (Hill, 1993). In fact, it was not too long ago that newspapers used to carry labour news pages in the same way that they carried Parliamentary pages.

But while the fortunes of the industry/labour correspondent declined, the fortunes of the industry/business correspondent have flourished since the 1980s, reflecting the increased news interest in finance and business as that sector of economic activity blossomed. Furthermore, interest in industry segued into interest in business and finance, sometimes without a clear line of demarcation. Wayne Parsons quotes from *The Economist* to argue that

> financial journalists have increasingly had to compete not only with each other, but with in-house economists and analysts employed by City firms. They have also had to survive the specialization of their own profession: where once only a financial editor wrote, there are now industry correspondents and banking reporters and energy editors and Euromarket reporters. (1989: 208)

The changing fortunes of specialisms and the absence of 'clearly defined boundaries' between them raise many interesting questions. It is unclear, for example, why the fortunes of areas of interest change, how areas of inquiry acquire or lose their respective boundaries, and how the responsibility for covering any particular event is distributed to different specialists either within a single newspaper or across newspapers. As we have seen, the news organization does play a part in designating specialist areas and in allocating specialist correspondents. It may build up an area (education, media, law) because it wishes to bring in new readers and/or advertising revenue; it may decide which of its reporters is best suited to cover that area; it might decide which areas are of interest to its readers and in keeping with the traditions of the paper. All these decisions are in the main made by executives, though specialists will retain some power to determine the actual contours of their designated area. One reporter described how he became a specialist:

> One day I was called in by [news executive] who said, 'I think we need a general team of reporters. We are missing a lot of stories because things are falling between specialisms.' And I was given the job to run a team of general reporters. Within three weeks, I was called back and told, 'I have changed my mind. There are more pressing things. I really need a third person to back this [area] up. I'd like you to do that.' (specialist correspondent, national broadsheet, 1994)

Sometimes, though, specialists will be able to exercise some control over their future careers and remain in their specialist area – but only if news executives consent.

Apart from sound organizational reasons for creating a system of specialisms within a news organization, does the designation of specialism have any other meaning or advantage? Common-sense understanding of the designation of someone as a 'specialist' suggests a degree of knowledge and expertise usually gained through long-term study or training. This is akin to the set of attributes usually associated with the idea of professionalism –

systematic theory, authority, community sanction, ethical codes, culture – but which are clearly missing in journalism (Tunstall, 1971: 69). In other words, the non-routine nature of journalistic work and the unsystematic, personal, experiential and intuitive nature of the 'search procedures' (Tunstall, 1971: 27) make it unlikely that the common-sense understandings of 'specialist' will apply fully. Stephen Hess' research into American news organizations confirms this since, as he reports, only in 'two beats – diplomacy and science – does a majority of the reporters list among the magazines read regularly the specialized publications that are related to assignments', and 'less than a quarter of the law beat reporters regularly reads law journals' (Hess, 1981: 64). Ericson et al.'s court-beat 'reporters repeatedly demonstrated that they lacked knowledge of the court and legal system' (1989: 39). However, Hansen's study of the coverage of science in the British media suggests that there can be significant variations between specialists in news organizations, as there can be across news organizations in different countries (Köcher, 1986). The reporters who covered science in Hansen's study did 'regularly scan a range of science journals and publications for relevant material' (1990: 14) and some – 12 of the 31 surveyed – had 'a qualification and a primary qualification in science' (1994: 113) though the rest either had an arts/social science background or journalistic training. Köcher's comparison of British and German reporters suggests not only that British journalism is a 'younger' profession but that it is made up of fewer academically qualified people than the German equivalent (1986: 50).

Such variations may be significant in understanding the organization of journalism within, as well as across, different countries but they also foreground the dilemma between creating a breed of professional, experienced and intellectually competent reporters as opposed to a breed of news-hungry and journalistically skilled ones. There are certainly strong elements of the latter in British journalism. In this respect, a specialist is a particular category of journalist who 'has developed an expertise interest' rather than one who comes to his/her (original) specialism with that expertise or interest already developed. As they acquire contacts and experience in one field they become specialists and/or experts in that field. It may then be possible for them to carry those skills into a similar specialism in another media organization or into a cognate specialism (as we shall see below). Indeed, some news organizations do encourage journalists to experience different areas of work and even possibly move from one specialism to another in order to prevent them from settling into too comfortable an existence and from atrophying in it. As one section editor on the *Financial Times* explained:

> No, I have no particular expertise in [my current] area. I think you would find pretty much everywhere in the FT that what counts is people's journalistic expertise rather than their subject expertise. In fact, the person who becomes too expert is moved on because we don't want people to lose sight of the fact that they are journalists. (1994)

There is, then, a tension between privileging the specialist side of jour-nalism by allowing for expertise to develop and having to guard against the risk that reporters will become too dependent on, or get too close to, their source or privileging journalistic skills which would allow for almost total interchangeability of roles. In other words, is the specialist a specialist with the skills of a journalist or a journalist with specialist knowledge? As Golding and Middleton put it, 'there is still in journalism widespread regard for the traditional skills of the general reporter' (1982: 134), a point made equally forcefully by Seymour-Ure: 'Most Science correspondents have "science" somewhere in their background. "Back-ground" is the right word: *their journalistic skills are what really matter*' (1977b: 62; my italics).

With the skills of the reporter under their belts, correspondents become mobile, flexible and they can be substituted as, or when, necessary: all journalists, in theory, can then ask the right sorts of questions irrespective of the area under investigation. However, what distinguishes one from another will be experience in journalism (and of reporting a particular area) and the contacts built up over the years of practising journalism. Hence, it is much easier for specialists to move across media or into cognate areas rather than into very different areas of specialism, though this can happen. In the early 1970s Clare Dover was interviewed by Seymour-Ure in her capacity as a science correspondent for the *Daily Telegraph* and some years later by Golding and Middleton in her capacity as a reporter of social and welfare issues for the *Daily Express*, and more recently for Hansen's (1992a) study of science coverage in her capacity as a medical correspondent. In fact, it is possible that the 'revolving door' nature of such movement is in no small part helped by the 'youthful' nature of the British journalistic profession compared to others (Köcher, 1986) although there is insufficient comparative work in this area to provide definitive answers.

Nevertheless, the importance of the transferability of skills cannot be underestimated since it does permit specialists to delve into areas about which they may not have in-depth knowledge even though these fall within their remit. A science correspondent is unlikely to be equally well con-versant with all aspects of science, just as the social affairs correspondents have significant gaps in their knowledge of the whole field of social security and welfare issues. Expertise, according to Golding and Middleton, 'is spread thinly' (1982: 136), though they had to admit that the correspon-dents were well informed. Wayne Parsons' view that financial journalists are not so much involved in the generation and discussion of ideas as in 'retailing information' (1989: 8–9, 206–8) usually culled from other sources also suggests that they possess a thin layer of expertise.

The definition of a specialist's job by the news organization, however, goes beyond simply setting out the general area of operation and includes the expression of preferences for certain types of news and 'knowledge'. Just as Golding and Middleton's journalists avoid the more un-newsworthy aspects of reporting the welfare state, including detailed information about benefits, on account of the 'perceived dullness and unimportance of social security' (1982: 136), the labour correspondent 'may want to cover a story about industrial health, but will be told that a current strike has more news "strength"' (Tunstall, 1971: 126). In this way, the 'experienced' specialist internalizes the needs of the organization and comes to define his/her own specialist area and 'knowledge' in relation to what he/she has experienced in his/her work as a specialist correspondent within a particular news organization.

> If am writing for the business pages, I won't worry about making it too technical but if I am writing for the Home page I'll write more about the politics, the domestic aspects of the story. (labour correspondent, national broadsheet, 1994)

> As you academics would say, I have internalized the value system of the newspaper. More practically, I know what I can get in and what I would not. (specialist correspondent, national broadsheet, 1994)

Overlaps and divisions of responsibility

Although some areas of reporting have natural boundaries, news stories often cut across them. Rarely are news stories complete in themselves and, as the term implies, they provide a narrative structure for relating a number of different and interconnected themes. A story about coal mines could focus, for example, on productivity, on employment, on devastation in coal communities, on political controversies over closures/redundancies or on a combination of all of these and more points of interest. In cases such as this it is common to find several reporters providing the coverage.

> When you have a major [industrial] policy decision like that and it affects a specific area, you will always have the specialist correspondent. You would probably have some political input as well. What you will never have is just the political journalist. (section editor, national broadsheet, 1994)

The sorts of overlap described above usually occur most often in areas where the story in question has a strong political angle. In such cases, the political angle appears to gain precedence; it could also be that the political implications of events/issues dominate British news judgements. According to Golding and Middleton, 'all news about social policy, social security and welfare news is above all news about politics. By politics is meant Westminster' (Golding and Middleton, 1982: 114). The same would probably apply to certain areas of fraud, e.g. the Bank of Credit and Commerce International (BCCI), political crime/violence, business matters. Even a study of the coverage of 'mad cow disease' (BSE) was forced to conclude that

> the agenda for news coverage of science is set, not by the scientific community as such, but by developments in the forum of formal political activity. [Also] . . . science and scientific discourse have to contend with a range of other discourses,

primarily political discourses but also legal, economic, and ethico-moral discourses. (Hansen, 1992b: 7)

If there are overlaps, are there frictions over the way such overlaps are resolved and decisions about coverage made? The way such work is allocated to different reporters and the way reporters have work shared out between them does not appear to be a source of major friction. Certainly there is no documentation which would support a contrary view. In the course of research on the 1988 BAe–Rover takeover (see Chapter 2) and the pit closure announcement of 1992 (see Chapter 4) some 30 reporters were interviewed and none voiced anxieties over allocations. When asked about such issues, reporters resorted to explanations such as 'It's simply the way it works', 'It's related to what I had covered before so the news desk will obviously send that sort of thing to me', and even 'it's all *ad hoc* and there is a lot of co-operation.'

What comes through quite clearly is the fact that the specialist is an employee of the news organization and consequently has his/her room for manoeuvre limited by news executives. Admittedly, that role as employee has to be counterbalanced by the 'power' to define the nature of the news stories (Tunstall, 1983: 188–91) but it further feeds the ambivalence of the role and power of the specialist journalist.

Does the content of the news stories differ according to which specialist reporter is involved? Discussions of specialists have provided many insights into the ways such reporters work and the differences that exist between different specialists, differences which have an impact on their careers, ability to generate their own stories, ability to control their own operations, and so on. What has remained under-researched is the internal working of news organizations and the ways in which decisions about who covers what stories are made and, more particularly, whether such decisions actually impact on the content and nature of news stories.

In essence, there are two positions with respect to the above set of questions. At one extreme, we find the following:

> I think who writes the story makes an enormous difference particularly on a paper, like ours, where there isn't massive sub-editing. Our stories are often edited and cut back but there is not a massive rewrite or the selection of what to write about. (Labour correspondent, national broadsheet, 1994)

At the other, the following: 'You can't look at each and every story and say only I could have done that. What does create a difference is the stories I generate myself' (media correspondent, national broadsheet, 1994).

These two positions would perhaps apply to all journalism and they trace the sorts of difference which would be evident in all news organizations: the more autonomy reporters have the more 'individualized' the story; the more the story is the product of particular individual endeavour, the more it will reflect its author's interests – yet there is always in the background the interest of the news organization and fellow professionals to consider.

But cutting across these dimensions are other considerations which permit one to note differences between reporters working in different media. National and local media vary enormously in how they cover particular stories: the local journalist would be much more concerned about giving the local angle (Deacon and Golding, 1994: 150). Unlike the national reporter – again it may depend on which national medium he/she is employed by – the local reporter may not have access to national figures. There is a hierarchy in the media which ranks media and of which sources are aware and respond to in different ways (Hess, 1986). One outcome of this national/local divide can be found in Deacon and Golding's study of the coverage of the 'poll tax'. Whilst political specialists on national newspapers mentioned parliamentary and political actors in 93 per cent of their stories, local government specialists mentioned them in only 71 per cent of theirs. By contrast, local councillors featured in 22 per cent and 63 per cent of stories respectively. 'News stories by political specialists reported a narrower range of political views than local government correspondents, mainly focusing on parliamentary actors. By doing so, they also emphasized different themes in their reporting.' The former focused on party political responses to the poll tax, the latter on such things as the implementation of the tax (1994: 160–1).

So there are important differences within journalism and its organization which make it difficult to generalize. Yet generalized statements are common in this field of study and they often have a bearing on whether this form of organization makes for better or worse media. One could argue, for instance, that a news medium built around the expertise of its reporters would be more sensitive to their needs and their judgements about the value of its content and the content of their news stories. It would also be sensitive to the needs of its specific audience. At the other extreme, a heavily edited paper such as a tabloid would be more concerned with producing an entertainment package in which expertise and knowledge of specific areas is of little specific value.

A different analysis altogether would suggest that it is not the expertise, professionalism, integrity or honesty of journalists which is (or should be) really the issue 'but rather the choice of topics and highlighting of issues, the range of opinion permitted expression, the unquestioned premises that guide reporting and commentary and the general framework imposed on the presentation of a certain view of the world' (Chomsky, 1989: 11–12). In this view, the research problem is not the complexity of news organizations but the overriding conception of news and news values which direct attention away from critical questioning of positions.

Such a view may have some merit but it cannot overlook the need to make sense of the daily work routines of reporters in their search for information to make sense of events. To suggest, as Chomsky does, that reporters are professional yet somehow select the 'wrong' topics for analysis *is* a contradiction which needs to be resolved: for a British journalist, being professional is being a 'bloodhound', always 'hunting for news' (Köcher, 1986: 63).

So how do the 'bloodhounds' hunt for news, and how successful is the hunt? These questions are explored in the next section.

Who covers what: the performance of the broadsheet press in their coverage of the British Aerospace takeover of the Rover group in 1988

The long-drawn-out saga of the BAe–Rover affair has already been described in this book. For our present purposes, it is only necessary to note the period under investigation for analysis. That period stretches from March 1988 – the initial announcement – to February 1991 and the preliminary conclusion of the affair, though, in fact, it was not until May 1993 that BAe finally agreed to repay some of the 'sweeteners' (£57 million) given to it in 1988 (Waller, 1993).

During this protracted period there was not one event or one story but a series of related occurrences each of which could have been dealt with – and often was dealt with – as a separate one. One such series of occurrences could be the select committee hearings; another could be the European Commission judgment; another the domestic political furore, and so on. Each of these occurrences could therefore be covered either by the relevant specialists (politics, motoring, Europe) or by a single specialist following the takeover from beginning to end. However, both options are beset by problems. As for the first option, in high-profile areas such as this more than one specialist is often called in to offer a 'rounded coverage' and to explore a variety of angles. Such a co-operative exercise can sometimes produce blind spots as the distinct parts of the whole remain unconnected. As regards the second option, allocating one specialist to the story is organizationally difficult: what about holidays, clashes of events that may need to be covered? Which specialist should be chosen – motoring (if there is one), politics, industrial affairs? How long a commitment is involved? As will be argued below, each newspaper covered the story in a way which reflected specific organizational solutions and its own way of defining what the story was 'about'.

Before turning to the quantitative exploration of these issues, it is important to make one further observation. When the proposed takeover was first announced by Lord Young in March 1988, few could have known – or could have guessed – that the affair would rumble on for so long. At that point the decisions of different editors reflected a decision about the nature and content of the 'BAe-Rover' story. But, even here, surface appearances can be extremely deceptive; news editors did not have a free hand. As it happened, on the day of the announcement (1 March 1988), most of the motor industry correspondents were attending the Geneva Motor Show! Thus, the *Financial Times* found that its specialist was not available to report the story but had to send snippets of information on the first day and then provide longer pieces on subsequent days and once he had had an opportunity to digest the news from London.

Analysing news content

For the purpose of this analysis, all news items in the *Financial Times*, the *Guardian* and *The Times* which focused on the BAe–Rover affair as their primary concern in the period March 1988 to February 1991 were clipped and coded. (A decision was made to exclude the tabloids on the grounds that their coverage was minimal. In March 1988, for example, the *Sun* carried only five stories compared to the *Guardian*'s 25!) The authors of each news item were identified and so it was possible to follow the 'career' of the story over the three-year period as it moved in and out of focus. Unfortunately, even such a simple exercise as identifying the author of an item is fraught with problems. First, though it is easy to identify the author by name, it is less easy to denote his/her specialism. Sometimes the name is followed by a byline, sometimes not; there is no consistent pattern across the papers. This may not be a problem in the case of correspondents who are obviously specialists but there is a whole category of infrequent contributors who have no designated specialism.

Second, even though there may be no designated specialism, it is clear that certain named journalists contribute to particular sections of newspapers. Thus, journalist X may not be designated as a specialist but he/she writes on the financial aspects of company policies, say. Whilst strictly speaking journalist X may not merit the specialist tag, he/she 'specializes' in certain types of story. An example of this would be the way the *Guardian* currently (1994–5) deals with the media field: its media correspondent (Andrew Culf) would deal with a range of media stories but when such stories have a strong business angle they are covered by others (Lisa Buckingham, Ben Laurence) from the City office of the paper.

Third, like other institutions newspaper offices experience change. Between 1988 and 1991 there was a turnover of staff in the three news-papers selected for the content analysis. This change was of two kinds. There were migrations; and journalists changed their designation. Thus, in the course of about two years one correspondent moved from being an industrial correspondent to industrial editor to business editor. He then moved to another paper! Another moved from being labour correspondent to business correspondent. Whilst these changes may be reflecting a concern to drop the labour/industry labels in favour of business ones, it also impacts on the broader question of the whole meaning of specialisms. Are they merely labels which can easily be exchanged? And is this so for all fields, e.g. including politics, or just for some?

All these factors make it much less easy to link up a specialist field with a particular story. Nevertheless, by locating the author of the story in the appropriate 'specialist' field, e.g. politics, industry, motor industry, it becomes possible to examine the way in which different newspapers handled the story. Tables 4.1a–4.1c look at the way in which three broad-sheet newspapers treated the story. These tables identify the first-named journalist on every news item over three years. Where a journalist

Table 4.1 *Number of stories on the British Aerospace–Rover group takeover written by first-named correspondents in a selection of newspapers*

(a) *Financial Times*

	March 1988		1988		1989		1990	
	n	%	n	%	n	%	n	%
Done	7	24	27	35	13	28	6	12
Griffiths	4	14	5	7	3	6	2	4
Riddell	3	10	3	4	–	–	–	–
Owen	2	7	3	4	3	6	3	6
Dawkins	1	3	8	10	–	–	–	–
Lynch	–	–	3	4	–	–	–	–
Leadbeater	–	–	–	–	7	15	6	12
Cheeseright	–	–	–	–	2	4	–	–
Atkins	–	–	–	–	–	–	5	10
Kellaway	–	–	–	–	–	–	7	14
Smith, A.	–	–	–	–	–	–	5	10
Stevens	–	–	–	–	–	–	2	4
'Lex'	4	14	10	13	4	9	–	–
'Leader'	2	7	3	4	1	2	1	2
Others	6	21	11	14	13	28	4	8
No named reporter	–	–	4	5	1	2	8	16
Total	29		77		47		49	

* Percentage figures are rounded up or down as appropriate.

(b) *The Times*

	March 1988		1988		1989		1990	
	n	%	n	%	n	%	n	%
Brewerton	5	17	6	9	3	9	3	8
'City staff'	2	7	3	4	1	3	–	–
'Leader'	1	3	2	3	–	–	–	–
Ward	4	14	9	13	–	–	–	–
Fletcher	1	3	7	10	–	–	–	–
Narborough	–	–	3	4	2	6	–	–
Gunn	–	–	–	–	5	15	7	18
Ford	–	–	–	–	3	9	3	8
'Political staff'	–	–	–	–	–	–	2	5
Other	10	34	22	33	10	29	16	41
No named reporter	6	21	15	22	9	27	8	20
Total	29		67		33		39	

* Percentage figures have been rounded up or down as appropriate.

(c) *Guardian*

	March 1988		1988		1989		1990	
	n	%	n	%	n	%	n	%
Smith	6	24	16	25	1	3	1	2
Cornelius	6	24	15	24	8	20	2	5
'Leader'	2	8	4	6	3	8	2	5
McRae	2	8	4	6	–	–	–	–
Palmer	2	8	5	8	–	–	3	7
Hencke	–	–	–	–	15	38	23	54
Nettleton	–	–	–	–	3	8	–	–
Travis	–	–	–	–	–	–	3	7
No named reporter	–	–	5	8	2	5	4	9
Others	7	30	14	21	8	20	5	12
Total	25		63		40		43	

* Percentage figures have been rounded up or down as appropriate.

contributed only one story per year, he/she was included in the 'Other' category.

One central point stands out: that across the three broadsheets no single correspondent played a dominant role in reporting the BAe–Rover story over the three years. For the *Financial Times*, Kevin Done, its motor industry correspondent, was a key figure in 1988 (35 per cent of all stories), and in 1989 (28 per cent) but by 1990 his contribution, though still important, had plummeted to 12 per cent of all stories (Table 4.1a). The same is true of *The Times* where Daniel Ward, its motor industry correspondent wrote 13 per cent of all primary stories in 1988 but his replacement (Kevin Eason) rarely featured in 1989 and 1990 (Table 4.1b). For the *Guardian*, Andrew Cornelius, industrial correspondent, was a key figure in 1988 (24 per cent of all stories) but less so in 1989 (20 per cent of all stories) and by 1990 he wrote only 5 per cent of all stories (Table 4.1c). The overall (1988, 1989, 1990) contribution of these three correspondents amounted to 26 per cent, 7 per cent and 17 per cent respectively.

Part of the explanation undoubtedly lies in the changing character of the story. In March 1988, the takeover discussions involved BAe and the government principally. The industrial and business dimensions of the affair were overlaid with political considerations since the whole affair was part of the government's privatization programme. Moreover, Rover always seemed to cause political 'headaches' for successive governments, and BAe was a major defence contractor. But by 1990 the location of the story had switched to an overtly political one. BAe had by then been in charge of Rover for nearly two years and so there were no industrial or business considerations to take note of. More critical was the political furore surrounding alleged government help to BAe in 1988 which was in contravention, so it was believed, of EC judgments. This furore began in

November 1989 and related to the publication of a critical report about the sale of Rover to BAe, and the leaking of the 'sweeteners' memo to the *Guardian* (see Chapter 2 for more details).

The other factor which helps explain this pattern is that since newspapers usually attempt to give a 'rounded' account, they call in different contributors. This inevitably decreases the dominance of any one contributor. In actual fact, a total of 22 different named reporters were coded for the *Guardian* over the period 1988–90; 34 for *The Times* and 32 for the *Financial Times*. Many contributed no more than one story but that, in itself, casts some doubts on the validity of the case made out for specialist correspondents. If the story could be covered by anyone, including stories written by but not credited to any reporter, where is the case for specialism?

Tables 4.2a–4.2c identify the location of the author of the news item by category, e.g. political, industrial, City. The *Guardian*'s political reporter, David Hencke, became the major storyteller as the focus of the story became overtly political in 1989. The story had originally been covered by the industry/business correspondents (the *Guardian* has no motor industry correspondent as such). The *Financial Times* also demonstrates the shift towards the political angle and away from the motor industry background of the story. For *The Times*, the shift is also towards the political aspect of the story, but in this case it also represented a shift away from a City/ finance story, rather than a motor industry story *per se*.

It is quite possible to justify this pattern; it parallels the twists and turns of the story and the shifting locations of interest. However, it does raise a fundamental question about the nature of specialism in journalism. If the strength of the specialist system lies in the opportunity which it affords journalists of standing to use their background knowledge and expertise to discuss events that take place in the socio-political sphere, how does one explain the patterns identified in the tables?

The initial announcement of the story is covered by different reporters: in the first month of coverage (March 1988), the *Guardian* placed it in the business/industry field; the *Financial Times* emphasized the motor industry perspective whilst in *The Times*, the City and finance correspondents dominated the coverage even though the paper had a motor industry correspondent. Clearly, the announcement of the BAe proposals *vis-à-vis* Rover crossed easily definable boundaries. It was a complex story over which many different correspondents could claim jurisdiction. Each could bring their own expertise and each would contribute something unique to the story, though the question remains whether these different perspectives give an adequate all-round coverage. Does the motor industry emphasis play down the political aspects of the story? Does the City/business emphasis play down both the motor industry and political perspective?

It is difficult to draw any firm conclusions from the available data, for two reasons. First, because of the changing nature of the story over the three years, it becomes impossible to find a pattern that would allow us to identify gaps in the coverage which can be accounted for by reference to a

Table 4.2 *Designation of correspondent and number of stories contributed to specific newspapers on the BAe–Rover affair, 1988–90*

(a) *Financial Times*

	March 1988		1988		1989		1990	
	n	%	n	%	n	%	n	%
Motor industry	11	37	33	42	16	32	8	16
Politics/Parl	6	20	10	13	6	12	16	33
Industrial	1	3	3	4	7	15	6	12
Aerospace	1	3	1	1	–	–	1	2
'Lex'	4	13	10	13	4	8	–	–
EC/Brussels	1	3	8	10	4	8	7	14
Leaders	2	7	3	4	1	2	1	2
Others	4	3	6	8	11	22	2	4
No reporter named	–	–	4	5	1	2	8	16
Total*	30		78		50		49	

* Percentage figures have been rounded up or down as appropriate.

(b) *The Times*

	March 1988		1988		1989		1990	
	n	%	n	%	n	%	n	%
City/finance	11	42	17	25	7	21	4	12
Politics/Parl	2	8	10	15	10	30	14	42
General reporters	–	–	5	8	3	9	–	–
Motor industry	4	15	9	13	–	–	–	–
Industry	1	4	1	2	2	6	–	–
EC/Brussels	1	4	3	4	–	–	4	12
Air corresp.	1	4	1	2	–	–	–	–
Leaders	–	–	2	3	–	–	–	–
Others	–	–	4	6	2	6	2	6
No reporter named	6	23	15	22	9	27	9	27
Total*	26		67		33		33	

* Percentage figures have been rounded up or down as appropriate.

(c) *Guardian*

	March 1988		1988		1989		1990	
	n	%	n	%	n	%	n	%
Politics/Parl.	–	–	7	11	22	55	35	71
Industrial	12	48	31	51	11	28	4	8
City/finance	2	8	4	7	2	5	–	–
Leaders	2	8	4	7	3	8	2	4
EC/Brussels	2	8	4	7	–	–	3	6
Others	7	28	6	10	–	–	–	–
No reporter named	–	–	5	8	2	5	5	10
Total	25		61		40		49	

* Percentage figures have been rounded up or down as appropriate.

specialism or a specific journalist. Second, over a longer period information surfaces in very different ways and what may seem an omission, or a gap, in the course of one month's coverage may be anything but in the course of a longer period of study. For example, a piece about a Rover subsidiary appeared in the *Guardian* some three months before a similar story appeared in *The Times* (Negrine, 1992).

There are, however, other ways in which one can begin to offer some clues as to how different specialisms relate to this news story. This can be done by examining the way these three national broadsheets covered the Trade and Industry Select Committee hearings on the Rover takeover.

Specialists and the coverage of select committees

Which reporter/correspondent has legitimate calls on covering a Parliamentary select committee looking at a complex mosaic such as the BAe–Rover affair? Does the committee deserve the attention of the specialist concerned or of the political reporter? And does this make any difference?

During 1988, there were four Trade and Industry Committee sessions. Three took place in May and the fourth in November. Witnesses appearing in May included Professor Roland Smith (then Chairman of British Aerospace), Graham Day (then Chairman of the Rover group), Lord Young (then Secretary of State for Trade and Industry) and assorted trade unionists. In the light of events taking place between May and September 1988, such as announcements of plant closures, the Trade and Industry Committee recalled Graham Day in order to ascertain whether or not he had misled it when giving evidence in May. As a result, the period prior to November was punctuated by newspaper stories which previewed his appearance in front of the committee. But, as Table 4.3 shows, apart from the *Financial Times*, there appears to be no consistency in the coverage of these sessions.

If one carries out a similar analysis for 1990, the results are equally interesting, if a bit more complex (Table 4.4). It is important to recall that 1990 saw the political dimension of the story gain precedence over everything. David Hencke's role in the *Guardian* coverage is without doubt one of the most obvious features here but the other papers are less consistent. *The Times* coverage is very limited and the political reporter, Sheila Gunn, dominates it. But the *Financial Times* coverage is puzzling: of the five sessions two were covered by the motor industry correspondent and two by the industrial editor even though the overall coverage surrounding these occurrences was written by political reporters. What we have then is a number of set pieces within the Palace of Westminster which are covered by a range of specialisms: industrial editors, Westminster correspondents, motor industry correspondents, political reporters and others.

What of the coverage itself? There are obvious variations in the level of coverage. For example, coverage of the first session ranged from 312 words

Table 4.3   *Trade and Industry Committee sittings on the Rover sale in 1988, and the designation of the correspondent covering that particular sitting*

	11 May	18 May	26 May	2 November
Financial Times	Motor industry	Motor industry	–	Motor industry
The Times	Political*	–	–	Political*
Guardian	Industrial	News in brief	–	Economics

* These were two different political correspondents.

Table 4.4   *Trade and Industry Committee hearings on the Rover sale 1990, and the designation of the correspondent covering select committee sessions in 1990*

	17 January	28 February	7 March	14 November	18 December
Financial Times	Motor industry correspondent	Industrial editor	News in brief	Motor industry correspondent	Industrial editor
The Times	Political reporter	–	–	Political reporter	–
Guardian	Westminster correspondent	Westminster correspondent	Westminster correspondent	Westminster correspondent	Westminster correspondent

in *The Times* to 525 in the *Financial Times*. The second session was ignored by *The Times*, merited 80 words in the *Guardian* but 548 words in the *Financial Times*. The third committee session was completely ignored by all three broadsheets. There were similar variations in 1990.

It is perhaps inevitable that with this variation, specialisms notwithstanding, the reports of the committee sessions would also differ, if only because of the different number of words devoted to them. But are there any variations which could be attributed in some way to the specialist reporters involved? To examine this possibility it is necessary to look at the coverage of individual sessions. The first session will be examined in some detail. This session was held on 11 May 1988.

All three broadsheets examined here carried accounts of this session under three very different headlines:

BAE ASSURES MPS ON ROVER PLANS (*Guardian*)
BAE PROMISE TO INVEST £1BN IN ROVER (*The Times*)
ROVER GROUP PLANS £1BN INVESTMENT IN NEXT FIVE YEARS (*Financial Times*)

The lengths varied, which may be a contributory factor as to why their coverage differed. In fact, all three versions made a point of noting some common points – that British Aerospace wanted to support Rover, that it would invest in Rover, that the deal was conditional on EC approval and that certain information about new models had to remain confidential.

There were different pieces of information which could be found in some but not all three versions. Thus, the *Guardian*'s industrial correspondent included several points about the likelihood of 'hirings and firings'; the *Times* reporter referred to the Rover group's profitability and whether or not it was being asset-stripped by BAe, and the *Financial Times* motoring correspondent discussed the shortfall in investment funds which would be made up by BAe.

The point of noting these similarities and differences is really to illustrate how the accounts have slightly different foci but this cannot easily be put down to different specialisms. The *Financial Times* account is certainly fuller and more detailed but that could be due to the nature of the paper and its business orientation as well as to the length of the article. Similar arguments could be made with respect to both the *Guardian* and *The Times*. Replicating this sort of exercise in respect of other sessions throws up an identical set of problems: are the differences due to the different nature of the papers? The lengths of the pieces? Do they arise in the sub-editing process? and so on. Perhaps as interesting as the differences are the similarities and the fact that different specialists ended up with not very dissimilar news stories. Thus, when it comes to set pieces the specialists remain primarily able journalists.

Looking at the coverage of set pieces such as these may not be the best way of pinpointing differences that can be attributed to specialisms. But there are too many variables to take into account before one can begin to identify that extra something that specialist experience can bring to stories.

Summary

In the introduction to this chapter, three key questions were set out:

- Which specialists cover which areas and why?
- Does the content vary according to specialisms?
- Does specialization lead to 'better' media?

Whilst an answer can be offered to the first question, the answers to the last two are ambivalent. The evidence offered above suggests that when it comes to set pieces, there are often great similarities in accounts despite the fact that different specialists may be involved. Journalistic skills are the greatest consideration here. Beyond that, one could argue that the differences arise when specialists generate their own stories: because they focus on one area and follow up their own interests they will be able to offer things which colleagues who do not 'plough the same furrow' cannot.

The data above confirm a more central point: that we know little about the organization of journalism on a day-to-day basis, and not only within one country but also across countries. As the data show, a large number of journalists were involved in writing the BAe–Rover story in the period 1988–91. Sometimes, a specialist was involved; at other times, a non-specialist wrote a news item. For the *Guardian* the pattern was more straightforward on account of David Hencke's involvement, but this was not so for the other two newspapers. Yet Hencke was not a motor industry correspondent and one could argue that he lacked the detailed expertise to analyse the best deal for Rover. It is at this point that collaborative work with other specialists is crucial.

Whether this arrangement of newsgathering practices makes for good or bad media is impossible to determine. On balance, specialists argue for the strength of the system and the fact that it does offer continuous monitoring of specific fields by people who build up knowledge of events and personalities. This strength outweighs the weaknesses of getting too close to sources and of compartmentalization, which can create gaps in coverage. As to the future, greater specialization for the purposes of organizational convenience cannot override the need for careful and insightful accounts of events, their causes and their effects. Such reportage may be difficult to institute in carefully managed, commercially run and deadline-obsessed organizations.

Two other general conclusions seem appropriate. First, there is a sense in which many of these correspondents were interchangeable. In reporting select committees, for example, there were no apparent disadvantages to having different correspondents involved. The resultant reports or 'accounts' may be simply 'put together after the manner of literature according to a sense of what is necessary and appropriate' (Elliott, 1981: 171). This, however, may not be true for longer journalistic pieces in the opinion columns, where prior knowledge may be a definite advantage. But, as always, this line of inquiry requires more research.

The second general conclusion is not dissimilar. The data suggest that the involvement of so many journalists, specialists and non-specialists, may have as much to do with the organization of newsrooms as with the essential nature of events or happenings. Specialisms may provide an easy way of organizing journalists and giving them responsibilities, but it is only one factor amongst many to explain how a story gets covered, and by whom.

How the specific British factors outlined in this chapter stand up in relation to journalistic practices in other countries is more open to debate largely because there is so little comparative material, particularly about other European countries. The available European material is suggestive of some differences – between traditions of journalism, for example – but also of similarities. But detailed studies of the sorts of issue explored in this chapter are more difficult to find. What also remains to be explored is whether the differences in journalistic traditions and practices which have been documented in the past will continue to mark one country's reporters off from another country's in the future. As Hallin and Mancini have pointed out, the 'standard conventions of journalism' which have dominated for so long 'may prove inadequate to the challenge of an increasingly multilateral and interdependent world' (1992: 137). This may produce a convergence of practices and a growing similarity between reporters in one country and another as the preference for a form of 'neutral' and 'objective' journalism takes root in increasingly media-dominated democratic systems (see also Mancini and Swanson, 1994; and Chapter 7 for a fuller discussion of this point).

Notes

1. Unless otherwise stated, all quotations with reporters are taken from a series of interviews with the author in 1994. This research was funded by the Social Science Faculty Research Committee at the University of Leicester.

2. The term 'journalist' is used interchangeably with the term 'reporter' and often with the term 'correspondent'. A stricter use of terminology would perhaps retain the term reporter (and correspondent) mainly for those journalists who gather news. News procesors and news executives would thus be journalists. Usage here and elsewhere, however, is not consistent.

5

Public Opinion, the Media and the Democratic Process

The 'audience' or the 'public' has a kind of phantom existence that the sociological study of news production has yet to consider in its theoretical formulations. (Schudson, 1991: 156)

It is not usual to connect a discussion of public opinion with studies of news production, yet there are some important reasons why the topic of public opinion should also be considered as part of the news production process. News media need audiences, and preferably paying audiences. If they do not cater well for that audience their very survival is at stake. But catering for an audience has to be understood much more broadly than in simple economic consumerist terms. News media need to reflect, and respond to, the concerns and life-styles of their readers or viewers: in the words of Smith, the media need to be in a position 'to hear, and then to articulate . . . what [their] readers [are] feeling and thinking' (1975: 241) if they are going to engage with them in any meaningful way.

But the task of coming to know one's audience is a tricky one. There are no ready-made mechanisms by which journalists working for mass media come into contact with their audiences (although they may have access to data about their audiences' habits and preferences). So how do journalists come to speak *on behalf* of their audiences? Do they simply *assume* a knowledge of their audiences? Or do they ignore their audiences altogether and only *claim* to speak on their behalf? Moreover, for their part, individuals do hold opinions and do have views even about complex issues (see, for example, Gamson, 1992; Neuman et al., 1992) so how can *they* vocalize these and make them known either within specific and limited localities or within larger communities? The need to connect these bits of the puzzle is the main theme of this chapter.

The first section will look briefly at some of the ways in which public opinion has been conceived and analysed. The second section, which explores some of the ways in which public opinion is assessed, forms an introduction to the third section which considers the nature of public opinion in relation to two specific case studies: the coverage of the death of Jamie Bulger, and the pit closures announcement of October 1992. This last case study focuses primarily on public opinion as a force within the context of political decision-making.

Public opinion

Studies of the news production process have long acknowledged the 'phantom' existence of the 'public' or the 'audience' but have done so at the cost of a thorough analysis of the consequences of this for the media representation of public opinion. To point out that there is a 'missing link' of one sort or another (Schlesinger, 1978; Tracey, 1978; Gans, 1980) does little to enlighten us about the ways in which the media come to express public opinion. But it should be obvious that such issues reflect back on questions of the media and the democratic process because they attempt to highlight precisely how the citizen, as an individual but also as a member of many publics, can come to have his/her voice represented in public discourse. Admittedly, individuals in democratic systems are rarely 'faced with a decision whether or not to obey [the state]' (Barker, 1990: 166). As Barker goes on to argue, 'the historical starting point is with legitimacy as the normal condition of government' (1990: 167) yet, if democratic politics is about anything it is about the level of argument and debate which is permitted to take place on all subjects short of the issue of the legitimacy of the state itself. At all these levels, democratic politics assumes individual and collective rational participation in argument, debate and even peaceful physical demonstrations of opposition or support.

But if there are no physical manifestations of public participation in politics, and no mechanisms which connect the individual, or collections of individuals, to the mass media does one assume that silence is the order of the day? Does one have to assume then that the public has no 'opinion'? Or are there, in reality, other mechanisms by which that public voice is often heard: sometimes as vocalized protest, sometimes in demonstrations, and sometimes even through the mass media?

Two major difficulties confront anyone attempting to provide answers to the above questions. The first relates to the almost impossible task of isolating something which we may wish to call 'public opinion' from its manifestation and expression in the mass media. When the press speaks of 'public opinion' is it referring to something that exists separately from it, or is it simply claiming to speak for it and for something that may not even exist? The media and the opinion of the public undoubtedly interact in complex ways, and the media may even help frame the opinion of the public (see Gamson, 1992; Neuman et al. 1992) but does this also suggest that there can be no opinion without the media?

Hall et al.'s work offers some clues. In *Policing the Crisis*, the media are given a prominent role in actively shaping public opinion, yet Hall et al. acknowledge that there is a level of public experience – 'an interplay of knowledge, rumours, folk-lore and opinions [which] constitutes a critical, and primary, level at which opinion begins to shape about an event' (1978: 135) – which exists independently of the media. However, according to Hall et al., this 'primary' level of opinion formation remains within the 'private world' of the citizen unless, or until, the means of mass communication make it part of the public discourse. 'The crystallising of "public opinion" is thus raised to a more formal and public level by the networks of the mass media' (Hall et al., 1978: 135).

Significantly, what happens during this process of crystallization is the articulation not of a 'spontaneous' public opinion but of a public opinion which 'underpins and supports the viewpoints already in circulation' (1978: 137); it reproduces dominant viewpoints rather than giving voice to alternative or independent viewpoints. As they ask, perhaps rhetorically, 'exactly what is involved in this apparently spontaneous *rendezvous* of dominant interpretations passing down and "public opinion" passing up? . . . it is not quite the spontaneous, miraculous process it at first appears to be' (1978: 137).

Clearly, how views come to be crystallized is a question which cannot be ignored. Nonetheless, the distinctions made above between private and public views, or between 'informal' and 'formal' channels, suggest that it may be valid to talk of the opinions of the public as something separate from, though not entirely independent of, the mass media. That is, they are not simply *creations* of the mass media or mediated expressions of dominant ideologies, and through the public expression of this public opinion the public comes to participate in the political process. In this case the media can be said to act as a megaphone for the public, rather than simply 'taking the public voice' or mediating the public mood. Hence the potential power and influence of 'public opinion' as something which those who govern, or who seek to govern, have to be aware of (Lang and Lang, 1983: 19).

The second difficulty is, in some ways, an extension of the first in that it raises the issue of definition: the phrase 'public opinion' is open to different interpretations. From the seventeenth century onwards, there have been a number of different ways of conceptualizing the nature, content and significance of public opinion. Price (1992), offers a summary of the ways in which public opinion has been understood throughout the last three centuries: these include references to the 'common will', to opinion polls, to the general public, to something which 'transcends individual opinions', and so on. Susan Herbst's (1993a) categorization of definitions of public opinion also covers some of the same ground and we can see in her schema the quite different meanings which are often attributed to the term. Briefly, she lists four, not mutually exclusive, definitional categories:

1. the aggregation principle of public opinion, where opinion polls, surveys, elections and referenda are taken to reflect, by aggregating, public opinion;
2. the majoritarian principle, 'where the opinions that *matter* are those associated with the greatest number of people' (1993a: 439);
3. the discursive/consensual definition, 'based on the notion that public opinion evolves through public discourse' (1993a: 439). Herbst here cites both Habermas and Noelle-Neumann in order to argue that

through discussion and conversation opinions can fluctuate, and need
not remain static;

4. the denial of the existence of public opinion. Here public opinion 'is a
   reification or fictional entity', a 'rhetorical tool used by the powerful to
   achieve their goals' (1993a: 440). To quote Bourdieu, 'the politician who
   yesterday said "God is on our side" today says "Public Opinion is on
   our side"' (1979: 125; see also Ploman, 1962).

On closer scrutiny, one can identify two obvious weaknesses in this listing
of categories. The first is that it evacuates the individual, as a member of a/
the public, from the scene. His or her opinions in reality do not exist
(category 4) or, if they do exist, are only considered if they are aggregated
in some way (categories 1 and 2), or if they emerge 'in the course of
rational/critical discussion in the public sphere' (1993a: 440) (category 3).
What has been left out is the more abstract notion of public opinion both
as an expression of public sentiment which, as it were, exists in a formless
state, and a view of public opinion 'as something that transcends individual
opinion and reflects an abstract common good rather than a mere com-
promise of individual interests' (Price, 1992: 11; see also Herbst, 1993b).
Although this may need to be given a 'visible' form – be articulated and
reflected – that articulation and reflection need not necessarily involve
elements of intentional distortion or mediation.

The second weakness lies in the 'reification' category (category 4) and it
returns us to the first difficulty discussed above. By adopting the reification
position, one explicitly denies that public opinion exists independently of
the agencies which articulate it; public opinion is thus no more than
something manufactured by powerful interests. It denies that something
which we may wish to call public opinion exists apart from the mechanisms
that reflect or mediate it. One can observe the implications of this position
in Hall et al.'s *Policing the Crisis* where the press is said either to act on its
own behalf, i.e. 'the editorial which actively *claims* to speak for the public',
or to speak up for public opinion by 'articulating what the vast majority
are *supposed* to think' (my italics). In both instances, although the public is
taken 'as an important point of reference', it is actually bypassed (1978:
63). The 'representations of public opinion are then often enlisted *by the
controllers* as "impartial evidence" of what the public, in fact believes and
wants' (1978: 63; my italics).

Whilst Hall et al. are correct to draw attention to the part the media play
in 'actively shaping public opinion' since public opinion is 'dispersed' (1978:
63), there is a risk of devaluing and even ignoring the content of the
dispersed opinion. Simply put, its dispersed nature does not empty it of
content: content which may on occasions cohere and form independently of
the media. To deny that possibility is to deny the public any part in the
political process, and to leave it as an entity to be manipulated by the
powerful.

What seems to be lacking from many of these categorizations is a more political and dynamic conceptualization of public opinion which avoids both the terminological debate – i.e. is it opinion polls, is it an aggregation of views – and the more static and politically disengaged analyses of its manifestations. For one of the things which binds the many different conceptions of public opinion together is a common concern with the relationship between the public/citizens – in reality, and perhaps more correctly, public*s*/citizen*s* – and those who govern or who seek to govern it. Here also lie the term's historical roots, as Price puts it:

> The combination of *public* and *opinion* into a single term, used to refer to collective judgements outside the sphere of government that affect political decision making, occurred following several large scale social, economic, and political trends in Europe [from the eighteenth century onwards]. (1992: 8)

The fact, or perception, of members of the public making or being able to make a 'collective judgement' about public affairs signified their *active* involvement in the political process. The public was no longer entirely passive 'bystanders' (Lang and Lang, 1983: 22) and what it 'thought' and expressed as a collective opinion was of importance to those who sought to govern. The linking of the public to elements in the political process was an important departure from earlier days when its 'opinion' may not have mattered very much.

One can find an extension of this interpretation in Habermas and his argument that in the eighteenth century the 'free exchange of information and critical, open reasoning, became the instruments of "public self-assertion" in political affairs. With the growth of a politically active public sphere, public opinion emerged as a new form of political authority – one with which the bourgeoisie could challenge absolutist rule' (Price, 1992: 10). Although the notion of the public sphere has come in for sustained criticism (Keane, 1991; Thompson, 1990; Calhoun, 1992), interest in the public sphere has also turned our attention to that period in the eighteenth century when rational and critical discussion in the public sphere began to flourish: in letters and novels, in the generation of discussion and debate in coffee houses and salons, in the emergence of an independent, market-based press, in openness of access to discussions, and in the way the emerging free press stimulated and encouraged new ways of thinking and new forms of social organization.

In Britain, the changes taking place could also be seen as a response to what was happening within the British Parliamentary and political system and the changing relationship between Parliament, the emerging political press and the public. As Tom Burns has argued, two 'fundamental principles were established' in the eighteenth century which came to redefine the relationship between public, press and Parliament.

> First, the very existence of newspapers, and the nature of their contents, presumed the existence of a public, political, opinion external to the small enclosed world of parliamentary politics. Second, their role was assumed to be that not merely of purveying information but of articulating and expressing public opinion; in so far as they were successful – i.e., in so far as their sales

grew, and their views were taken seriously by government ministers – they were not only the 'independent and responsible organs of public opinion' they claimed to be, but *organizers* of public opinion. (Burns, 1977: 48)

The distinction which Burns draws between newspapers 'articulating and expressing public opinion' and 'organizing' it is of central importance in that it does raise significant questions about the means by which these two roles, especially the former, come to be fulfilled. Examples of powerful interests colonizing and controlling the content of the press can most certainly be interpreted as attempts to organize public opinion, to mould it. But it is more difficult to conceive of the press/media 'articulating and expressing public opinion' given

- their centralized and commercialized nature;
- the growth of public relations as a crucial part of the news production process (see Deacon and Golding, 1994: 4–7; see also Chapter 1);
- newsgathering processes which privilege powerful elites;
- the often stated simple point that 'journalists communicate with an audience they cannot see or hear. It is a one-way conversation' (Neuman et al., 1992: 3); and
- the general nature of mass democracies.

In these circumstances, and in the context of mass representative democracies, how can journalists come to know or articulate the opinion of the public? How can they give a concrete reality to public opinion?

How does public opinion crystallize? Public opinion and the democratic process

In their account of the career of the poll tax, Deacon and Golding suggest that there are 'four feed-back mechanisms: audience correspondence, opinion polls, public demonstrations and electoral outcomes' (1994: 175). In the context of their study, each one of these operated and so the media, and politicians, were able to gauge movements in public views. But what if there are no opinion polls, if correspondence is not particularly overwhelming? If there are no demonstrations? How do journalists then sense the public mood? How do they begin to gauge public opinion?

One view, put forward by Leo Bogart, is that 'the journalist who assesses the popular temper is much like the artist who translates his own personal experiences and observations into intuitions of a deeper and more generalised truth' (1972: 16). This finds some resonance in Smith's suggestion that 'journalistic "flair" is (or is believed to be) an intuitive ability to judge . . . how things are shifting, opinion is moving, new interests are emerging, in what direction society is evolving' (1975: 247). More recently, Deacon and Golding have written of how 'journalists trusted their own judgements about what their audiences would find relevant' in covering the poll tax

(1994: 195). The journalist here abandons any notion of being an objective and dispassionate observer of events! Little wonder then that journalists prefer to claim that they are simply reporting public opinion even though their reactions often imply that they are assessing the situation intuitively. One political correspondent, quoted by Deacon and Golding, illustrates this when he identifies the problematic nature of the poll tax: 'And it stepped up and at each stage it became £200, £250, then, you know, you thought "Jesus, this is big trouble"' (1994: 165).

It is perhaps more usual to rely on public opinion polls as a summary of the public's verdict on events, and where such polls exist there is often little argument about what 'the public thinks'. In fact, the media regularly report public opinion polls on a variety of contemporary issues and they 'have become a mechanism through which the public becomes sensitised to its own needs and self-conscious about its own collective stance' (Bogart, 1972: 15). They have also become means by which politicians can gauge the public mood.

But where such polls do not exist, how do the mass media find out what the public thinks, and how does the public become aware of what it thinks, of 'its own collective stance'? Who claims to 'speak' on behalf of the public, and the form which that public expression takes become critical issues in the analysis of the relationship between 'public opinion and the democratic process' (Lang and Lang, 1983: xi). Such a concern sidesteps interest in the development of an adequate definition of public opinion *per se* since it seeks to explore the relationships between the public/s, their opinions, the mass media and the political process. More specifically, it seeks to explore the role of the mass media

- as an important link between the public, and the opinion of the public, and the decision-making processes of government;
- as a key player in the construction or creation of 'the public' and of public opinion;
- as a means by which the public can come to play a direct and indirect part in the democratic process.

By playing these roles – amongst many others – the mass media can provide that 'central place of assembly' (Peters, 1993: 566) which modern societies in the age of mass communication cannot provide for their dispersed and disaggregated communities. In this respect, and borrowing from Habermas and his interpreters, the media can not only enable informed discussion but they can represent that discussion to those who govern. This fits in well with Peters' description of democratic government, as government which 'rests on a posited link between the people and the state via the public sphere: the state opens itself up *via* publicity, and the people respond with *public opinion*' (1993: 549), though perhaps that description is incomplete since it does not offer a discussion of how that 'public opinion' links up with the state and with the exercise of power.

In pursuing this line of discussion, an interest in a *working* definition of public opinion is perhaps of greater value than a fully adequate conceptualization of it. The Langs, for example, provide a number of clues as to how public opinion can be understood. Thus:

> public opinion is a collective representation, a shared image of the likely response that elite actors see themselves forced to take into account. It is, in essence, the dominant opinion. Quite often this is indeed the opinion of the majority, but it can be less if the minority view has sufficient logic, prestige, resources, or commitment to carry the day. (1983: 17)

In effect, the Langs define public opinion not as an aggregate of all opinions or even a 'scientifically determined' artefact but as something which has an influence on political processes and decisions. For them, public opinion is a form of 'social control' which 'comes into play in problematic situations where none of the rules of law apply or where there is a dispute about their suitability' (1983: 12).

Such a way of looking at public opinion is preferable to conceptualizations which offer a static definition of it and it provides a dynamic model for exploring the ebbs and flows of opinions and the mobilization, or not, of such opinions by the media and by political actors. Finally, it also connects these elements with the political process. It does not, in other words, expend resources on determining whether or not:

- one can discuss public opinion without, at the same time, paying considerable attention to the means of communication through which that opinion is reflected, amplified, manufactured or mediated;
- there is something which one can call public opinion. If there is, how would we describe it and what would it consist of?
- it has an existence which is separate and distinct from the mass media either as a contributory factor in its formation or as a means for its expression, e.g. via the mass media.

It is more interested in the dynamics of the process, and the ways the mass media come to 'connect' with their audiences or publics, and how public opinion becomes a mechanism of 'social control'. The two case studies explored below amply illustrate the usefulness of this approach.

Case studies

The sense of public opinion as something which is ever-present and not necessarily coherently articulated takes us back to earlier conceptualizations of public opinion as 'diffuse, shapeless, shifting . . . and elusive currents of thoughts' (Bogart, 1972: 15) which have tended to be overlooked more recently. The reason for reintroducing the idea of public opinion as a shapeless, unformed public sentiment is precisely to provide a corrective to the reification category. One can point to numerous instances when public sentiment – itself surely a manifestation of public feeling and opinion – is reflected rather than simply mediated by the mass media even though it may not have been 'aggregated' or measured. We may wish to consider, for example, the support given to Band Aid in the 1980s in this category; or, more recently, the coverage of the murder of a two-year-old boy, Jamie Bulger, in England in 1992.

The real question is: can the mass media act as the 'organs of public opinion' or are they merely there to organize, control and direct that opinion? Two other questions follow on from this: can such public expression of public opinion – assuming that it is strong, united and singular – have any influence on patterns of decision-making and on decision-makers? Can it bring about a change of policy? If it cannot, and does not, what does this mean for our understanding of the relationship between public opinion as a form of censure, as a political force, as a political act and those who govern us?

We need a better understanding of the relationship between the public, the mass media and political actors if we are to be able to contribute to contemporary thinking about the public sphere, and the role of the 'ordinary' citizen in modern political life.

The case of James Bulger

The case of James Bulger is a particularly sad case since it began with the disappearance, in 1992, of a little boy from a shopping centre, and the eventual conviction of his 11- and 12-year-old killers in 1993. Two aspects of the case have given it special notoriety. The first is undoubtedly the age of Bulger's killers. This factor created a sense of unease since it gave rise to a panic about the morals of young people in Britain. The second aspect which caused some concern was the fact that several people had seen the little boy with his abductors but had not intervened. Again, this was seen by many as indicative of the way British society had become less organic, with people less willing 'to get involved' in matters which did not directly concern them.

Interest in the case was enormous and the media gave it extensive coverage. Although it would be possible to argue that this interest was generated by the media – creating a 'moral panic' – a contrary case can also be put forward. This would stress the way the press reflected a sense of communal involvement in a tragedy, of communal mourning and incom-prehension in the face of the crime. Here, in other words, is an instance of the press acting as a voice of the public, expressing public opinion, and making that voice echo across many other publics. The piles of flowers placed on the spot of his abduction which featured on the front pages of several of the national daily newspapers can be read as an expression of that sense of communal participation in a sad tragedy. This was most

powerfully expressed on the front page of the *Daily Mirror* which carried a
picture of the mound of flowers sandwiched between a top strap line which
read JAMES BULGER: BORN 16 MARCH 1990, KILLED 12 FEBRUARY 1993,
and a quote placed at the bottom which read 'Goodnight, little one.
Nobody can ever hurt you again' (2 March 1993).

If the Bulger case illustrates the role of the press as a reflector of public
sentiment and opinion where that opinion has never been actively measured
– that is, with the journalist acting as 'artist' with an intuitive 'flair' – it
also illustrates the role of the press as 'organizer' of public opinion. Thus,
for the *Daily Mail* , the Bulger case was no less a tragedy but it was also
symptomatic of something much deeper. The *Daily Mail* used its front
pages to connect the tragedy with political shortcomings in government. Its
front-page lead on 1 March 1993 was the Archbishop of York's statement
to the effect that juvenile crime was linked to unemployment. The headline
read ARCHBISHOP BLAMES MAJOR. On the following day a more direct
injunction was placed above a photograph of the young boy's coffin being
carried by relatives: FOR JAMES'S SAKE, MAKE THE WORLD A BETTER PLACE
(Plate 5.1).

It would be unjust to suggest that the *Daily Mail*'s mediation of the
event in calling for political action was no more than a manipulation of
public opinion. The sentiments it expressed, it could be argued, were in
tune with a public at a loss to explain a tragedy and to ensure that it would
not be repeated. This has echoes with the analysis by Smith of newspapers
in the post-war period.

> When the traditional rhetoric of a newspaper flows in the same direction as the
> emergent experience of social change, the convergence – in terms of confidence,
> coherence, mastery of language and presentation, inner assurance – is striking.
> When such convergence does not take place, the newspaper seems to go to pieces:
> the central organising core is not there. (Smith, 1975: 245)

Had the *Daily Mail* not been in tune with its public, the tone of its rhetoric
would have sounded very hollow.

There are interesting parallels here with the analysis of 'moral panics'
offered in *Policing the Crisis* in that the latter also featured public concern
over 'senseless crimes', namely, thefts or muggings for small sums of money.
But whereas the authors of *Policing the Crisis* (Hall et al., 1978) suggest that
the public concern was hijacked by powerful forces so as to legitimize
judicial actions, I wish to stress the ways in which public concern was
articulated, drawing on fundamental public perceptions of more enduring
themes and divisions between rights and wrongs, between the permissible
and the prohibited. This is not to suggest that these divisions are static or
that they cannot be manipulated but that they exist as residues which can be
made to react to different contemporary elements (see the discussion of
'scroungerphobia' in Golding and Middleton, 1982; Negrine, 1994: Ch. 7).

Although the Bulger case throws up some interesting issues with respect
to the relationship between public opinion and the media, it is a case which

Plate 5.1 *Funeral of James Bulger, in the* Daily Mail

is largely 'apolitical'. Would the press be able to voice public concern in cases which were overtly political and party political to boot? How would the general lack of diversity both in ownership and content of the British press deal with such instances? Would the intervention of the press, as in the Bulger case, be no more than a temporary lapse into a vicariously participative role within a political system in which the public is usually on the outside? And how would that intervention connect with the full machinery of the democratic process at work?

'Miners look to public opinion to save them' (Financial Times, 1992a)

On Tuesday, 13 October 1992, British Coal announced that it planned to shut down 31 pits (of the remaining 50) and to make over 30,000 miners redundant. The closures were to start that very week and were to continue for several months. Immediately after the announcement, Michael Heseltine, the President of the Board of Trade, announced a package of redundancy and other measures which were designed to soften the blow.

These announcements, not unexpectedly, featured prominently in the following day's newspapers under a variety of different front-page headlines all of which were, more or less, critical of British Coal's plans. For the usually loyal Conservative *Mail*, this was 'THE GREAT MINE DISASTER'; the *Financial Times* led with 'Anger erupts at coal pit closures', and for Murdoch's *Sun* the miners were 'Heroes in the morning . . . sacked in the afternoon'. Whilst this reflected the sense of devastation which the closures heralded, there was something very peculiar in the press getting worked up about events and closures which were neither a secret, nor unexpected.

The coal industry has been in rapid decline for many years. There were over 130 pits open in 1985–6 but only 70 or so in 1989–90; after the Second World War there were over 700,000 working miners; by the mid-1980s that figure had shrunk to about 150,000, and by 1990 to some 80,000. At the beginning of 1992 there were only 50 mines open, and just over 40,000 employees. The proposed closures would undoubtedly have enormous repercussions on the size of the industry. Nevertheless, such closures had been taking place for many years and it was likely that this process would continue or accelerate in the wake of the privatization of the electricity industry. Moreover, as the electricity companies' need for coal lessened, the coal industry was increasingly at risk.

As one labour correspondent put it:

> we knew and had written repeatedly in the paper that there was going to be this savage pit closure programme, and a very rapid acceleration of what was going on before . . . so it was completely bizarre to me why . . . this massive eruption [of feeling] had taken place. Why it had not been such a dramatic event two or three weeks earlier . . . [There was] this sudden [media] intensity and focus on something which had not been focused on for years . . . and suddenly it disappears from the public domain.[1] (Reporter A; see Figure 5.1)

In fact, knowledge of these closures was quite widespread both inside and outside the industry. As far back as September 1991, there were newspaper stories about plans to restructure and privatize the coal industry. Some were based on material made public by the Coalfields Communities Campaign which had long been attempting to publicize the danger to the industry; others were based around a government report on the privatization of

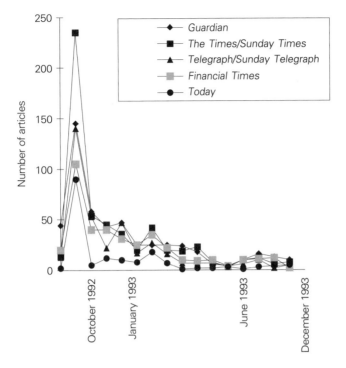

Figure 5.1   *Number of articles on 'pit closures' in selected newspapers, January/September 1992–December 1993*

the coal industry (*Guardian*, 1991). Such stories continued to rise to the surface throughout the intervening months, and came to a head with leaked reports of the government's plans to institute a closure programme which were published in several national newspapers on, or around, 18 September 1992.

The absence of a negative response to the leaked information and the fact that the plans to restructure and then privatize the industry were an open secret, may have led the government and British Coal to believe that the formal announcement of the pit closures in October would be largely uncontroversial. But, as it turned out, what started off as a run-of-the-mill press conference to announce a change in industrial policy, that is, to speed up pit closures, turned within a matter of days into 'the gravest political crisis since Suez in 1956' (*Daily Mirror*, 1992). Yet a week later, the whole affair seemed to have blown over, the crisis dissipated and the miners, once more, were left to their original fate.

By examining the press coverage of this affair, one can begin to identify not only the origin and genesis of a 'crisis' in government but also the mechanisms by which public opinion is gauged and is fed through to Members of Parliament. In this respect, public disenchantment is an important ingredient in the generation of a crisis but it is one that can often be used instrumentally; for example, MPs may decide to back their government even though disenchantment may persist. Similarly, the press can cease to reflect or mediate the public disenchantment even though it persists. This coupling, and uncoupling, of public disenchantment and Parliamentary protest has implications for our understanding of the role of public opinion in the democratic process.

Announcing the closures   As one journalist who covered the announcement for a broadsheet paper observed:

> the fact that there wasn't any controversy when the thing was originally leaked I think goes a long way to explaining part of the government's behaviour as to why they were so taken aback when precisely the same piece of news was officially announced, and the reaction was so much stronger . . . I was surprised by the strength of the political reaction it is because it seemed to me that there was nothing in the announcement when it was made that was shatteringly new. I suppose what it did though was that it reinforced the message in the public's mind and particularly touched that chord of sentimentality that exists about the coal mining industry in this country. (Reporter E)

Two points arise from this statement. First, the sense that the existence of rumours or even of leaks does not, of itself, generate controversy. In certain circumstances this may clearly not be so: for example during the economic crisis over the ERM, rumours about pit closures could simply be left to one side. Second, and this became more pronounced with time, there was growing criticism from many quarters not so much of the policy itself but of the *manner* of its announcement, and of the speed of the closures and job losses.

But there are two things missing from the press coverage on 14 October. The first is any sense of a looming political crisis *in* government. The headlines express anger and dismay but do not yet highlight major political dissent. The fact that Parliament was in recess at the time may have contributed to this, just as it may have contributed to the way the coverage developed over the next few days. Clearly, by not announcing the plans in the Commons there was no easy way for the government to gauge back-bench opinion. Consequently, backbench reaction would have to follow on after the announcement, leaving no opportunity to make feelings known to government advisers. The manner of the announcement may also have allowed for a public response to manifest itself before Parliament colonized, and channelled, reaction.

The second omission is any reference whatsoever to the public or to the public sympathy which was to become so central to the coverage in the following few days: by the 19th – only a week after the announcement – the role of the public in this unfolding crisis was not only well defined, but also a contributory factor in giving rise to John Major's 'greatest crisis' (*Daily Telegraph*, 1992a).

How, and why, did the announcement become a 'crisis'? Four factors contribute to our understanding of that transformation. The first was the continuing unpopularity of John Major as Prime Minister. The second, and related, factor was the perception of the government as unable to lead or to find solutions to the country's problems. One political correspondent admitted:

> I think the government was vulnerable in our eyes [given the panic over ERM]. And when a government looks vulnerable, it emboldens journalists, I think, to make judgements that they might not make otherwise. (Reporter F)

The third factor was the press using the 'mishandled' announcement as an opportunity to be critical of the government and of ministers (Plates 5.2–5.4).

The fourth factor was the fairly immediate, and largely negative, public response to the pit closures announcement itself. Miners are a powerful political symbol the potency of which has not declined in tandem with the shrinkage of their industry. They have played an important historical role in Britain's industrial and political heritage, and they generate strong emotions. Winston Churchill, MP, reminded his readers in the *Mail* of Macmillan's words about the miners: 'The enemy could not budge them. The only way they could advance was by cutting them down on the ground where they stood!' (Churchill, 1992: 8). Or as a *Daily Mail* leader put it, 'Miners are different. They live in communities. Thus, through their despairing solidarity, they somehow released the anger and frustration bottled up in the whole of Britain' (1992b).

All these elements were welded together in the ensuing days' coverage as the media began to turn up the heat on the government by exposing it to attack from all quarters. But how, and why, did the press stoke up the flames? How did it begin to make sense of the crisis?

Mediating the public mood   The press, and television also, had to reflect the political mood if it was to play an active part in this unfolding story. But it also had to echo the public mood, and the political symbolism of the miners, if it was to remain in tune with the public. It would have been inconceivable, for instance, for the press to announce the closures as well timed, well conceived and justified at a time of growing unemployment and economic depression. Clearly, there are occasions when the press simply ignores public sentiment, but this is likely to be rare when at the same time there are divisions in government. It is that combination of public and political dissent which is significant (see Negrine, 1982). But how did the press come to gauge that public mood?

That 'a pall of gloom has descended over Britain' (*Financial Times*, 1992b) was never much in doubt for the press. Although on the 14th, the anger referred to in most stories is an institutionalized one expressed in the main by trade union leaders and opposition MPs (Table 5.1), in the following days phrases such as 'a nationwide wave of protests', 'public

Daily Mail

WEDNESDAY, OCTOBER 14, 1992   30p

★ £1 MILLION ★

YOU ARE ENTERING A MADONNA FREE ZONE

£1billion payout as 31,000 jobs go in massive pit closure

THE GREAT MINE DISASTER

THE LIST OF VICTIMS

Easington, Durham	(1,394 lost jobs)	Cotgrave, Notts	(620 lost jobs)
Vane Tempest/		Rufford, Notts	(806 lost jobs)
Seaham, Durham	(936 lost jobs)	Silverhill, Notts	(817 lost jobs)
Westoe, Tyne and Wear	(1,230 lost jobs)	Betws Drift, Sth Wales	(113 lost jobs)
Sharlston, West Yorks	(749 lost jobs)	Bolsover, Derbys	(494 lost jobs)
Bentley, Sth Yorks	(654 lost jobs)	Markham, Derbys	(1,296 lost jobs)
Frickley, Sth Yorks	(1,002 lost jobs)	Parkside, Merseyside	(782 lost jobs)
Grimethorpe, Sth Yorks	(957 lost jobs)	Point of Ayr, Nth Wales	(478 lost jobs)
Houghton Main,		Shirebrook, Notts	(1,005 lost jobs)
Sth Yorks	(441 lost jobs)	Silverdale, Staffs	(701 lost jobs)
Kiveton, Sth Yorks	(774 lost jobs)	Taff Merthyr,	
Markham Main, Sth Yorks	(730 lost jobs)	Mid Glamorgan	(410 lost jobs)
Rossington, Sth Yorks	(873 lost jobs)	Trentham, Staffs	(1,544 lost jobs)
Bevercotes, Notts	(807 lost jobs)	Wearmouth, Tyne & Wear	(989 lost jobs)
Bilsthorpe, Notts	(935 lost jobs)	Prince of Wales, W Yorks	(701 lost jobs)
Calverton, Notts	(752 lost jobs)	Hatfield/Thorne, S Yorks	(459 lost jobs)
Clipstone, Notts	(967 lost jobs)	Maltby, S Yorks	(1,301 lost jobs)

By PAUL EASTHAM, Political Reporter

MORE than half of Britain's coal industry was swept away yesterday in a devastating shutdown that will cost £1billion in redundancy payouts.

British Coal is axeing 31 of its remaining 50 deep mines, wiping out 31,000 jobs, in the next five months.

It is the most sweeping closure programme since post-war nationalisation.

Bitter coal bosses blame the breathtaking losses on power generating companies moving away from coal

Why it had to happen — Page Eight
Fury of Scargill — Page Nine

because gas-fired stations are cheaper to build and less vulnerable to industrial action.

The move could well lead to higher bills for electricity consumers — gas-produced power is more expensive.

The demise of King Coal will be swift, with the first six closures this Friday. Twelve pits will close this month, three in November and four in December. It means 19,000 jobs will have gone by Christmas.

NUM leader Arthur Scargill condemned the announcement as 'the most savage, brutal act of vandalism in modern times' and called for a national rail and coal strike.

But miners tempted to heed his call to arms were given a stark warning. Anyone taking any form of industrial action will lose redundancy entitlement worth up to £37,000 for men with 30 years' service.

The cash is being offered under a specially-improved emergency package unveiled by Board of Trade President Michael Heseltine last night. He also announced a huge

Turn to Page 2, Col. 1

Revealed: Two women in Dimbleby's life

THESE are the two women in the life of David Dimbleby. The age gap is the difference between the broadcaster's girlfriend Belinda Sykes deft and his wife Josceline. Otherwise, from their dazzling smiles right down to their choice of hairstyle, the resemblance is uncanny. However, while 47-year-old cookery writer Mrs Dimbleby is an unrepentant 'home bird', go-getter Belinda, 34, has carved a career in the tough world of television. And that, say friends, is where she and Dimbleby — also a workaholic — became romantically involved.

Full Story — PAGE THREE

INSIDE: Weather 2, World Wide 10, Femail 12, Diary 21, TV and Radio 32-34, Entertainment 36, Letters 38, Coffee Break 40, City 42-44, Sport 45-52

Plate 5.2

Plates 5.2–5.4   *The 'pit closures' announcement as covered in selected newspapers*

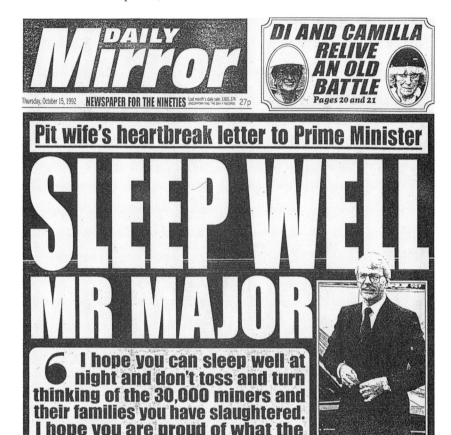

Plate 5.3

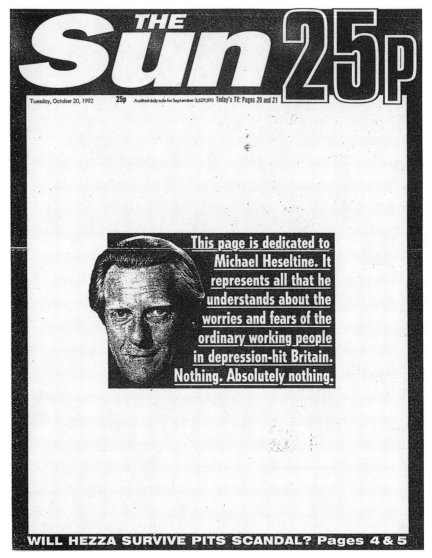

Plate 5.4

furore' and 'a tide of protest' did not seem out of place. This fact was underlined in the *Financial Times* on Saturday, 17 October:

> As cabinet ministers admitted privately that they had simply failed to foresee *the scale of the popular backlash* against the closures, the fate of 31,000 miners replaced Europe as the lightning conductor for the deep disquiet among Tory MPs. (*Financial Times*, 1992c; my italics)

The *Daily Mail* was no different in the way it perceived the opposition to the government, nor in the way in which the public mood was mediated. Its

Table 5.1   *References to selected actors in the* Financial Times, *the* Daily
Mail *and the* Daily Mirror *in stories about the pit closures on 14–17*
October 1992, inclusive

Actor	Financial Times	%	Daily Mail	%	Daily Mirror	%
Political (Conservative)	90	35	83	48	55	25
Political (Labour)	12	5	4	2	19	8
Political (Lib. Dems)	2	1	–	–	2	1
Miners	9	3	9	5	18	8
Miners' wives	1	–	1	–	10	4
Individual miners	–	–	3	2	21	9
British Coal	20	8	9	5	14	6
Trade unions (all)	46	18	25	15	34	15
Church/judges	4	2	1	1	14	6
Local politicians/ business people	21	8	1	1	4	2
Companies (assorted)	19	7	9	5	9	4
Taxpayers/consumers	–	–	3	2	–	–
Public	–	–	5	3	–	–
Total*	224	87	153	89	200	88
Total references	258	100	172	100	224	100

* Percentage figures are rounded up or down as appropriate.

columnist Graham Turner used the personal form to address the PM
directly: '*Has it yet struck you that you have managed to do in one day what
Arthur Scargill failed to do over the course of many years – to unite the
British people against the Government on the issue of the future of our coal
industry?*' (Turner, 1992: 6).

And so gradually, and in the following few days, the press took on '"the
public voice" [to articulate] what the vast majority of the public are supposed to think' (Hall et al., 1978: 63). But a closer analysis of the coverage
in the period up to, and including, Saturday, 17 October does not reveal
any particular mechanism through which the press was able to gauge that
public mood or opinion. There are no opinion polls to report, no vox pops,
no interviews with the person on the proverbial 'Clapham omnibus'.
Indeed, an analysis of actors referred to in three national dailies reveals the
absence of comment from individual members of the public; the majority of
actors referred to were directly involved in the unfolding drama (Table 5.1).
So, in 'taking the public voice' was the press shaping and structuring public
opinion 'while actually bypassing [the public]' (Hall et al., 1978: 63) or was
it somehow – perhaps at the same time – also channelling a public mood
which was independent of it? These questions are clearly problematic since
they touch on the rather mysterious way by which news organizations and
journalists come to gauge the public mood and they also highlight the
complex nature of public opinion itself.

Unfortunately, the formulation of the above question, and the dichotomy
between editorial comment which voices a newspaper's own opinions in

contrast to the newspaper 'taking the public voice' (Hall et al., 1978: 61–4) is notoriously simplistic in its understanding of a very complex communication process. As Table 5.1 reveals, there are few instances in which the public voice, however defined, finds an expression but this should not necessarily lead to the conclusion that the press is actively shaping and structuring public opinion, and no more. Such public opinion may exist, and may be manifested in a variety of ways which, *when taken together*, come to represent something which we may call the opinion of the public, and which the press can report.

The most obvious visible manifestation of the public mood could be a march or demonstration, and more precisely, a particular type of march – like the one which took place in Cheltenham on Sunday, 18 October 1992, the first Sunday after the announcement. Reporting this march, the *Financial Times* (1992d) noted that among the '3,000 miners' supporters', there were 'many prominent Conservatives and Socialist Workers Party supporters. Mr Tony Hilder, an executive member of the right-wing Freedom Association, marched alongside Mr Quentin Tallon, Chairman of the Cheltenham Trades Union Council'.

The symbolic significance of the march was not lost on the *Daily Mail*; it explained to its readers (and to the government) what was happening in Cheltenham.

> Tory shires stood shoulder-to-shoulder with mining communities in the fight to save the pits yesterday. The Gloucestershire gentility of Cheltenham was swept away as a 3,000-strong 'non-political' protest march brought the Regency spa town to a standstill. (1992b)

The roster of Tory 'stalwarts' was impressive: Lord Neidpath 'whose uncle Lord Charteris is a personal friend to the Queen', assorted former MPs, church leaders and business folk, one of whom, Mrs Lorraine, a local hotelier who had helped organize the march, was quoted as saying, 'This is happening in Cheltenham, not Nottinghamshire or Yorkshire. It must surely show the government the strength of feeling that exists' (*Daily Mail*, 1992b).

The marchers of Cheltenham thus came to represent the public mood in the country. This was 'The revolt of Middle England' (*Daily Express*, 1992a), or, as the *Guardian* put it,

> Shire toffs transformed into militants. Maev Kennedy reports from Cheltenham on how 'Middle England' reached a crossroads. It was waxed jackets, pearl earrings and golden retrievers for Cheltenham miners' day . . .
>   And to ringing cheers from as motley a crowd as Middle England ever assembled, and wild barking from hippie lurchers and country terriers, he [Lord Neidpath] read out the phone number for No. 10. (1992a)

By Monday the 19th, then, the weekend marches *confirmed* to the press the public mood it had already hinted at the week before but had not been able to verify empirically. And it was a sombre mood: according to MORI poll findings based on field work carried out on Tuesday, 20 October, two days after the Cheltenham march, 88 per cent of those questioned said they were dissatisfied with the way the government was handling the coal industry. Over three-quarters (76 per cent) also disagreed with the statement that 'There is no realistic alternative for the coal industry to the pit closure programme', a statement which encapsulated the government's position (MORI, personal communication, 1994).

The Cheltenham march was, however, only one piece of the puzzle of public opinion. The problem for a news organization is that there are often very few such visible pieces of evidence. What other mechanisms allow journalists to write of 'a nationwide wave of protests', of a 'public furore', of 'the tide of protest', of 'anger' and 'fury'?

The simplest answer, if a very general one, is that one can piece together very different bits of evidence such as phone calls, letters, faxes, and conversations with political actors and others. All these are then fed into the news organization, and to journalists, and are, as it were, recycled. To give an example, one political reporter pointed out that his own news organization would be aware of 'its readers' (Reporter B); another said that he would be made aware of what other reporters were doing, what they were picking up, and what they were finding out, and that this would help him build up a picture of what was going on (Reporter C). A different correspondent explained how that network impacted on his own work:

> You get a lot of phone calls, a lot of letters, obviously organized lobbying by the particular constituencies involved but you have to discount that to some extent. And you also get it indirectly through the way other people react to it. The Labour party, for example, sensed a tremendous amount of groundswell and they put up a great big performance about it. Newspapers are at the receiving end of a tremendous amount of material . . .
>
> It was one of the busiest times of my life. The phone never stopped ringing. Faxes came pouring in, and I had piles and piles of faxes from organizations, Labour councils and so on. [It was] very very unusual. (Reporter E)

The instinctive journalistic reaction was given support by other bits of evidence that the event was causing enormous public and political concern. Letters to newspapers added another pillar of support. Though there are some real problems in using these as indicators, the selection of letters to represent different points of view can sometimes throw some light on the state of public opinion. Letters were used by the newspapers in a variety of ways and, in some cases, featured on their front pages. The *Daily Mirror* illustrates this technique well (Plate 5.3, p. 117). The *Guardian*'s technique of printing an extract on the front page achieves a number of different objectives at the same time:

> Why, on the evening following the news of closure of 31 coal mines, was I, a middle-class, somewhat more than middle-aged, housewife living in a nice house in leafy suburbia, crying into the washing up? (*Guardian*, 1992b)

The more traditional use of letters was also in evidence as broadsheet newspapers carried selections from their postbags. How representative these were is impossible to say so long after the events themselves but it is clear that the vast majority of letters were critical of the pit closures announcement and the plans for coal. The *Mirror* devoted a full page to letters on Saturday, 17 October, the only time it carried letters about the pit closures. Its rival, the *Sun*, adopted a different technique by which to gauge and mediate public opinion. In addition to carrying 'just a few of your letters' against the closure of pits (*Sun*, 1992a), it gave front-page space to a story about the '1,000 letters of hate for PM. Tories bombard No 10 over pits.'

> Hundreds are from party supporters showing their outrage at the way the mine closures have been handled. One insider said: 'Some express their disgust in very stark terms. *There has been nothing like it before . . .*'
> Scores of Tory MPs reported similar fury when they faced party activists at the weekend. (*Sun*, 1992b)

In keeping with technological change, the *Sun* also introduced a new method by which the public could express its opinion. 'Send Roy [Lynk] stacks of your fax', it urged on 17 October. Roy Lynk was the President of the Union of Democratic Mineworkers which was formed as a breakaway from the NUM during the 1984–5 miners' strike. The UDM, the 'moderate' face of mining, received much credit for precipitating the collapse of the strike in the mid-1980s. That it found itself targeted by the Conservative government in the 1990s, alongside the NUM, was a great cause of concern, not least to Lynk who felt betrayed. But the *Sun* came to the rescue:

> hero miner Roy Lynk is fighting the pit massacre with a sit-in protest 1,200ft below ground – but you can join his dig for victory with the *Sun*.
> You can show . . . that Britain cares . . . by faxing a message of support to his colliery. (*Sun*, 1992c)

Predictably, the *Sun* then carried some of the 'hundreds' of messages of support: Roy Lynk was 'overwhelmed' (*Sun*, 1992d).

It is not possible to determine the degree of cynicism, enthusiasm or sincerity that lay behind the *Sun*'s coverage of protest. Along with the telephone polls which it encouraged – a 7,009 to 541 majority vote deciding that the government was wrong to close 31 pits (*Sun*, 1992e) – everything was an occasion for public participation.

Perhaps the greatest oddity, and the most suspect way of gauging the public mood, was the reliance on the electricity-generating industry as a monitor of protest. According to several national papers, the 'National Grid Company said 2m lights were switched off at 9 p.m. on Sunday in protest at proposed pit closures' (*Financial Times*, 1992e).

Some of these methods of gathering public opinion are clearly dubious but they nevertheless help the press to make sense of reactions to unfolding events and they lend support to individual newspapers. But there was one other source of information about public reaction to the closures announcement which not only alerted the press to the depth of public reaction but also played a significant role in helping determine the nature of the coming crisis in government. This source of information can be best described as public comment directed at MPs and then redirected to the press. When it comes to gauging the public mood, MPs are often at the sharp end of public comment. As one political correspondent explained:

> The press and Tory MPs and public opinion all feed off each other. It's a terrible chicken and eggs situation, really. Something happens . . . now what comes first, the public outrage, the outrage of Tory MPs or the outrage of newspapers/ television? Well in fact they were all, I would guess, inextricably linked.
>
> What is clear is that if Tory MPs are cross about something then it appears on *News at Ten*, and *News at Ten* says well here are a dozen people up and down the country who unexpectedly do not support the government. So Tory MPs on the next day would be slightly more cross, and then it appears on the front pages, so there is an indivisible critical mass that builds up. That's what happened over coal. (Reporter F)

> We were taking our lead from what we were feeling was the view in the Commons. If all Tory MPs had just said we don't care and it had only been confined to Labour then we would not have seen all these stories.
>
> The thought of a march through London, with Conservative marchers joining the marchers, was unheard off so they [the press] had to reflect that. I don't think people were being pushed into the street by our screaming front-page headlines. (Reporter C)

How much any of this public mood would have counted for without the threatened backbench revolt is open to debate, though as the *Daily Express* admitted, the government 'had been prepared for a bitter reaction from opponents and mining areas, but not from Tory supporters and Middle England' (1992b). Crucially, the opinions of both 'Tory supporters and Middle England' found their way to Members of Parliament, the traditional and constitutional representatives of the public!

They too are open to persuasion, with letters and comments from constituents and local party activists being particularly important. These local views are, in turn, fed to the media. As interviewees admitted:

> Our office here got 3,800 letters within about eight days . . . I had quite a lot from constituents . . . but most of those came from all around the country. (MP 1)

> I think this was not an instance where the press was leading the opinions of Members of Parliament or indeed of the public. I think it was rather an instinctive reaction both from MPs and from the public.

> *Q*: What response did you personally get from the public?
> *A*: Some letters from constituents, some fairly active members of my constituency party who just didn't understand why it was being handled in this way. And if there was a well reasoned justification for it, if there was a sensible reason behind it, that was not being explained.
> *Q*: Did you get many letters?
> *A*: Yes. I don't normally get a large postbag on issues from constituents, so 20 or 30 letters would be quite a lot as far as I am concerned . . . It did actually go on for quite a long time . . . and of course once I had been quoted in the press or on the radio or had appeared on television that tended to generate letters from other parts of the country as well. (MP 2)

The connection between local party members and MPs was also referred to many times in the press and it contributed to a picture of loyal party members disenchanted with their government. In 'the beautiful village of

Normanton on the Wolds', according to the *Daily Mail*, 'telephone lines at the Rushcliffe Conservative Association have been jammed since last week as even die-hard Tories, already reeling from the recession, register protests over the proposed closure of Nottinghamshire pits' (*Daily Mail*, 1992c).

Similarly, after surveying one MP's surgery, the *Daily Telegraph* quoted a constituency branch chairman as saying 'I've never seen anything like this on a Saturday morning in nearly 20 years' (*Daily Telegraph*, 1992b). The *Express* also noted how on 15 October Tory MPs and Conservative Central Office were 'besieged by calls from outraged supporters' (1992c). MPs, according to one political correspondent,

> were picking up in their own constituency just a general feeling that the govern-
> ment is incompetent, it's out of control. I think the MPs were picking up
> throughout all their constituencies this general feeling of complete and utter
> chaos . . . MPs are the conduit very often for us picking up what we perceive is
> going on in the country. And they were quite quick on this one. I think a lot of
> them had got a lot of phone calls, the Downing Street switchboard was
> absolutely mangled on the night of the announcement, letters were coming in.
> You talked to Tory MPs in Esher and places like that, they were getting letters
> galore. People who just regarded it as unfair. (Reporter C)

Another political correspondent explained why the media had gone on the attack it this way:

> what was also clear was that Tory MPs, who are a pretty good conduit for public
> opinion, they are quite well plugged in . . . they were being called by their
> Association chair and whatever and they were told, 'We are not going to put up
> with this.' And that fed through quickly. (Reporter F)

Resolving the crisis, and ignoring public opinion?   In the face of this barrage of critical comment and a threatened revolt by a sufficient number of Conservative MPs who could put the government at risk, the government decided to backtrack on its plans. Initially, it promised a reprieve for 21 mines out of the original 31, in anticipation of a review which it would also set up. The other 10 mines would, however, be shut down following the proper closures procedures. This so-called U-turn appeased some but not all the potential rebels and abstainers; consequently, other promises were made about the possibility of including all the threatened pits in the review procedure. In the end, all but one of the rebellious Conservative MPs came to heel and the government won the vote by a majority of 13.

As the political furore in Westminster died down, coal lost its attraction as a front-page industrial story (see Figure 5.1). However, the marches of support for the miners, and against the government, were not quite over yet. The march on Wednesday the 21st – coinciding with the debate in Parliament – attracted over 70,000 protesters and very favourable coverage from unexpected quarters such as the *Sun* and the *Daily Mail*. The march on the following very wet Sunday attracted between 150,000 and 250,000, and received equally favourable coverage. But to all intents and purposes, the political crisis was long over. The miners, and their supporters, were once more relegated to the fringes of the political process. Public opinion was uncoupled from its political representation.

By June 1993, British Coal had managed to halt production at 19 of the 31 mines on the October 1992 closure list, with other mines closing soon after. By the end of 1994, fewer than 20 mines were still open.

As usual, there is no single explanation for the withering of media support for the miners and for the ensuing calm in middle England. One reporter gave the following explanation of some of the factors at play:

> I think once the governmental crisis was over most of the media just did not consider it a story. On the contrary, they considered it boring. From the miners' point of view, when the actual pit closures took place . . . they became convinced that there was a news blackout, a formal news blackout, and that somehow the government had made an arrangement with the media to stop coverage. They could not understand why there had been this total coverage at one point . . . [but] when pits were actually closing against the will of the miners and as they saw it against what the court had decided and so on, there was no interest at all. They found it totally baffling and it was very, very hard to convince people that there was not such a blackout.
>
> You can perfectly well understand why people thought there was such a blackout and maybe in the level I am talking about, i.e. of not being encouraged, it may be true that there was a sort of blackout. I have heard stories of government ministers having conversations with their more friendly newspapers to say this business is dealt with, we are doing our best, there is no good in dwelling on it . . . I am sure that kind of thing went on, but no more than probably is usual.
>
> [But] it wasn't just the fact that the media lights were switched off that the thing ran out of steam. I think it was also because there was no political mechanism to channel that mood and to turn it into some lasting political movement. (Reporter A)

What this lengthy compilation reveals is the uncoupling of those elements which brought the crisis into being, elements described by McCrystal as the 'triple alliance' between 'miners, politicians of all parties and the media' (1993: 3).

The accounts given above contribute something to the explanation of the ensuing silence. Yet, and this is significant, public concern about the coal industry did not wholly disappear. In spite of the dramatic decline in media coverage of the pit closures after October 1992 (see Figure 5.1, above), MORI found that in January 1993 as many as 97 per cent of the quota sample said they were aware of the closure proposals and that 75 per cent opposed or strongly opposed the proposals to close the coal mines. Furthermore, whilst the public had a more negative view of most Conservative politicians, it had a more positive view of Arthur Scargill, the NUM President and media *bête noire*, and this had gone up 22 per cent (MORI, personal communication, May 1994).

The press, by giving publicity to the issue, created an opportunity for public outrage to manifest itself. Because the announcement came during the Parliamentary recess, it was not possible for MPs to monopolize and colonize outrage and dissent. To reinterpret Peters slightly, the media did provide a 'central place of assembly' perhaps *because* the state inadvertently opened 'itself up *via* publicity, and the people respond[ed] with *public opinion*' (Peters, 1993: 549). Had the announcement been handled differently, and presumably better, then the Westminster–Whitehall–Downing Street triangle would not have been exposed to either internal (backbench MPs, ex-ministers, etc.) or external (public opinion) sources of pressure. There would have been no place for that, since the important sources of pressure would have been anticipated and dealt with.

The collapse of the 'triple alliance' does, paradoxically, point the way to a better understanding of the role of the mass media in political communication. As we have seen, and the various tables lend support to this, the political content of newspapers, especially broadsheets, is dominated by the Westminster–Whitehall–Downing Street triangle. Nevertheless, it is not an impervious triangle: Westminster is open to public communication and public opinion, and both Downing Street and Whitehall are open to communication from Westminster via well established channels such as the Whips and, in the case of the Conservative government, the 1922 Committee. During the period 14–21 October, all these channels of communication were open and were being used to convey opinions.

The final observation which is worth making relates to the relationship between what I have called the Westminster–Whitehall–Downing Street triangle and the media. The interviews, and the analysis of the coverage of this episode, reinforce a traditional view of the nature of political communication with the political elite and the journalistic elite, i.e. political correspondents, dominating the discussion about the nature of British society. The Westminster view of the world overrides all and pushes other coverage off the front pages; when there is a crisis in Westminster, there is *via the media* a crisis in the country; but it does not follow that when there is a crisis in the country, there is a crisis in Westminster. If the idea of the public sphere is to gain greater purchase, it must somehow take account of the manner in which power is exercised, and political and institutional arrangements feed into it. Otherwise, informed discussion in the public sphere may be no more than discussion for its own sake.

Note

1. Unless otherwise stated, all quotes from reporters are from interviews conducted with the author. This research was funded by the Social Science Faculty Research Committee of the University of Leicester.

6

The Construction of Politics

Most of the chapters in this book focus, in one way or other, on the production and dissemination of political information and on the interaction of political actors and media workers. Little attention is paid to the role of the public in this conception of the political communication process. On those occasions when the public is considered, as we have seen in Chapter 5, it is as no more than an imagined collectivity that is, more often than not, constructed and acted upon rather than acting. An even more obvious gap in this book, and in much of the literature on political communication, is the absence of commentary on the public's general comprehension of the outcome of the political actors–communicators interaction. Does the public understand the political content of the media? What sense does it make of that content? How does the content of political communication help the public understand (or not) the nature and the importance of issues? What part does it play in the way the public makes sense of events?

One of the many reasons for these omissions is that the study of political communication is very often bounded by a certain view of where the main focus of research is or ought to be, with different researchers pursuing different areas of interest (see Blumler et al., 1990a). However, there is another reason why the whole question of the public and political communication is so difficult to deal with and this relates to the controversial issue of the public, as audience, in mass communication research. In brief, the earliest of traditions had been to explore the audience, in reality *audiences*, as being composed of individuals upon whom the mass media were acting. So a considerable amount of effort was spent on the 'effects tradition' in order to demonstrate or support/deny increasingly sophisticated versions of the ways in which the audience was/was not influenced by the mass media (see Neuman et al., 1992). As Swanson put it, 'the effects tradition's model of voting viewed voters' *understanding* of political communication as unproblematic' (1981: 172; my italics).

So although it has long been acknowledged that we should really study 'what people do with the media' rather than, more simply, what 'the media do to people', it is not a task which has attracted a large number of students of political communication. In the main, attention has been devoted to exploring behavioural and attitudinal changes and not the trickier question of how the media have contributed to the ways in which individuals come to make sense of their world. Admittedly, such an exploration does involve passing some judgements on the efficacy and influence of the media but the linkages between the two are more complex than simplistic causal relationships would suggest. If the media are only one amongst many sources of information and influence it would be unwise to either overestimate or underestimate their influence, as simplistic formulations of the relationship tend to do. Furthermore, as Robinson and Levy (1986) have argued, it is even necessary to question the efficacy of different media as sources of information and as tools of learning.

The primary focus of this chapter, then, is on how individuals, as members of the wider public/s, come to make sense of their world. Inevitably, some attention will have to be paid to the more specific question of the contribution of the mass media to this process of understanding but this is, as it were, a secondary concern. In taking for granted Blumler's statement that the media provide 'the informational building blocks to structure views of the world . . . from which may stem a range of actions' (quoted in Negrine, 1994: Ch. 1), this chapter seeks to flesh out in more detail what 'the informational building blocks' are and how these come to 'structure views of the world'.

The first part of the chapter will explore the 'constructionist' approach, an approach which has a great deal to contribute to this field of study. The second part focuses on how children make sense of the political world while the third part concentrates on studies of adults. The conclusion identifies a number of other issues that need to be considered when exploring the ways in which individuals make sense of their world.

The 'constructionist' approach

One useful approach to the study of how persons come to understand political communication and to act politically is the 'constructionist' approach. Neuman et al. describe this as 'a new theoretical perspective' which 'focuses on the subtle interaction between what the mass media convey and how people come to understand the world beyond their immediate life space' (1992: xv).[1] On the one hand, then, we have 'people', and on the other the media, and it is the interaction of the two which is in focus. Thus, 'rather than thinking of them as a set of stimuli to which individuals respond, we should think of [the media] as the site of a complex symbolic contest over which interpretation will prevail. This cultural system encounters thinking individuals, and political consciousness arises from the interweaving of these two levels' (Gamson, 1992: xi–xii).

Although much of this sounds fairly straightforward and uncontroversial (and perhaps even familiar) both Neuman et al. (1992) and Gamson (1992) attempt to move away from simply identifying the nature of this complex interaction. What they propose is that individuals make sense of the media's menu of issues by 'framing' them in ways which draw on past personal, and other, experiences. An individual's understanding of a news item will be framed within that individual's understanding of similar issues, of personal experiences, of other information, and so on. Such an approach is in the long tradition of work which takes it for granted that media content can be 'read' in different ways and that audiences can 'negotiate the meaning of what they are told' (Philo, 1990: 154) but, unlike much work in this tradition, the work of Neuman et al. (1992) and of Gamson (1992) is based on an analysis of both audience frames *and* media frames. In other words, just as the audience frames issues in particular ways, the media also frame news items and issues in particular ways and the task of the researcher becomes one of exploring the extent to which these frames coincide or differ.

In this way, the 'constructionist' approach looks at the issue of media influence and media power from a different perspective, a perspective which draws our attention to the many ways in which influence can be exerted. It also points up other questions. What part do the media play in helping (or hindering) the audience to make sense of events in particular ways? Do different people understand political messages differently, and if so why? Do the media communicate efficiently and effectively? Are some media better than others in helping individuals understand issues? Does the audience reproduce media frames? Can the audience go beyond the boundaries of media frames and make sense of issues in very different ways?

But if the 'constructionist' approach draws our attention to the need for a better understanding of the ways in which the public interacts with political messages through a variety of media, it also has a research agenda and a methodology which sets it apart from the more quantitative and survey-based tradition that often accompanies studies of political communication. Four features of the approach are noteworthy.

The first is that studies which adopt what can loosely be termed a 'constructionist' approach focus on individuals (children, teenagers, adults) rather than on collectivities. They concentrate on what those individuals 'think and how they structure their ideas, feelings, and beliefs about political issues', that is, on what Neuman et al. call 'common knowledge' or 'what people *do* know about public affairs' (Neuman et al, 1992: 3). 'Common knowledge' is distinct from 'public opinion': the former has more to do with 'what people think and how they think about public issues than narrowly defined valence-oriented "opinions" concerning an issue or candidate' (1992: 18). There is also, one should add, a certain suspicion of survey work which cannot always distinguish between different interpretations of events or issues and often conflates them into one response for the sake of methodological tidiness (see Neuman and Fryling, 1985: 223–5).

The aim of the 'constructionist' approach, then, is not to pass judgement on how well informed members of the public are/are not but, more simply, to find out what they think and how they think about issues in the public domain. This approach inevitably raises questions as to how people come to 'construct (possibly different) meanings' even if they attend to the same media content and whether there are factors – personal, psychological, dispositions, media specific, or whatever – which can account for broader patterns of public interpretations.

The second feature is that studies which adopt the constructionist approach can be linked to what David Buckingham describes as the 'cognitive revolution' of the 1960s in which television viewers were seen 'as having an active role in constructing meaning from television: rather than merely responding to stimuli, they are consciously processing, interpreting and evaluating what they watch' (1993: 12). Despite Neuman et al.'s suggestion that 'constructionism' is 'a new theoretical perspective', it has some important elements in common with a series of earlier studies of children and politics (Stevens, 1982; Connell, 1971); studies which in their own way throw considerable light on the ways in which children draw on the mass media for information that enables them to make sense of the 'political'. In fact, there is an ongoing and wider debate about the extent to which the concern with the public and the public's understanding of media content is novel (Curran, 1990: 149–50). Nevertheless, the focus of interest in the 'constructionist' approach when combined with the methodology employed (see below) does permit for a more detailed and sophisticated approach to the understanding of how the public thinks about issues.

The third feature is that studies which have shown an overriding interest in the ways in which individuals come to make sense of contemporary issues usually adopt a methodology which permits individual 'respondents' to discuss those issues at length and in their own ways. The usual practice is to conduct in-depth interviews with a small number of respondents either on their own or in small groups. Neuman et al. carried out in-depth interviews with 43 different people, Doris Graber looked at the responses of 21 individuals (quoted in Neuman et al., 1992: 24), Gamson's researchers recorded conversations with 188 people (Gamson, 1992: 13) and Connell spoke to 149 children (1971: Appendix). With such small numbers of interviewees involved, there is a real problem over how far the findings can be generalized to larger populations.

Fourth, studies which adopt the constructionist approach suggest that individuals rely on 'frames' 'to convey, interpret, and evaluate information' (Neuman et al., 1992: 61). Entman, drawing on the work of Gamson, illustrates how a frame comes to (a) define a problem, (b) diagnose causes, (c) make moral judgements and (d) suggest remedies. His example is the 'cold war' frame which highlighted 'certain foreign events – say, civil wars – as problems, identified their source (communist rebels), offered moral judgements (atheists aggression), and commended particular solutions (US support for the other side)' (Entman, 1993: 52). Children also employ certain strategies in order to make sense of the political world. For instance, through their (however imperfect) understanding of hierarchies in, say, a school or community context, they come to make sense of the complex and detailed nature of power structures by reducing their essential characteristics to more simplified schemas. (Connell, 1971, uses the term 'schemas' rather than 'frames' in his work.) An example offered by Connell is the way children can often make sense of a president and of presidential power by using such ideas as 'the boss', ideas often acquired from television cartoons. Bosses, like presidents, control and order others around (Connell, 1971: 24–9; see also Moore et al., 1985: Ch. 3).

From these examples, we can see that frames are 'conceptual tools' and that they simplify a complex issue in order to enable it to be grasped and manipulated. But, according to Neuman et al., they do not 'predetermine the information individuals will seek but [they] may shape aspects of the world that the individual experiences either directly or through the news media and [are] thus central to the process of constructing meaning' (1992: 61).

Although the suggestion here is that frames do not guide or direct individuals to bits of information or cause individuals to select pieces of information to sustain their framing of issues, Swanson's version of 'constructivism' and people's use of 'constructs' – a term which can be likened to frames – points in a different direction. That is, 'constructs' can be used to 'discriminate among political actors and events in the process of perception' (1981: 177). For Swanson, the act of framing or of 'discrimination' is an act of selection of information and would thus, to some extent, 'predetermine' the information sought. To define a problem is to select information and to construct it in a particular way; it may, in other words, predetermine the information which will be sought so as to sustain that version of the problem. However, what is absent from both versions – intentionally absent, one should add – is any attempt to relate frames or constructs to the more 'traditional' explanations of class, partisanship, etc.

How do these features of the constructionist approach help us to understand the ways in which people come to make sense of the political? The next section explores this topic in relation to studies which have specifically focused on children.

Children and politics

A considerable part of the literature on 'children and politics' can be found under the general heading of 'political socialization', that is, 'the process of social learning whereby individuals acquire the knowledge, skills and dispositions that enable them to participate as more or less effective members of groups and the society' (Dowse and Hughes, 1972: 179). Although this sort of definition is open to accusations of being too concerned with an individual's 'induction into norms and the stability of [political] systems (Connell, 1971: 234) it does have the merit of drawing attention to the process of social and political learning and to the agencies which contribute to that process.

Interest in political socialization, however, is more often than not directed at finding out how children become socialized into specific political systems rather than how they come to make sense of the world around them and what sense they make of it. Partly for this reason, the focus of interest revolves around the question of which agencies are the most powerful ones for political learning and how these come to shape children's political learning. At this point of the analysis, though, the discussion which ensues is usually replete with generalizations and qualifications. Thus, 'much political socialization is both non-political in its origins and latent in its process'; there are numerous agencies of socialization and one cannot determine their levels of importance; the relationships between attitudes, opinions, etc. and political behaviour are problematic (Dowse and Hughes, 1972: 183); longitudinal studies are rare so findings are problematic; learning theories are sometimes inadequate in explaining how children learn, and so on (Moore et al., 1985: 6–8). To quote Atkin: 'despite the outpouring of studies in the past few years, the body of knowledge about communication and political socialization is modest in scope and unimpressive in quality' (1981: 322).

That said, there is some logical structure to the processes of socialization often referred to. According to Dowse and Hughes, the primary agencies of socialization include the family and the school, with other secondary agencies (the mass media, peer groups, and the like) exerting their influence on the child as she/he grows up and becomes immersed in a larger environment. Two specific criticisms can be levelled at this account of political socialization. The first is that we need to understand the process of political learning not in some narrowly focused context, e.g. familiarizing the child with practices within a specific society, but in a broad setting where children learn about local, national and international practices and traditions. Connell gives the example of Australian children learning about the (British) Queen as the head of many states. In this way they come to relate their immediate experiences of the Queen (of Australia) with the knowledge of other nations in which the Queen is head of state. Children can then be thought of as learning to be 'members of a number of overlapping groups bearing various traditions and subject to different sets of influence' (1971: 236). So there needs to be a better awareness of the way political learning takes place and the breadth and depth of such influences which transform it into a longer-term and more open-ended process.

If the first criticism points to shortcomings in the way the processes, and constituents, of social and political learning are conceptualized, the second focuses on the distinction drawn by Dowse and Hughes between primary and secondary agencies of political socialization. Although one can justify the decision to designate the family as the primary agency of socialization, including political socialization, it would be wrong to relegate the mass media to a secondary role. Even when they were writing their book in the late 1960s, there was sufficient evidence to suggest that the role of the mass media was actually more significant than the secondary designation warranted. By then, radio was well established and television had become widely available so that a child could be easily exposed to *non-familial* influences from a very early age. Today, this would be even more true with videos, satellite channels, and round-the-clock television transmissions filling up the 24 hours of the day. Any child growing up in the 1980s and 1990s is exposed to a wide range of televisual content from birth as her/his parents intentionally (or unintentionally) place them in front of the electronic child-minder.

The covertly political outpourings of television can often cause considerable anxiety. In recent years, there has been some concern about the way television programmes such as cartoons or more general features have highlighted the issue of environmental problems. Some have seen this as producing a 'green bias'. One cartoon programme which has come in for heavy criticism is *Captain Planet*. It has been said to present 'an unquestioning acceptance of a link between population growth and environmental degradation' (T. Young, 1992: 27). This, and other programmes, provide information, ideas, images and the like about the environment and environmental issues but in a one-sided way. If this is a valid concern with respect to the environment – and, at the time of writing, there is no reported research work on this topic – its wider implications cannot be overlooked. They point to the way that television may help young people to come to understand, and view, environmental and other topics but outside the context of the adults' 'balanced' programming.

If the importance of television has been underestimated in the past, it is not valid to conclude that the importance of the family has been overriden by television. After all, the family setting continues to provide the context within which much media activity takes place and within which media content is sometimes explicated. Indeed, there is a strong argument for saying that the study of television and its influences should be conducted within the family setting and should take account of family interactions (Morley, 1990). Nevertheless, television introduces an independent and uncontrolled stream of images and sounds which can often contribute much to the process of learning about the world. One can see this very clearly in Connell's work on 'the child's construction of politics' (1971). Here we find material taken from in-depth interviews with 149 Australian children. With this interview material, Connell explored the ways in which children came to understand and interpret politics. This aspect of the work will be examined in more detail below. Of more interest here is the extent to which the mass media were the points of reference for the children's comments about events and issues, that is, the extent to which television was the source of much of what they used to make sense of politics.

As far back as the late 1960s – Connell's field work was carried out in 1967–8 – it could be claimed that 'the children's main point of contact with the political world is the television news . . . [and that] no other medium has anything like the breadth of coverage or the immediacy of impact that the television has for them' (1971: 120–1). In fact, television was the most often cited source of information on a range of topics (1971: 119). Connell also claims that 'the global network of mass communications' is 'breaking down parochial tradition and bringing up the children as citizens of a global *polis*' (1971: 128) as they become exposed to the (uneven) international news flows. They thus become familiar with events taking place, say, in the US but not in other nearer or equally distant lands. Although children become involved 'in world politics it is an involvement of emotional reaction, not an involvement of action or potential action . . . Television can show things to fear, things to be shocked by, things to amuse, things to like and things to hate, but it does not show the children things to do, forms of engagement' (Connell, 1971: 129).

The idea that television informs but does not involve is one to which we shall return. As Stevens comments in relation to her own study of children and politics, children are not only open to the stimulus of television but 'from this source, children may acquire not only information and images, but *vocabulary organized into models of description, argument and discussion*' (Stevens, 1982: 14; my italics). Stevens' point here is suggestive of 'frames' being made available, and being acquired by children.

Finally, although these researchers do indicate that television/the media are an important source of information for children, they also introduce a qualification to this statement. Simply put, a 'person learns from exposure to the media in proportion to the level of knowledge possessed prior to the media exposure' (Moore et al., 1985: 133). Once children have enough background knowledge of roles, issues or people – usually at the age of nine or ten – they can supplement that with information gleaned from the media, more so if it is 'reinforced' by parental and other figures. Without that prior knowledge, exposure to the media does not necessarily lead to an increase in knowledge.

An example drawn from Connell's book illustrates many of the above points. It is taken from a conversation with a 13-year-old boy. Connell asked him how he heard about the death of Harold Holt, an Australian prime minister who disappeared, believed drowned, in 1967. The boy replied:

> I was watching a TV show news flash came over, and I went and told Mum and, it's funny but, he was an own Australian I liked him and everything but it didn't seem as quite a shock to me as, when, Senator Kennedy was killed, never felt quite, not as much sad over it. (Connell, 1971: 128)

Although Connell comments that this, and other, conversations show the ways in which television is important, how information about politics is gleaned and how emotional involvement can take place one could go further and note the way in which this child also recognizes the differences between ordinary people and people whose fortunes merit a news flash. It shows how, in other words, children begin to distinguish between ordinary people and people in positions of importance and authority.

But how do children construct the world of politics and what do they learn about it? According to Olive Stevens, 'a child constructs his political concepts, initially, through relating his "here and now" world to the "out there" political world, and finds important parts of it reflected there. In this way he brings external events under conceptual control' (Stevens, 1982: 171). In this way, that which is familiar to the child can often be used to understand that which is unfamiliar; the former becomes a simplified way of comprehending the complex and distant. A head teacher, for example, would be seen as a figure of authority like other, more distant, figures of authority and just as the head teacher can use his/her position to get things done, so too with other figures of authority. What is involved here is a process by which children arrive at their understandings of different aspects of the political world. So to examine children's thinking about politics involves 'looking at the ways in which they arrive at conclusions on such matters as the functions of government, their expectations of government, their perception of social principles, and the ways these are expressed in different parties' policies' (Stevens, 1982: 6).

According to researchers, children are able to achieve different things at different stages of their lives. They also develop different abilities and acquire and process information in different ways. In brief, since how children learn is not of direct concern here, children come to think about politics (and other things) in different ways at different stages. At the early age of five or six, political consciousness 'is a collection of scraps of information, unrelated to each other' (Connell, 1971: 17) but by the age of seven children come to 'distinguish a political and governmental world from other areas of life, and to see relationships among the figures in it' (Connell, 1971: 18). At the ages of eight and nine, more information is collected but children remain, by and large, confused about different people and their roles and tasks, different institutions, and so on. Despite this continuing level of confusion about, for example, political actors and their tasks, Connell believes that children have nevertheless accepted a distinction between the public at large and those who are, loosely speaking, in government. Children have developed a conception of 'the governmental' (Connell, 1971: 27).

From her own work, Stevens points out that at the age of nine and ten children develop a vocabulary which 'can be used to organize everyday speech into political meanings' (1982: 147). As children grow older they acquire a larger vocabulary, can articulate their thoughts better and have a better grasp of the political world. So that by adolescence most children 'have a fair idea that different political positions have different tasks associated with them, even if they cannot describe them accurately' (Connell, 1971: 137). Once they understand this, children can then relate ideas about political tasks to ideas about political structures and institutions.

A graphic example of this is given by Moore et al. from one child's responses to the same question, 'What does the President do when he goes to work?', over a period of five years. In kindergarten, the answer was 'I don't know'; in first grade, 'Sometimes makes speeches and works in his office'; in second grade, 'Makes speeches and does laws'; in third grade, 'He signs bills and all that; he signs laws'; in fourth grade, 'He signs bills, goes to meetings in Congress, signs laws' (1985: 90).

This brief exposition of the stages of development gives an idea of how children's capacity to deal with politics changes with time. In essence, as they move into adolescence or become adults, individuals are better able to cope with different amounts and complexities of information (not that they necessarily do!). Whether children's confusion at an early age could be removed if they were actually taught about government and politics – usually a taboo subject in schools – instead of picking information up along the way is a point that merits serious consideration (see Stevens, 1982: Ch. 6).

The above approach acknowledges age as a factor in a child's learning – other factors such as sex and social grouping (Stevens, 1982: 7) may also be significant – but it is far removed from the approach criticized by David Buckingham as comprising a 'rigid series of "ages and stages" which lead inexorably towards the achievement of adult rationality'. In other words, it does not 'regard the child as a deficit system . . . as more or less "incompetent" when compared with adults' (Buckingham, 1993: 14). Whilst this rigid approach can certainly be found in the literature it is a far cry from the approach of either Stevens or Connell which seeks to understand how children learn and what they learn about the world of politics.

How do children come to organize the available information? Conversations with children, as with adults, often produce vast quantities of material and it is up to the researcher/s to make sense of it. One way in which Neuman et al. (1992) do this is by exploring the 'frames' used by people to make sense of the world. Connell does something similar with his conversations with children although he does not use the idea of 'frames' as such. Instead, he places parts of the conversations under four headings which reflect how 'four parts of the whole political field come to be organized' by the children. The four parts are: hierarchy, conflict, elite–mass relationships, and political parties. What we have then is the 'organization and interrelating of political information' under four separate headings (1971: 38).

Hierarchy As we have seen, 'young children apply to political figures the same simple idea of command they apply to "bosses" of all kinds, the idea of one person giving instructions to others' (1971: 38). However, by the age of 11, children do begin to develop some sense of where power lies and of hierarchies of power.

Conflict Even very young children become aware of violent conflict (wars, riots, etc.) and this sort of conflict can often incorporate the idea of there being 'goodies and baddies', 'attackers and defenders', and so on. The idea of conflict over issues, however, is a very different and a more sophisticated one. Issue conflict is 'commonly mastered at the age of twelve but, more significantly, understanding issue conflict presumes an understanding of both alternatives and alternative policies' (1971: 50).

Elite–mass relationships Young children accept that certain people may be important – the Queen, the Prime Minister – even if they do not always comprehend why they are important. With time, they come to develop their ideas about the institutional nature of political power. To an extent this would also apply to knowledge about laws, or perhaps more appropriately rules, where children would be aware of their existence but not of their origin. Similarly with voting and the electoral process. Though children become familiar with the idea of voting and elections from an early age, they do not always relate these to political offices. Very few kindergarten children in Moore et al.'s sample, for instance, knew anything about voting and the electoral process and nearly two-thirds (61 per cent) could not say how the President was chosen (1985: 50). By the age of 9 (fourth grade) nearly two-thirds of Moore et al.'s sample described an election as a process that decides between competing forces (1985: 92; see also Connell, 1971: 52–9).

Connell draws our attention to what he sees as a significant feature of this acquisition of knowledge about the electoral process and voting: that children do not acquire a 'conception of popular sovereignty' (1971: 59), or of the mass public having any calls to make on the élite. Rather it is an act by which the institutional process is legitimized and not a means of making demands on the élite.

Political parties As with voting so too with political parties. By the age of 9 (fourth grade) over three-quarters of Moore et al.'s sample claimed to have heard of both 'Republicans' and 'Democrats' compared to less than a tenth five years earlier (1985: 103). Connell's findings are not dissimilar, though he goes on to suggest that from the age of 12 onwards children come to see political parties as 'connected with elections, that they are in conflict with each other, that they produce leaders, and that they are in one way or another units of government' (1971: 59).

From these illustrations of how children organize information about the political world, we can see the ways in which they begin to grasp the nature of political structures and organization. The details and the complexities of the political whole may not always be present but the sense of there being a political whole made up of specific component parts certainly is. Moreover, ways of thinking about the political world – about the nature of authority and hierarchies, the framework of rules, the distinction between the important and the ordinary – are already established in the minds of children.

Two further comments need to be made before we turn to the transition from child to adult. The first is that all these studies tend to suggest that children to a large extent reproduce the ideas handed on to them by adults in family contexts, in schools and from the media. However, even this process of reproduction leaves room for the children to contribute something of their own. This leads on to the second point: that children are rarely able to escape the confines of the processed information. As Connell writes, 'when we consider the general tenor and the total content of the interviews, we must be impressed by the conventionality, the lack of *realized* freedom in them . . . the political outlooks become a rehash, sometimes an interesting rehash to be sure, of well-known themes from adult politics' (1971: 239).

So children learn to exist within a framework of politics produced by others and they reproduce it and its boundaries. Yet at the same time, children can introduce their own individuality into the material which becomes available to them. One has to acknowledge the child's own contribution to her own construction of politics. If one does not, the child becomes no more than a link in a chain which starts off with a family transmitting values to the child. Yet this is precisely the criticism of the political socialization approach to political learning, for it often sees the child as no more than part of the process by which values are transmitted from parent to child with the child playing no active part whatsoever. Clearly, the child does come to experience things directly, the child is open to non-familial experiences and the child can inject an element of individuality, so care needs to be taken when considering the relationship between parent and child in the process of political socialization. So what we need to consider when looking at this whole area is both the processes of social learning with their emphasis on stimuli, exposure to the media and so on, and the developmental theories which pay attention to the maturity and abilities of children. Unless both these features of a child's life are examined it will remain unclear precisely how a child comes to grasp the political world and to develop her own individuality when considering it. Yet this is perhaps what is necessary when looking at the whole question of the parent–child relationship in the context of political party preferences and voting intent.

Children, political parties and voting

The existence of a multiplicity of agencies which play a part in contributing to a child's and to an adult's political learning is beyond doubt and this creates problems for those who attempt to study voting behaviour in adults. How, for instance, does one begin to set a value on each and every agency, how does one distinguish between influences, and so on? There are similar problems when one seeks to understand how children come to express preferences about political parties and voting intentions. Do they simply take on the parental choice, given that the family environment provides a strong socializing context? Do they make individual choices? Do they do a little of both? At the heart of these sorts of question lies the issue of how children (and adults) come to make decisions, the stages at which they can begin to think about issue differences, the stage at which they become exposed to external influences and ideas, and so on.

As we noted above, children become familiar with the idea of voting from a very early age and Himmelweit et al. comment that party preferences develop early. Some studies even suggest that 'by the age of 10 primary schoolchildren could accurately name the country's main political parties and express a preference for one'. In the case of 'British school-children 80 per cent were able to do so' (Himmelweit et al., 1985: 51), though not all who expressed a preference could describe what the parties stood for. Moore et al.'s findings tend to confirm both the age criteria and the relative paucity of information known about the parties (1985: 103).

When Himmelweit et al.'s sample of 13-year-olds were asked in 1951 who they would vote for, 81 per cent were able to name the party of their choice. As for parent and child correspondence, Himmelweit et al. note that 'where the parents had voted Conservative or Labour over 60 per cent of the sons followed suit, while less than 20 per cent did so where the parents had voted Liberal' (1985: 51). Other studies cited by Himmelweit report a lower degree of parent–child agreement (1985: 52). The Jennings and Niemi panel study of 'young adults and their parents' also came up with only a 'modest' degree of parent–child concordance *vis-à-vis* a range of political orientations (1985: 114). That is, although there may be an element of similarity between the political orientations of a child and those of his/her parent, that correspondence is not so large as to point to a straightforward process of value transmission or transmission of party political preferences.

The significance of these findings, at least for Jennings and Niemi, led them to favour what they called a 'life-cycle' model of political learning which 'holds that while persistence [of values] is the rule, certain orientations are very amenable to alteration at given life stages . . . it lays great weight on the reactivity of the individual to alterations in social circumstances, alterations which commonly, though not invariably, accompany the ageing process' (1985: 20–1). Once more, we return to a description of a process that is open to external influences, to learning and increased (or different) knowledge, to maturation.

There are other, perhaps contributory, explanations as to why the level of concordance was only 'modest'. One reason put forward for the lower level of agreement in one 1980 study was that the sample for the study grew up in the 1970s, a period in which there was a 'decline in strong party identification' (quoted in Himmelweit et al., 1985: 52). This sort of account can also be found in Moore et al., where they pinpoint the 'weakening party system . . . and the dramatic lowering of party identification among adults in the late 1970s' (1985: 107). Societal factors such as the impeachment of the US President in the 1970s, and governmental incompetence and duplicity can also lead to individuals becoming less trusting of political institutions – a factor which may explain differences between parents and their children who were maturing during the 1970s (Himmelweit et al., 1985: 63).

Despite the low level of correspondence between child and parent *vis-à-vis* political orientations, it is important to ask why there should be an expectation that correspondence would be of a high order. Several reasons can be put forward. These include the following: that children identify with parents and so would take on their parents' choices, or that children imitate their parents, or identify with/imitate one or other parent, and so on. Connell questions this interpretation of the supposed processes at work on several grounds. First, he argues that the whole notion of 'identification' is not particularly well thought out. What is being proposed is that a child comes to identify with his/her parents and in so doing 'picks up a commitment to a party as part of a bundle of the parent's traits; and his party preference thus has an unconscious, emotional basis' (1971: 78). Yet a number of different versions of identification can be elaborated. For example, identification need not necessarily lead to a wholesale transmission of values. Second, support for the idea of identification cannot be derived from large-scale surveys since these do not reveal the existence of identification. Rather they identify coincidences of voting preferences between generations. Third, he suggests that we need to understand the family environment if we are to understand the development of political orientations. Thus, he argues,

> we can regard the typical nuclear family as a political monopoly of one party and, from the child's position, analogous to a totalitarian state where all communications about parties point the one way. Given that the bulk of communications to the children about party preference come from their parents; and given that the children do not widely distrust their parents' judgement, then the grounds for choice available to any child will usually make a reasonable decision coincide with his parents'. No emotional basis for correspondence need be assumed . . . So it can be seen as a 'reasonable act of political choice'. (1971: 82–3)

Although this position is not articulated by other authors, other studies contain some clues which can validate Connell's account. It is important to recall here just what the process of socialization is seen to do. As Himmelweit et al. observe, the family is the primary socializing agent and its success as such depends on

> the political involvement of the parents, their agreement on matters politic as well as the relation of child to parent. Where both parents are actively involved in politics, share the same political outlook and have good relations with their children, influence should be maximal, *particularly where the wider community provides supporting cues.* (1985: 51; my italics)

Not only is this a good description of Connell's 'totalitarian state' but it goes one step further in emphasizing the extent to which the 'wider community' reinforces what takes place within the family setting. It follows that as the supports that can be found in the wider community weaken, so too will the nature of party identification within the family, and therefore of children, unless other circumstances mitigate this. Here one need only recall Parkin's (1971) argument that it is only in those settings which have strong occupational and traditional community ties that alternative value systems can be maintained. Only under such conditions can they withstand the onslaught of the dominant value systems. Obviously, as these settings (mining communities, steel communities and the like) decline or disappear and as political parties shun strong ideological positions then the basis of support for alternative and oppositional value systems narrows considerably.

Just as the weakening setting reduces the likelihood of strong attachments developing, adolescents and young adults leaving the family environment has the same effect. As they enter adulthood, experience the vicissitudes of the labour market, develop permanent relationships, have children, etc., other considerations will come to have a bearing on the direction of their political development. Certainly, the life-cycle model favoured by Jennings and Niemi and derived from their panel study of young people and their parents does lend support to this view.

So the transition from child to young adult is marked by a decline in parental influence, more so if a young adult moves away from the family home. Although research has sought to explore parent–child influences, what remains unclear is the relationship between a child's own early political development, her/his construction of the political and her/his political activity in later life. The period of transition is much less researched than periods of adulthood. This is the subject of the next section.

Adults and the construction of politics: are there parallels with the child's construction of politics?

Although one would expect adults to have a more rounded appreciation and understanding of the complexity of the political system and of the political process, are there similarities between the ways in which adults and children frame political issues? It may be that just as children work with simple notions of 'goodies' and 'baddies', so too do adults; indeed, even an adult attempting to make sense of the war in ex-Yugoslavia would be hard pushed to go much beyond an account of transgressors ('baddies') and those transgressed upon ('goodies'). If this is the case, one can hypothesize that there is indeed a limited number of ways of framing issues and that these recur with enormous regularity irrespective of generational differences. Before we turn to this hypothesis, it is important to dwell a little on both Gamson (1992) and Neuman et al.'s work (1992) in order to explore their findings about the adult's construction of politics.

As noted above, Neuman et al.'s concern is with the way individuals frame issues. For example, in relation to the 'Star Wars' project (SDI) – one of the five explored in the study – individuals could think about this as an economic issue (i.e. cost would be uppermost in their minds), or as an issue about conflict (i.e. us and them), or as something which alerts us to the human impact of such developments, and so on. In other words, one does not need to know the full details of the 'Star Wars' initiative in order to be able to say something about it. Individuals draw on past experiences, past events to make sense of the present and so 'when we refer to making sense of the news or constructing political meaning, the corresponding micro level process for the individual is, in effect, linking a news story (by definition, new information) to a news issue and an interpretive frame (what they already know)' (Neuman et al., 1992: 39).

Another example would be the pit closure announcement which generated a great deal of anxiety and public disquiet (see Chapter 5, pp. 112–25). Coming at a time of economic depression and high unemployment, the announcement of an immediate cut of 30,000 jobs and the closure of an industry was unlikely to be welcomed by anyone. The details of the government's plans were, as always, important but it was the piecing together of a government decision to make many workers unemployed, the manner of the announcement, the unfair treatment meted out to a particular group of workers, and so on that permitted individuals to pass judgement on this case. How well thought out or consistent these responses were cannot now be known, but that there could be a response on the part of individuals is beyond doubt. This example, only sketched out here, offers another reason why it is important that we understand better the interaction of people and the media.

The fact that responses can be elicited, as the above two examples suggest, leads on to the question of whether such responses can be infinitely variable. According to Neuman et al., this is not so and only a handful of frames dominate. They identify five:

frames which

- involve economic themes,
- involve divisions of protagonists into 'us' and 'them',
- involve perceptions of control by powerful others,
- involve a sense of the human impact of issues,
- involve the application of moral values. (1992: 62)

Several frames can be used at one and the same time when looking at a particular news story. The interesting question, and this is one pursued by Neuman et al., is whether or not the public frames used correspond with media frames or the official media discourse. If they do, then one could see an obvious link between the ways the media framed issues and the ways the public thought about them; if they do not, the correspondence will be much weaker, so leaving considerable room for individual and public multiple readings of the news story and comprehension of the news issue. The comparison of audience frames and media frames revealed significant differences: 'the most dramatic difference is the heavy emphasis on conflict in the media (29 per cent) compared with only 6 per cent in the depth interviews ... the human impact (36 per cent) and moral values (15 per cent) frames are more prominent in the discourse of the mass public than in the media (only 18 per cent and 4 per cent, respectively)' (Neuman et al., 1992: 74).

Whilst accepting that public discourse is much richer than media discourse what is less clear in Neuman et al.'s work is the extent to which alternative frames can be found in public thinking about the news. Put another way, does the public simply reproduce a much richer version of the media discourse rather than formulate a different one altogether? Or, and this is another possibility, is the public discourse one that reveals the audience's limited comprehension of news and limited grasp of detail? Some answers to both of these questions can be found in the works already cited. We have seen that children tend to reproduce, albeit with some amendments, adult versions of events and their interpretations. And in the work of Gamson we can also see the limited range of frames employed by adults. He identified his frames differently from those cited by Neuman although there are some important similarities.

Gamson is much more interested in how people decide to take part in forms of collective action such as protest and what it is in their use of sources of information, experiences and the like which spurs them to take action. In pursuing this research agenda, he suggests that individuals must adopt a 'collective-action' frame if they are at all likely to act. The collective-action frame has three components: the injustice component 'refers to the moral indignation expressed in this form of political consciousness'; the agency component refers 'to the consciousness that it is possible to alter conditions or policies through collective action'; and the identity component 'refers to the process of defining this "we", typically in opposition to some "they" who have different interests or values' (1992: 7). Significantly, though, he goes on to argue that 'none of the visible frames on any of the issues considered here promote or encourage citizen action' (1992: 62).

Two things follow on from this. The first is the suggestion that media content may inform but not seek to engage. As with the study of children, television 'simultaneously draws them in and holds them at a distance' (Connell, 1971: 129). Second, and in spite of the absence of 'collective-action' frames in the media, people do consider taking part in collective action and do take part in collective action. Much of this can be explained by referring to experiences other than media ones, e.g. personal experiences, experiences with relatives, and the like.

So even though media discourse, intentionally or unintentionally, sets boundaries of interpretation what one finds is a much more complex picture: 'interviewees freely mix together exemplary events and ideas drawn from their own life experiences, books, motion pictures, and entertainment television as well as the traditional news media as they explain their thinking on political topics' (Jamieson, 1992: 112; see also 117–18, 180). This is a veritable heady brew but, significantly, one which involves the continuous replaying of media images and interpretations of events. Perhaps not surprisingly, Gamson could claim that in his transcript material one could find 'plenty of evidence of gaps in knowledge, confusion, and passivity if one is looking for them'.

Part of the reason for these gaps may lie in the nature of media discourse and even in the very different qualities of the media in question but there is one other point that is worth pondering. Both Gamson (1992) and Robinson and Levy (1986) note the importance of discussing the news as a way of beginning to comprehend the content in question. One of Gamson's interviewees is quoted as saying, 'Yeah, this has an effect on us, just talking, because you don't even, you don't even think about it until you're *asked* about something' (1992: 64). Or, as Robinson and Levy point out, one of their five conclusions to their study of news comprehension is that 'Interpersonal discussion of news may be at least as powerful a predictor of comprehension as exposure to news media' (1986: 234). Though they are referring in part to news transmitted by word of mouth, they also note how at this stage in the processing of news 'we see the real diffusion of information, because it is here that the media accounts are "introspected," discussed and even challenged' (1986: 24).

From a different perspective, what is interesting in juxtaposing these two is the degree of similarity one can find between them and, going one step further, between these and the points made by Connell concerning the way children came to organize the parts of the political field, namely an appreciation of power structures and hierarchical role structures, the idea of conflict ('us' and 'them') and others which are present in the text but are not drawn out. For example, several of Connell's child interviewees refer to the Aborigines and their condition in Australia. Sometimes parallels are drawn with the case of blacks in the USA – the research was conducted during a period of upheaval in the USA – but at other times the children draw on a sense of 'injustice' to account for the state of the Aborigines: 'I think they should get the same rights, I don't think they get Housing Commission, all that they've got a reserve down at La Perouse' (15-year-old boy, 1971: 87). As Connell comments, in ways reminiscent of Gamson, the boy's argument 'relies on the idea that people unfairly deprived of what is due them have a right to disruptive protest. Though Sam never states it in so many words, *a concern for social justice runs through his observations*' (1971: 88; my italics). Whether or not such a 'general attitude' (Connell, 1971: 88), an 'injustice component' (Gamson, 1992: 7), or a 'moral values' frame (Neuman et al., 1992: 62) is a theme which is very commonly expressed is an important question. It could be that an idea of what is fair and just develops at an early age as children come to interact with others in a rule-bound social environment such as the primary school and the playground. There may be limitations to the extension of this argument since it is obvious that those who hold 'racist' views would regard comments concerning 'injustice' to ethnic minorities differently. So the context in which such positions are allowed to develop may be significant.

Summary and conclusion

This chapter has covered a great deal of ground and it has highlighted a series of questions which have not been as adequately researched as they perhaps should be. Central to much of the chapter is the view that we need to understand better how individuals make sense of the political content they confront in their daily lives. This forces us to consider the sense made of news programmes, of current affairs programmes, but there is no reason why a broader definition of political content should not be adopted here so as to include other media content whose content can also be deemed political or which may contain information or images about the social and political world.

It may be that the 'constructionist' approach is the best one currently available to offer answers to some of the questions posed above. It is not beyond criticism, though. Can one safely identify the frames used by individuals, and to what extent are these frames accurate reflections of public sentiments, of public thoughts? There is an ever-present danger that the positions may be inappropriately categorized and that slight, but significant, differences in perceptions will be ironed out for the sake of neatness. Other criticisms of the method, particularly the statistical aspect of it, have also been voiced (Gavin, 1994). Having set out these points, one still returns to the overriding concern of this chapter with the task of exploring how people think about their world and the part the media play in it all.

In exploring this sort of area, we clearly need to pay particular attention to whether different media have different properties which can make for better communication, and whether enough effort has been made to look at this in order to improve the situation. Are there better ways of covering politics than the clip from Prime Minister's Question Time, a round-table interview with representatives of major parties, or a leaden interview with a politician? In view of the importance of the mass media for political communication and for the public's understanding of politics, this is a task which requires some attention

Note

1. David Swanson also uses the term 'constructivist' approach. There are many similarities between his account of that approach and the 'constructionist' approach used by Neuman et al. One of the key differences between these two accounts is that Swanson seeks to move from an account of interpretations to an exploration of subsequent political behaviour (see Swanson, 1981).

7

Political Communication and the Americanization of Politics

Election contests have often provided an important setting for the analysis of the changing nature of the relationship between politics and communication. In such settings one can, for instance, explore the possible influence of the media on voting behaviour, on political party organization and parties' communication strategies, and on the nature of the political system itself. What is beyond doubt, though, is that the presence of the mass media, particularly television, has altered the whole process of political communication to such an extent that political activities and strategies revolve around them.

Indeed, individual country studies of political communication during election contests appear to emphasize very similar points. Whether the examples are drawn from southern Europe, or from South America, matters little: the constituent parts of the election process in whichever country one is investigating have a sense of familiarity to them, as these recent comments on two electoral contests illustrate.

> For Boris Yeltsin's referendum campaign, Saatchi and Saatchi were invited by . . . Yeltsin's pollsters, to accompany Gallup Poll and Matrix Public Relations on a research study among Russian voters. We were then asked to present recommendations to help Yeltsin. (Hilton, 1993: 24)

> The victory of Ernesto 'the bull' Pérez Balladares in the Panamanian presidential elections . . . marks the second time in a fortnight that Saatchi & Saatchi has won an election in central America.

> Saatchi and Saatchi 'had a very disciplined client who accepted all their recommendations', says Alberto Conte of the rival PR firm McCann Erickson. 'It was a well-structured campaign with attention to detail. The experts did their job and the "product" followed the instructions to the letter.' (Gunson, 1994: 11)

Whether Ernesto 'the bull' Balladares, or indeed, Yeltsin, are aware of it, or not, their political activities contribute one more piece of evidence to a growing body of literature on the evolution of electoral practices around the world and their seeming convergence, and, perhaps more critically, on the implications of that convergence not only for the practices of political communication but also for the future patterns of socio-political development which these countries are embarking upon. It is this very broad topic – and one that has far-reaching implications – which is explored in the first part of this chapter. In addition to looking at the evidence for this convergence, it will outline the argument that this process of convergence has an American origin and that it could therefore be referred to as the 'Americanization' of politics and political communication.

The second part of the chapter will look at shortcomings in this conceptualization of change in political practices. It will also suggest that the notion of 'Americanization' needs to be considered within a broader appreciation of the 'modernization' of societies. The conclusion will draw the themes together and outline some of the major concerns about the present trends in political communication. In adopting this approach to the topic of political (election) communication, this chapter seeks to avoid making specific and lengthy references to individual countries, preferring to concentrate on the seeming similarities in practices that are emerging across countries. Whether or not similarities outweigh differences is a theme that runs throughout this chapter.

Political communications and elections

The above examples drawn from Russia and Panama resonate with electoral communication practices across the Western world: the presidential debate, the attention paid to the polls, the use of Anglo-American PR firms, the advice of experts, and so on. As Mancini and Swanson (1994) have recently suggested, we can see around the world many common practices despite great differences in the political cultures, histories and institutions of the countries concerned. These are practices such as political commercials, candidates selected in part for their appealing image on television, experts advising candidates on strategies, media professionals hired to produce campaign materials, mounting campaign expenses, and mass media moving to centre stage in campaigns.

This close resemblance to electoral practices developed in other settings such as the USA or Europe raises some fundamental questions about the nature, and patterns, of change that are being experienced in countries far from these centres of media, political and economic power. Are these countries copying Western practices wholesale? Are they adapting them to local needs? Are these countries becoming more like the Western countries they are emulating? Are they becoming more alike in their media practices during electoral, and other, periods?

It is perhaps easier to document the existence of similar practices, such as the use of 'experts', than to make sense of the significance of those practices in different political and social settings. One example of such difficulties would relate to elections and electoral practices. Whilst all elections comprise similar elements – candidates, media practices, voters, etc. – the way these elements are grouped together and their significance varies from one political system to another. In some countries, for instance, voters have to choose between candidates for President as well as other representatives (USA, France), whilst in others the choice is between different political parties (Britain, Greece) (see Table 7.1, pp. 155–6). Even where there are apparent similarities, differences of detail may exist. Thus, American presidential candidates can appear almost out of nowhere and can make themselves into viable contenders for national office through careful and extensive use of the mass media (e.g. Ross Perot), whereas French or Greek presidential candidates cannot progress far without extensive party political support – or at least up to now! So even a comparison of electoral communication practices in the context of presidential contests requires sensitive analysis of the political processes under investigation. Such problems inhabit the very nature of comparative work. What is being compared, and are the institutions or practices compared similar or do they play similar parts in different political and social systems?

Such problems notwithstanding, the reasons for carrying out comparative work have become stronger as the sorts of similarity in communication practices described above have become more obvious across countries. Not only do we need to document and explain the similarities in electoral (and other) communication practices but we also have to pay attention to the differences. Only by addressing the issue of similarities – and how they have come about – and differences – and how these continue to persist and possibly outweigh the superficial semblance of similarities – and the significance of both, can we develop a proper understanding of the processes of communication and politics in contemporary societies.

This task is implicit in Blumler et al.'s (1992) support for comparative (political) communications research. They cite three main reasons for pursuing this line of research. Comparative research, they argue,

- permits us to explore 'patterns and problems . . . in our own spatial and temporal milieux' (1992: 3) which are usually taken for granted and are treated unproblematically. By making comparisons, one can come to appreciate the extent to which they are either fairly common, or unique, and the possible reasons why that should be the case;
- can often allow us to transcend the specificity of single country studies and to generalize 'theories, assumptions, and propositions' across time and space. As Blumler et al. comment, 'most election studies are culturally blinkered . . . they cannot distinguish those features of campaign communication that are common to all democratic polities from those that are nationally exceptional' (1992: 3–4). Here too, comparisons begin to permit one to make sense of the emergence of similarities, and the entrenchment of continuing differences;
- can 'explore and reveal the consequences of differences in how communication is organized at a macrosocial level' (1992: 4).

Comparative research allows us, then, to view domestic practices not in isolation but as a set of practices which may have similarities with sets of practices in other countries. We can then begin to explore how such similarities have come about, why they have come about, and the meaning of this convergence for the future social and political development of the societies themselves. To return to the example at the start of this chapter, is the political system of Panama becoming more like that of the USA or Europe, or is the resemblance superficial, with real differences persisting at other levels of analysis, say, at the level of routine domestic politics? Furthermore, if some sort of convergence is taking place, what are its implications for the practices of communicators, and of politicians?

The Americanization of election communication

Although the idea of Americanization is not a new one – it was first used in the 1830s as a term of abuse (Rose, 1974: 10) – it has gained greater currency as the mass media, and television in particular, have moved to centre stage in social and political life. Indeed, as television becomes the main source of information for most people, the fact that its development has been greatly influenced by the American experience or format increases the connections between practices in the USA and elsewhere. In this respect, the American experience cannot easily be overlooked, nor should it. Butler and Ranney (1992), for instance, identify a range of practices including the use of computers, fax and direct mailing, which originated in the US but which are currently widely used outside it. As they point out, even phrases such as 'sound-bite', 'photo-opportunity' and 'news management' have an American origin, yet they are commonly heard today 'in every election strategy conference in Western Europe' (1992: 8). So much so that Mancini and Swanson (1994) have suggested that campaigning in democracies around the world is becoming more and more Americanized as candidates, political parties and news media take cues from their counterparts in the United States.

But can the notion of Americanization be defined more precisely? Does it simply refer to the adoption of practices first used in the USA? Does it refer to the take-up of technological developments? Does it refer to imitation and importation of practices and values? Does it contribute to our understanding of the significance of the transfers being alluded to? And what significance does one attach to the adaptation of imported practices? For, as Jeremy Tunstall observed in relation to the press, 'all other nations in the world have borrowed American press models and then subsequent media models; but this does not mean that more or less American-style media "fit" so neatly into, or constitute such an important part of, other political systems' (1977: 263).

One can begin to see the relevance of the notion of Americanization if one considers the nature of modern election campaigning. Without doubt, modern election campaigns in most Western democratic systems revolve around the medium of television. To an extent, all electoral campaigns force candidates to communicate with their electorate and so it is not surprising that television will be used extensively. But the modern election is seen by many as being significantly different from past elections in the extent to which the whole process of political communication has become professionalized. At its simplest level, this means that political actor/s seeking election will co-ordinate their activities to ensure maximum publicity, but as political actors – *and their consultants* – become more adept at using the media, they seek ever more sophisticated ways of guaranteeing favourable publicity, favourable images, a news agenda reflecting their priorities, an uncritical media, and so on.

We can perhaps appreciate this sense of a qualitative shift in some recent writings on elections. Pfetsch and Schmitt-Beck observe that 'the election campaign is often viewed as a pure marketing problem . . . The application of the marketing approach to political campaigning . . . has been labelled as "New Politics"' (1993: 6). Philippe Maarek also works within that frame of reference, though he draws a distinction between political communication and political marketing. This distinction may be worth making when considering only one aspect of political communication, namely electoral communication practices. He suggests that political communication is a more general term which can refer to the means by which political actors 'communicated' with the public in the recent past, whilst 'political marketing' is a more recent phenomenon which involves 'a strategy of design, rationalization and conveyance of modern political communication' (Maarek, 1995: 2). As he goes on to explain, 'political communication no longer means merely designing and printing a message on posters without consideration of whom they are addressed to. It encompasses the entire marketing process, from preliminary market study to testing and targeting' (Maarek, 1995: 28).

Maarek, amongst others, is in no doubt as to the (American) source of many of the ideas that make up 'political marketing'. Gurevitch and Blumler note, for example, that 'American style "video-politics" seems to have emerged as something of a role model for political communicators in other liberal democracies' (1990: 311). Kaid and Holtz-Bacha develop this notion further. For them, the Americanization of campaigns can be judged according to the extent to which the characteristics of American campaigns take root elsewhere. These characteristics include the dominance of television, 'the predominance of images instead of issues', the personalization of politics, and the 'professionalization of political actors in the development of media strategies' (Kaid and Holtz-Bacha, 1995: 9).

We can see the relevance of these comments if we identify in a little more detail some of the tendencies in (electoral) political communication which gave rise to the idea of Americanization. Of all these, it is perhaps the use of the communications consultant which marks off modern electoral contests from the more traditional ones. And, as Kathleen Hall Jamieson has suggested, it was only relatively recently – in the 1960s – that firms specializing in political media consultancy came into existence. This was not so much a radical innovation as the evolution of a role which had existed for some time. What was significant in this new era, according to Jamieson, was that the role had evolved from 'one of technical adviser unwelcome in the strategy sessions . . . to campaign insider responsible for the strategy for all the campaign's advertising and, often, for its communication strategy, as well' (1992: 36). By the 1990s it was obvious that the communications adviser had come to play a key role in electoral contests both within, and outside of, the USA.

One can see a similar evolution in British electoral practices although one should also note the relevance of the American experience with television for the future of British electoral communication. As in the USA, the early involvement of publicists and advertising agencies from the immediate post-war period onwards was mainly in the design and publicity of political party material. It was much later that they came to occupy a more central position, particularly as the political parties themselves became more keenly aware of the importance of effective communication techniques. And it was here that the American experience was useful. Michael Cockerell records, for example, how John Profumo 'had been on a special trip to study the American presidential campaign of 1952' before producing a report for the Conservative party (1989: 15). The sense of learning from the American experience 'because they were much cleverer in their election propaganda' (ibid.) cannot be denied, though the details of that process of importation have yet to be fully documented. Accounts of the period, and of the early years of British television, suggest that everyone was learning the tools of the trade but that the American experience may have been the prime source of inspiration. It was probably in the late 1940s and early 1950s that these experiences began to gel, and that the lessons of advertisers and media experts both in the USA and in Britain began to form a sort of first-draft text on the practices of electoral communication via television (see, for example, Windlesham, 1966; Cockerell, 1989).

By the mid-1950s, British television personalities/producers such as Christopher Chataway and Tony Benn began to bring their own individual expertise of the medium to their respective political campaigns. In time, others were brought in to advise on campaign communications and so the nature of the electoral contest began to change. So much so that by 1966 Lord Windlesham could write that 'professionalism in communication techniques became the accepted ideal of party political organizers' (1966: 37) without fear of contradiction or ridicule. By the 1990s, and after the much commented upon techniques of Gordon Reece and Harvey Thomas in support of Margaret Thatcher's campaigns, campaign advisers had become an accepted feature of electoral contests, and their role as insiders could hardly be doubted though it left some of the politicians wondering whether (or if?) ideology should have been abandoned at the say-so of media experts, and for reasons of better imagery and effective communication (see Negrine, 1994; Franklin, 1994; Scammell, 1995; Kavanagh, 1995).

Even if we look at electoral communication practices in countries where the media are less well developed either historically or in terms of the legitimacy of their practices, it is possible to test the validity of many of the propositions discussed above. In this respect, Greece offers an interesting example. Ruled by a dictatorship until the mid-1970s, Greece has only in recent decades become a state with democratic practices. And it is only since the late 1980s that the broadcasting system has moved away from the control of the state. Some government control over the state broadcasting channels ET1 and ET2 is still in evidence but there is no overt governmental control of the plethora of private television channels which have proliferated since then.

As in other democratic systems, television has become the dominant medium. In a recent piece of research conducted by MRB Hellas, it was found that as many as 69 per cent of the sample obtained their daily information from television compared with 15 per cent who gave the press as their main source (1993). With such evidence, it is then hardly surprising that political parties would devote most of their energies to the medium of television. But this interest in television stretches beyond the contemporary decade; even in the late 1970s when television was a government monopoly political parties had already begun to tailor their conferences and rallies to its needs.

The current situation may then be seen as an *evolution* – to use Jamieson's phrase – along a path of greater sophistication (or professionalization) in the handling of the medium of television for, presumably, more 'effective' communication. Foreign experts, American and European, were first employed by the socialist party Pasok in the election campaign in the early 1980s, and this tendency continued right up to and including the 1993 election when foreign experts as well as domestic advertisers were used by the conservative party New Democracy. In addition, considerable sums of money were spent by the political parties on television: 94 per cent of the total advertising expenditure.

The sense of there having been a change in the nature of political campaigning is obvious from the many examples given above; similarly, the sense that this change is somewhat reprehensible cannot be overlooked. For many critics of 'political marketing', the fact that politicians are being 'sold' or 'packaged' like a bar of soap devalues the nature of political communication, of the political process itself, and of the role of the citizen now turned consumer. Yet this view of political marketing is not shared by all. Steve Hilton, who worked for Saatchi and Saatchi on Yeltsin's referendum campaign, points out that it is 'entirely appropriate that political communication techniques developed in the Western democracies are put to good use in Russia and elsewhere, as democracy becomes established. Advertising and communication is as essential for modern democracy as a ballot box' (1993: 24). For Hilton, the techniques are anything but reprehensible. They are the useful methods for enabling candidates to make their points to their electorates in the most appropriate way, using the most dominant medium of the day.

Hilton's position merits serious consideration but it is an extreme one if taken too literally. It may be true to say that the use of political marketing approaches is simply a modern development but it can only be useful and proper for both candidates and voters if it is counterbalanced by an active, inquisitive media system. As with a nation's diet, a stream of mass media commercials on the virtue and goodness of chocolate bars, crisps and sugary soft drinks may be taking the idea of properly informing consumers about food choices a bit too far. In a sense, Hilton's argument can be presented and discussed rationally because most of the sources for his experiences are Western democracies where an active and inquisitive media system is still in existence.

What is much less in doubt in Hilton's comments is the source of the many techniques of political marketing. It is taken for granted that they have a Western origin, or more precisely as with Maarek, an American origin. Yet if one looks closely at the developments in the USA, Britain and Greece or elsewhere, it is far from clear that they herald an inexorable drive towards Americanization. Does it refer to the use of similar – how similar? – *practices* during election contests only or to all forms of political communication? We know, for example, that in Britain, in contrast to the USA, broadcasters ensure equal distribution of time to major contenders and that air-time cannot be bought. In the case of Greece, paid-for political advertisements can be aired though broadcasters remain under the control of government or proprietors. Broadcasters are not the neutral observers so favoured by American commentators. So in what sense does the adoption, and adaptation, of certain American practices in Britain, Greece and elsewhere lead to Americanization?

We need to be fairly precise about the significance of two factors woven into the Americanization theme. First, we need to clarify the distinction between the adoption of practices and their adaptation in different settings. Writing about the influence of Americanization of Australian popular culture, White made a very similar point: that 'the examination of Americanization should embrace not just the impact of Americanization on popular culture, but also its effect on the culture as a whole' (quoted in Maguire, 1990: 216). The American impact both on specific techniques of political communication and on the environment of political communication needs to be considered. In this way, issues of similarities and differences – in techniques, approaches to political communication, to the nature of electoral contexts within different political systems – all become germane. Second, and by far a more general task, we perhaps need to question whether the Americanization noted above is any more than the professionalization of practices related to the growing dominance of television as a medium of communication; whether, in other words, the similarities which are much in evidence are somehow related to media-specific factors.

Similarities and differences

Even those who readily subscribe to the idea that Americanization of electoral communication is very much in evidence are careful to point out that differences between countries persist. Mancini and Swanson (1994), for example, draw back from a bold version of Americanization when they suggest that the processes described above do not always establish themselves elsewhere in identical ways or with the same consequences. Similarly, Kaid and Holtz-Bacha observe that although there are similarities, there are also important differences – 'in political structures and processes, in political culture, and in media systems' (1995: 10) which need to be recognized and which may give practices their individual country-specific and local characteristics. Gerstlé et al. remind us that

> While some of the above speculations [about Americanization] may indeed turn out to be accurate, the argument overlooks the power of other elements in the political milieu and grants to technology a power that it does not have. The emergence of privately owned television stations in France does not mean that they will be used politically in precisely the same way that they are used in the US and that 30-second spots will be the outcome. Many other options are possible. (1991: 281)

And Tunstall warns us against assuming that because things have the same name they operate in similar ways:

> the enormous proliferation of the media which the USA developed (and which is now found with modifications in all other industrialized nations) assumed the American type of political party – a loose coalition of local parties and factions which met together mainly for electioneering. (Tunstall, 1977: 264)

Parties across Europe clearly differ from this type, although – and this is an important question to which we return – there is an implication in the Americanization thesis that contemporary political parties are taking on these characteristics. Note, for instance, the current concern expressed about the 'modernization' of the British Labour Party and its move away from its more traditional roots and ideologies.

Some other differences which persist in the way political actors use the media during elections have been due to the 'nature of the media system/ political system interface', especially where 'the public media systems have dominated Western democracies' (Kaid and Holtz-Bacha, 1995: 207). It would not be an exaggeration to suggest that such public service institutions have limited the influence of political actors on the broadcasting system and that they have maintained a strong defence against broadcasting becoming responsive to commercial pressures alone. So, although those who write about Americanization acknowledge the existence of differences between political systems and practices, the issue of convergence, especially future convergence, remains. As Blumler succinctly put it, are non-communication factors such as culture and political and social traditions any more than 'brakes – the force of some of which may be gradually weakening – in the accelerating momentum of the modern publicity process?' (Blumler, 1990: 111).

That there are similarities and differences can be seen in Table 7.1. Interestingly, for the purposes of supporting, or otherwise, the Americanization thesis, it is difficult to know whether one should emphasize the similarities or the differences. More problematic is that the 'snapshot' offered in Table 7.1 offers no information about how these practices have developed historically. Nor does it identify the factors which can help us project future trends. It does not, in other words, enable us to disentangle the knot of influences which have come to bear on election practices across a broad range of countries; influences which can, in part, be accounted for as a response to the emergence and entrenchment of the 'modern publicity process'.

The 'modern publicity process'

According to Blumler, 'the modern publicity process involves a competitive struggle to influence and control popular perceptions of key political events and issues through the major mass media' (1990: 103). The significance of the American experience in the emergence of the 'modern publicity process' is not denied, but the emphasis is much more on the nature of television itself as a major factor in the changing nature of electoral communication and other political practices. As Butler and Ranney observe, 'It is the practices of politicians and the media, *exploiting technical innovations and marketing approaches*, that have altered the appearance of elections' (1992: 4; my italics). This comes about because politicians seek to communicate with and/or influence all the citizens and the primary way of doing so is via television, a medium which they rarely completely control. Hence both politicians and broadcasters devise strategies, including reliance on marketing approaches and images, to ensure that their preferred presentations dominate. Put more extremely, the medium of television has brought about a significant change in the ways in which political actors seek to communicate with their publics. This is also true in relation to the development of the press, and of the development of radio broadcasting.

This is not to suggest some deterministic power of television (or any other medium) but merely to point out that the existence of such a medium brings enormous changes in its wake. It is a point which Thompson underlines when he argues that 'new technical media *make possible* new forms of social interaction, modify or undermine old forms of interaction, create new foci and new venues for actors and interaction, and thereby serve to restructure existing social relations and the institutions and organizations of which they are a part' (1990: 225).

It follows that politicians as well as the public will inevitably interact differently once a new medium of communication is inserted, as it were, between them. Just as politicians will use television extensively because it offers them the opportunity to contact all members of the public simultaneously, so too the public will begin to rely on television for most of its information about the political world because of its comparatively easy use. There are obviously numerous other changes that one can use to illustrate what happens once 'the modern publicity process takes over' (Blumler, 1990: 104). An increased importance is attached to media strategies, to getting the

Table 7.1 *Selected features of electoral and political communication in the USA and some European countries*

	Britain	USA	Germany	France	Greece
Selected features of political system	Parliamentary Elections for members of Parliament	Presidential	Parliamentary Elections for members of Parliament	Parliamentary	Parliamentary Elections for members of Parliament
		Direct elections for President		Direct elections for President	
	Two-party system	Two-party system	Multi-party system	Two-party/bloc system	Multi-party system
					Two-party/bloc system
Can TV air-time be bought for political broadcasts?	No	Yes	No	No	Yes
Is there free and guaranteed air-time for all political contenders?	Yes: according to proportion of votes cast	No	Yes: according to proportion of votes cast	Yes: equal time for presidential candidates	Yes: according to proportion of votes cast
Are there restrictions on how that free air-time can be used?	No	No	No	Yes. Detailed restrictions on what images can be used, how, etc.	No
Who 'pays' for the political broadcasts?	Political parties	Candidates	Parties	Parties pay for presidential candidates	Parties

Table 7.1 (*continued*)

	Britain	USA	Germany	France	Greece
Where are the political broadcasts shown?[1]	Public channels, private channels	Private channels	Public channels; can be shown on private channels	Public channels	Public channels, private channels
Number of political broadcasts permitted	Limited	Unlimited	Limited	Limited	Limited free time, unlimited bought time
Length (most common)	5 to 10 minutes	30 to 60 seconds	2.5 minutes	1993: up to 4 minutes	Length can vary
Turnout in recent presidential/legislative election	77.7% (1992 elections)	55% (1992 Presidential election)	79% (1994 Bundestag election)	68.9% (1993 Assembly elections)	83% (1993 elections)

[1] An important consideration here, as in other questions concerning broadcasting, is the commercial vs. non-commercial nature of the systems, as well as the balance of power between them. For example, whilst the public sector remains strong in Britain and Germany, it is less strong in France and Greece. What remains unclear is how the emergence of new commercial terrestrial and satellite broadcasting systems will impact on the nature of political communication.

Source: adapted from Kaid and Holtz-Bacha, 1995. Other sources used include: Kaid et al. 1991; Haiman (1991) 'A tale of 2 countries', in Kaid et al., 1991; Mair (1995)

message 'right', to the personalization of politics on the grounds that the medium cannot easily cope with the abstract and functions best with personalities. All of these can be seen as emanating from the insertion of television into modern life and its increased importance as a medium of communication and culture, or, as Swanson has written, from 'adapting the institutions and practices of politics and government to the central role of mass media, particularly television, in modern life, producing what may be described as 'media-centred democracy' (1993: 2).

What is significant here is that one can treat both Blumler's account of the 'modern publicity process' and Swanson's account of 'media-centred democracy' *independently* of any real reference points in the USA. What both these accounts describe or document is the growing importance of television in modern life, or, in Thompson's words, the 'mediazation of modern culture' (1990: 3). In fact, there may be considerable advantage in not attempting to connect the 'modern publicity process' or 'media-centred democracy' to Americanization and not only because of the inherent difficulties of searching for the roots of practices in a world which is increasingly typified by exchanges of ideas, practices, travel and experiences. By simply focusing on the 'modern publicity process', one can, for instance, examine the routine strategies of politicians and practices in disparate political and cultural contexts (e.g. Mexico, Panama, Greece) without unduly worrying, at least initially, about the American connections.

However, there is also a danger in *underplaying* the American influence. It is worth noting, for example, that non-American options are perhaps less readily taken up: who has copied the British model, or the French (Table 7.1)? To paraphrase Schou's account of post-war modernization in Denmark, the 'modernization [of Denmark] occurred in a *specific*, American form not strictly inherent in the process of modernization' (1992: 157). A similar statement could be made concerning the development of contemporary media with the emphasis being, by and large, on the deregulation and liberalization of media systems – an American idea imported into other countries – and away from the creation of publicly funded and publicly run systems of communications (see Palmer and Tunstall, 1990).

We can see many of these points – the difficulty of pinpointing the origins of practices, the impact of new media, the influence of circumstances – in the development of some forms of British political communication, including election practices. In his study of broadcasting in Britain between the two world wars, Mark Pegg devotes a section to the impact of radio on 'local political activity' (1983: 186–91). In those early days of radio, one could only speculate about the way in which radio would influence politics and political activity. That influence turned out to be 'a great deal more complicated' than was generally believed (1983: 186). Many groups, including the local press,

> were looking at ways in which candidates could get their message across before broadcasting became a reality. For this reason, radio was seen to be an

absolutely essential *aid* to the traditional methods of expressing comment or debate and, normally, it was welcomed by the local press and certainly by the local community. (1983: 186; my italics)

Pegg goes on to show how radio at first supplemented other forms of political communication but then gradually brought about a change in the form of communication and audience participation during elections. 'Election nights', he writes, 'became a lot quieter' as people stayed at home, forsaking the town hall meetings. 'The close physical contact between the electorate and parliamentary candidates had been considerably diluted by the appeal from the party leadership, using radio to speak directly to voters over the heads of their party colleagues' (1983: 187–8).

This discussion by Pegg is given over to a period in the life of the BBC when John Reith was devoting his energies to the creation of a model of broadcasting far removed from the American one. In this period, Reith also began to create the framework for (party) political broadcasting, broadcasts by the head of state, and broadcasting during periods of emergency (such as the 1926 General Strike). It is easy to treat these beginnings as the foundations of contemporary political communication in Britain. Indeed, that is precisely what Grace Wyndham Goldie argued in her autobiography, when she wrote that, 'television in Great Britain, in fact, inherited all the rights, duties and responsibilities which had been given to, and won by, radio broadcasting as a result of the struggles of Sir John Reith and the . . . Committees set up from 1923 onwards' (1977: 20).

Goldie's book on the development of current affairs television in Britain tends, on the whole, to suggest an indigenous autonomous pattern of development rather than a wholesale or even partial imitation of American practices. The continuity with radio was one obvious aspect of that development. Another aspect is the way she readily contrasts British television with, and distances it from, 'the grosser forms of commercial exploitation' evident in the USA (1977: 21).

But the really curious aspect of her book is the absence of any significant references to American broadcasting, or to practices in the USA which were then to be used in the UK. This absence is also noteworthy in Geoffrey Cox's book on the origins of Independent Television News (ITN), the provider of news programmes for the commercial network which was established in the mid-1950s. And yet it is probably correct to suppose that there must have been some knowledge of US television and that some of that knowledge and experience would have been of significance. Cox had spent time in the USA and he relates very vividly his experience of watching the McCarthy hearings on television in 1953. This, he wrote, 'had convinced me that television could revolutionize news coverage' (1983: 19), though he does not elaborate on that.

The view expressed by Cox was not very different from that of Donald Baverstock, one of the pioneers of television journalism in Britain. He too had experienced the American approach to television. As Alasdair Milne writes:

Donald's visit to America had been both a shock and a stimulus to him – a shock that American television studios were far more competently run than ours by people of apparently less calibre than we had available; and a stimulus that Europe' had just as much to offer in terms of ideas as the United States. 'That place', he said to me, 'confirmed to me that I was a European' (1988: 15; for other examples of travel between Britain and the US, see Briggs, 1979; 1995)

How do we make sense of this sort of information in relation to the theme of Americanization? Does it point to a straight transfer of practices, to an adaptation of practices? To a combination of adoption and adaptation? Could it be that different individuals in different locations arrived at similar answers at about the same time in the same way, as Anthony Smith describes in relation to the coming of radio? Sarnoff, wrote Smith,

> hit upon the idea at a moment when others were making the same connections and separations within other societies which had acquired the appropriate technical expertise. *No single person 'invented' radio; nor did any single society.* The post-war world was in a number of partly identifiable ways 'ready' for a new piece of machinery which would disseminate the culture of mass society. (1976: 56; my italics)

The sense of there being some 'spirit of the times' element in the transfer and adaptation of practices is also to be found in Gurevitch and Blumler's longitudinal study of election practices in British television news. Although the two authors stress the extent to which the changes they identify in the period 1966–92 reflect 'changes in the overall culture of the BBC, derivative partly in turn from cultural changes in British society at large' (1993: 440), they go on to suggest that the 'processes of change that have played on the election role of the BBC in the period analysed may not be so uniquely British as a first look would imply' (1993: 441). They suggest, as an extension, that 'the notion of *zeitgeist* deserves to be taken seriously and to become part of the conceptual tool kit for tracing the impact of large-scale social and cultural change on mass media workings' (1993: 442).

The development of radio and television was influenced by many factors, with none of them being accorded a major and significant role. Is it possible, then, that these media, like others before them, encourage the use of certain practices because they seem 'appropriate' – although it is crucial to note here that, by and large, it is the Anglo-American practices that are being adopted/adapted/imitated, and not others. Whilst there may be other options, for example the British insistence on disallowing the sale of broadcast air-time for party political uses, these are not options that are widely accepted or readily taken up. Whether or not this points to a fundamental 'commercialization' of societies, where the legitimacy of publicly owned and run institutions is gradually being eroded, is a deeper and larger question which cannot be addressed here. (For a discussion of this, see Wernick, 1991.)

Americanization and modernization

If the first strand of the argument concerns the transfer of American communication practices into other countries, the second takes the argument in a somewhat different direction. At one level, the task here is to make sense of the reasons why similar practices have been taken up in widely different political environments, but at another, the task is to raise questions about whether all political systems are, in some way or other, becoming alike. Are similar practices being adopted because societies are becoming more and more alike in their make-up and in their structures and processes of governance?

One hypothesis is that when a country adopts American practices, it is a reflection of a wider and more general process which can be usefully termed 'modernization'. That is, as societies change and become more alike in make-up and in structures and processes of governance, they come to adopt communication practices of an American origin. In this way, a theory of contemporary social change – the fragmentation of society, the emergence of a mosaic of political groupings and interests – is made to connect with an account of changes in the practices of political communication (see, for example, Mancini and Swanson, 1994).

This picture of social change is, in itself, unproblematic since it merely describes the sorts of patterns that lie at the heart of accounts which document the shift from traditional to 'modern' societies. Keane, for example, connects social change with communication in his discussion of Tönnies' analysis of the transition from 'pre-modern societies' to 'modern societies [which] . . . are differentiated and associational and structured by three overlapping organising principles: markets, states and public opinion' (1991: 21). Such accounts fit in well with the discussion of modernization (and Americanization) since the sense that there has been a shift from one form of society to another – from the 'traditional archetype' to the 'modern archetype' – is ever-present in them (see, Mancini and Swanson, 1994; Kaid and Holtz-Bacha, 1995: Chs 1 and 2).

There is much here that parallels the current debates in social theory on the concept of 'modernity' and 'postmodernity'. In this growing body of work on past, present and future patterns of change the emphasis has been on understanding the ways in which Western industrial societies are fragmenting and producing new forms of association and action. Modernity is identified with periods of change from the Enlightenment onwards, through the periods of industrialization in the nineteenth century which brought about enormous social upheaval. By the twentieth century it 'became a progressively global phenomenon' (Hall et al., 1992: 2). It is, more precisely, 'constituted by political processes (the rise of the secular state and polity), the economic (the global capitalist economy), the social (formation of classes and an advanced sexual and social division of labour), and the cultural (the transition from a religious to a secular culture) (Hall et al., 1992: 2. See also Giddens, 1991).

The notions of fragmentation and of continuous social change permeate all the characteristics of 'modernity' in ways which are not substantively different from the idea of modernization. What we have here, then, is an account of large-scale social change where the older, more traditional 'ways of doing things' are superseded by newer social structures and cultural factors. One example which is particularly applicable to West European societies would be the demise of older class-based structures surrounding specific work and community structures (e.g. mining, trade unions, etc.) and their replacement by newer types of association based on, say, consumption, gender or cultural groupings. In this newer context, politicians can no longer simply rely on traditional values or allegiances such as class to garner loyalty. New methods need to be used, and new forms of communication are required to make contact with the remnants of traditional support as well as the newer structures which bind citizens together. Socialist politicians would, in this scenario, have to connect with their traditional bases of support (miners, the working class, etc.) but also with other groupings such as working women, salaried workers and so on.

This transformation of society will inevitably privilege those who can effectively connect with as many disparate groupings as possible in an electoral contest. Hence, one can argue, new ways of communicating need to be found to make that contact *in such a way as not to alienate supporters, and would-be supporters*. Herein lie the foundations for modern campaigning/marketing in modernized societies. And since modern campaigning is characterized by its use of techniques developed in the USA, here can also be seen most clearly the link between modernization and Americanization. Not surprisingly, then, the view that the more advanced the process of modernization, the more likely we are to find American innovations in campaigning is being adopted and adapted. Maarek, however, adds a qualification to this particular view: as he points out, 'many not-so-rich democracies, such as most of those of Latin America [which are less 'modernized' one presumes] do use many of the modern political communication techniques, and [make] campaigns in many European countries look quite pale in comparison' (1995: 21).

If this is correct, then we are exploring something which strongly relates to the emergence of television as a dominant medium of political communication even in less modernized countries!

So change notwithstanding, the real task must be to connect all these developments both with the exploration of modernization and with the themes of Americanization. It could certainly be argued that modernization – the transformation of society – has forced political parties to review the sources of their support. This has been graphically illustrated by Tim Delaney in his account of the 1979 general election in Britain when he noted that the Labour Party could no longer simply show a photograph of a man working at a lathe to illustrate the conditions of the working classes (1982: 27). As societies change, even become modern, images of society also need to be reassessed. Yet such a reassessment may be said to be independent of the growing importance of television *per se*, or any links with Americanized campaigning techniques. Admittedly, in wishing to make effective use of television someone like Tim Delaney may be using it in a way which owes something to the American experience, but all these links are tenuous, at best. The point is that modernization impacts on the way we communicate to each other face to face as well as via the mass media. For, as Graham Murdock has suggested, 'the constitution of modernity is inextricably bound up with the development of modern communication systems' (1993: 525). And he proposes that

> the organization of communications is not only constituted *by* the general dynamics of modernity but is constitutive *of* them, and that as we move to the present it comes to play an increasingly central role in shaping both institutional and cultural formations and the textures of everyday life. As a consequence, we cannot theorize modernity without taking formations of communications centrally into account. (1993: 522–3)

However, to argue that modernity and communications are constitutive of one another, and that communication is shaping everyday life ('media-centredness' by another name?) is a far cry from connecting modernity/ modernization to Americanization. Indeed, one of the crucial aspects of modernity is that it is not only a globalizing force but also that societies are 'shaped by both "internal" and "external" forces. The West forged its identity and interests in relation to endogenous developments in Europe and America, and through relations of unequal exchange . . . with "the Rest"' (Hall et al., 1992: 2).

As societies continue to make, and re-make themselves, they borrow, if not from one another, then from more dominant partners and influences. They continually transform themselves in myriad ways. In his recent work on 'post-war Americanization' Schou suggests, for example, that the study of '"Americanization" must not only deal with the study of *transmission* of values, ideas, images, and myths' but also 'with the process of *trans-formation*.' What is imported interacts with established cultural patterns. 'The American influence', he points out, '*revitalized* European culture' (1992: 143). A similar point about transformations and the interplay of cultures is made by Abu-Lughod. She gives the example of how 'oriental' and 'western' music mix in different cultural contexts. 'From an ethno-centric point of view, what *we* tend to see is the westernization of oriental music, but I would like to propose an alternative diagnosis. What we are seeing is the orientalization of western music' (1991: 133). Her point is not that there are not forces pushing towards a convergence in practices and institutions but that these do not define cultures and do not lead to a convergence of 'world views' and beliefs. Similarities abound but dissimilarities continue to inhabit the world. There is no real purpose in identifying the origin of change or the origin of practices since they have long melded together; knowledge of other countries and their institutions and practices circulates freely.

Conclusion

There is a certain lack of clarity about the precise nature of American-ization. There is also a need to identify more clearly whether one is describing a process simply of the adoption of techniques, philosophies and practices, or a process of adaptation. Similarly, we need to be clearer about the 'intensity' of the adoption or adaptation in question. One cannot deny the importance of America as a source of influence but other countries have also been important in other ways. Britain, for instance, has been the model for many a foreign broadcasting system. The obvious danger is to employ a simplistic notion of Americanization, implying, as it often does, a unilinear process of transfer from the USA to other countries.

But there are other difficulties with the Americanization thesis which also need to be considered. First, it is almost impossible to refute. We can see this problem clearly if we look at recent technological innovations such as the fax machine or the Internet. Both have been used in American elections, and they have been taken up in other countries. Some British politicians, for instance, can now be contacted via the Net. Is it valid, therefore, to argue that Britain is Americanized in its practices? What does the American influence actually mean in this sort of context? What if these innovations were used to foment revolutions and dissent? Would that still be considered part of the Americanization process? What, in other words, would a country uninfluenced by American (British, French, Portuguese, Spanish, Islamic . . .) practices and institutions actually look like, and is it possible to conceive of such a thing in the modern world? The problems inherent in the impossibility of disproving the Americanization thesis, or of making any real meaningful headway with it, is in no small way related to the increasing speed and wholesale manner in which modern practices flow across the world.

Moreover, although the Americanization thesis strongly implies that it is a one-way flow of influences, in reality we may be observing a more complicated process. Not only do some countries adapt practices from outside America – in Greece, for instance, European influences may loom larger than American ones; Panamanians used Saatchi and Saatchi, a British company, and so on – but America may itself import practices. As the *Guardian* reported in November 1992, 'the director and deputy director of campaigning for the Conservatives, flew to Washington to give the Bush campaign team seminars on how they had won from behind, in spite of adverse opinion polls and the recession' (Walker, 1992: 14). The Clinton camp made use of advisers from the Labour Party!

In these circumstances, to focus on specific patterns of importation and exchange of practices and to point to a single source would seem to undermine the complexity of the modern world and the sorts of inter-connections that the above examples make evident. It underplays 'the interpenetration of space and time' in the modern world.

A second criticism of the idea of Americanization is that it is perhaps too focused on only a small aspect of the process of political communication. It focuses on elections – and then only some and not all – and not on other ways in which political actors communicate with their publics. There is much more to political communication than a study of elections. So what does this mean for a thesis that appears to work with a definition of Americanization that applies to elections only? Once again, it may be more appropriate to view contemporary change as a product of technological, political, social change, etc. – and American (and other) influences.

Two final points need to be made. The first concerns the continuous evolution of technologies of communication, the second the implications of the discussion in this chapter for political communication in general.

The introduction of each new medium has altered the patterns of communication between political actors and publics (amongst other things). We are now entering a period in which other forms of communication are being established: cable television and satellite broadcasting, fax machines, the Internet, party phone lines, and so on. If the main media discussed here – the press, radio, television – led to the perception of the vast audience as an undifferentiated mass, these newer technologies are giving rise to ways of communicating with smaller publics. As with political marketing, the emphasis is, or can be, much more on the targeting of publics: different content and different practices to meet different needs. Political parties may then direct their 'messages' more precisely to entice different types of voter. To some extent then the evolution of campaign practices, of political marketing, takes into account experiences with new and different means of communication. New levels of sophistication are brought to bear, new practices copied or developed. Some will have been learned in America, others probably not.

The interesting questions relate to the evolving nature of the political system both as new means of communication are introduced and as existing ones become more commercial in orientation as a direct outcome of deregulatory policies. One of the arguments developed in Chapter 3 was that it is more likely that the political world will adapt to the media (and their needs) than the other way round. The more commercial the systems of communication, the less likely it is that the more traditional forms of political communication will survive intact. To give an example, having to pay for commercial political spots is likely to lead to the production of short, e.g. 30-second, spots and not the five-minute broadcasts common in Britain.

To return to Blumler's remark to the effect that the persistence of differences is being maintained by 'brakes' whose power may be weakening, the convergence which may take place in years to come may be driven by a changing media landscape. It may also be driven by journalists' changing perceptions of their roles, moving away from a position of dependency to a more powerful position in their own right. Journalists may then come to challenge politicians in a way that was less common when politics and political actors retained an aura of power. How this links up with the idea of Americanization with which we began this chapter, is something that future generations will have to look at.

Finally, Maarek has suggested that one of the consequences of the rise of political marketing has been short-termism: stress on the need to win and not the need to engage in debate. It leads to a pragmatic use of the media by politicians and their consultants in their search for victory but it does not engage with publics at large. It is one explanation, for example, of the 'drop in voter participation in most western democratic countries', or 'the demise of political ideologies' (1995: 225–6). But contemporary governments are all attempting to tackle similar problems – environmental, economic, political, social – with varying degrees of success. This too may be a factor in the explanation of a decline in participation, if such a thing is actually taking place. There is a danger then in oversimplifying the causes of the enormous upheavals that have taken place in Western democracies over the last 50 years and in pointing the finger at one part of a process of communication as the cause of much of it.

Note

This chapter is a longer version of a paper written jointly with Dr S. Papathanassopoulos which appears in *Press/Politics*, 1 (2), 1996.

8

Political Communication in the Age of Global Electronic Media

There was no place for journalists in the respectable world of diplomacy of half a century ago. Before the First World War, they were not allowed inside the Foreign Office until the doorkeeper had first satisfied himself that there was a bit of news that could be fed to them. If senior officials had decided that there was nothing they wanted to say, the journalists waiting in the courtyard would be sent away and told to try again another day. (Barman, 1968: xi)

The preceding chapters have covered a range of issues from the exploration of the way the mass media dealt with one particular topic to the way they cover Parliamentary institutions and their work, from the nature of journalistic work to electoral communication practices. Implicit in much of this text is a sort of ambivalence towards some of the issues and processes discussed and analysed. The specificity of the material has emphasized differences – across political systems, across different systems of communications – yet the material has often highlighted similarities, as in the convergence of election and communication practices, in discussions of the 'modern publicity process', and so on.

The ambivalence towards some of the issues and trends reflects a similar ambivalence which can often be spotted in discussions about the globalization of the means of mass communication. As we shall see in the first part of this chapter, although there are undoubtedly trends towards a globalization of media systems, there are also national and local forces which seem to mediate, or go against, such trends. Consequently, the political implications of these trends, at least as they impact on political communication, also display ambivalence. This theme will be explored through an analysis of 'media events' and through a brief exegesis of the role of the media in international diplomacy.

The second, and concluding, part of this chapter attempts to place the discussion of internationalization and globalization within a much more domestic and national concern with the adequacy of the mass media: 'adequacy' with regard to the provision of a proper supply of 'information' to enable political actors and citizens to fulfil their various roles in contemporary societies, 'adequacy' with regard to skills of investigation and clarification, and 'adequacy' with regard to surveying the local, national and global scenes. There are two implicit assumptions which guide much of the discussion. The first is a suspicion – sometimes more than that – that the media cannot always live up to the traditional demands made upon them. There are successes and failures, ups and downs. Nevertheless, and this is the second assumption, the media have moved to 'centre stage' both *in* modern Western democracies and in *connecting* Western democracies. Thomas Barman's comments, reproduced at the start of this chapter, on the life of the diplomatic correspondent in the 1910s, come from another age in more ways than one. One should take for granted the fact that much political activity is adapting, or has adapted, 'to the central role of mass media, particularly, television in modern life' (Swanson, 1993: 2; see also Chapter 6 for a discussion of 'the modern publicity process'). For all who are concerned with the 'health' of the polity, the implications of this are clearly immense.

The issues raised in the second part of the chapter transcend local and national dimensions. They are issues which have a universal importance. But their local and national focus continues to remind us that although the processes of internationalization and globalization are much in evidence, a considerable part of our political, cultural and social life is still bound up with more limited geographic, political and ethnic considerations. The media may have diminished the significance of temporal and spatial differences, yet we still attach ourselves to localities and different communities in a continually changing mosaic of allegiances.

For students of political communication, then, the significance of the international and global dimension of media matters needs to be tempered by the persistence of the nation-state and of domestic issues and concerns – admittedly alongside global ones – and the continuing importance of domestic media. We can observe all these things in the processes of media globalization, the imagery of 'media events' and the role of the media in international diplomacy.

The age of the global electronic media

In the last dozen or so years it has become commonplace to discuss the systems of mass communication as being part of larger, international or global organizations of communication (Smith, 1991; Negrine and Papathanassopoulos, 1990; Tunstall and Palmer, 1991). The basic facts to which such discussions allude are, at least on one level, fairly straightforward: certain media corporations straddle continents and operate across the international or global landscape.

This structural dimension of media globalization is easy to demonstrate and it reaches its apogee in Rupert Murdoch's media empire. With control over newspapers and satellite television organizations around the globe, Murdoch's interests literally span the world:

- in London, he owns or controls News International (*The Times*, the *Sun*, *News of the World*, etc.), BSkyB with a package of over 20 satellite channels (including sports) reaching over 4 million homes, HarperCollins UK, News Datacom providing conditional access for satellites;

- in Hong Kong, he owns Star TV and related satellite services;
- in Australia, he owns News Corporation and related newspaper interests, as well as airlines (Ansett);
- in Germany, he has a near 50 per cent interest in Vox;
- in South America, he has an interest in Canal Fox, and joint ventures with the Globo organization;
- in the United States, he has newspaper and magazine interests as well as control of Fox Television stations. (*Guardian*, 1995: 16–17)

Other 'media moguls' exist alongside him controlling such groups as Time-Warner, Disney, Bertelsmann, Viacom and Fininvest (Berlusconi). Lesser players, such as Canal Plus, can be added to this, albeit short, list.

Such a recitation of famous names and players, however, masks some features of globalization which also need to be considered carefully. First, although such systems of communication span the world, the content of many of them is not necessarily uniform. Even services such as CNN which cover the world with a news service allow for some variation. This is perhaps even more true of services that carry entertainment, sports and films. Second, the global systems of communication tend to focus their activities on those regions or areas where they are likely to make a profit. Third, the interests of these giant media corporations may differ significantly so that one (e.g. Murdoch's News Corporation) may focus on specific media sectors (newspapers, television) and not others (e.g. music recordings). This is not to say that there cannot be alliances and common groupings of interests but that their primary interests may lie in particular directions.

None of this should in any way detract from the observation that many media groups are increasingly operating internationally or globally. This is even true of the BBC, the British licence-funded public service broadcaster. As the British government recently observed, 'the BBC has scope to develop commercially its role as an international broadcaster, and should be encouraged to take up the challenge offered by the growing global market' (DNH, 1994: 8). But the fact that some groups are, or are desperately seeking to be, global should not be taken to mean that the process of globalization is complete and that we are somehow all part and parcel of a totally interconnected and communicating whole. As Annabelle Sreberny-Mohammadi has counselled, we have to contend with

the slippery nature of the linguistic terms used in international communications analysis: that 'global' rarely means 'universal' and often implies only the actors of the North; that 'local' is often really 'national' which can be oppressive of the 'local'; that 'indigenous' culture is often already 'contaminated' through older cultural contacts and exists as a political claim rather than a clean analytic construct. (1991: 134)

However, just as the uneven nature of globalization does not negate its importance, the linguistic fog does not detract from some of the many cultural implications of globalization which have so excited commentators.

As Giddens has noted, globalization refers to 'the intensification of world-wide social relations which link distant locations in such ways that local happenings are shaped by events occurring many miles away and vice versa' (1990: 64).

This not only throws up questions of power and the relations between the centre and the periphery, but also questions about national identity and cultural identity, and world cultures as against local cultures. With the technologies of communication currently at play, the global nature of such linkages and effects cannot be overlooked: satellite communications, for instance, make contact between localities instantaneous and force us to reconsider the significance of time and space. We can all be joined together to watch the final of the World Cup football competition live, irrespective of physical and temporal differences. The technologies of communication play an important part in compressing space and time because they enable international connections to be made with the greatest of ease. It follows that the ability to create such a complexity of relations within localities and between localities spread across vast distances can also have significant implications for the conduct of formal and informal international political affairs. A good illustration of the media creating such linkages and, at the same time, fostering an international forum of, and for, political communication is the 'media event' (Katz and Dayan, 1991). A different sort of example, but one which also brings to the fore the media's role in national/international political affairs, is the role of the media in international diplomacy.

Media events and media diplomacy

'Media events' are usually large-scale events which are planned and staged for national and/or international media audiences and which are broadcast live. Unlike 'pseudo-events', 'media events' have an existence in their own right but they are imbued with important symbolic, political, social and other properties which set them apart from the coverage of more 'ordinary' events. Typical examples would include royal weddings, inaugurations, state funerals and, more recently, signings of peace accords. Within a national *and* international context, then, we can all be participating guests or observers in a royal wedding, a presidential inauguration or a state funeral. According to Hallin and Mancini, media events are seen 'to dissolve or de-emphasize social divisions, and bring the members of a community together around shared values' (1992: 121).

Media events can also have an international political dimension if they involve events of international political 'significance'. Hallin and Mancini's analysis of US/Soviet summits in the 1980s suggests that they were seen as crucial not simply on account of any decisions reached but because of 'the "spirit" they created, by the sense of common commitment transcending political antagonism and presumably leading to further political accomplishment' (Hallin and Mancini, 1992: 121). A very similar 'media event' would be the signing of the declaration of principles of Palestinian self-rule in the West Bank between Israel and the Palestinians in Washington in September 1994.

The advent of sophisticated technologies of communication clearly makes such media events more easily available internationally and allows many more citizens/viewers from very diverse locations to participate in them in a variety of ways: as viewers, as keen observers, as direct participants, and so on . . . we are all invited to take part. But media events can also take place with a 'lower' level of technological development. Raymond Cohen has argued, for instance, that Richard Nixon's visit to China in 1972 was 'the first diplomatic encounter to be structured around the requirements of prime-time television' and that the effect of the live broadcast of the banquets had a dramatic impact on relations between China, the USA and Japan (1987: 8). The issue may not be so much the global availability of the images but the use of such events as part of the international 'theatre of power' (Cohen, 1987). The images become part of the diplomatic process because they provide clues to changing relationships. Thus, a cordial banquet attended by key political figures is meant to convey friendly and valued relations; low-level political figures in charge could convey the lack of importance attached to the event, or perhaps even a snub. Jarol Manheim documents in great detail the significance of official head-of-state visits as part and parcel of such politics and diplomacy. Foreign heads of state

> come to the United States to gain political advantage, sometimes in their respective domestic spheres and sometimes internationally. They come to Washington because it is, for them, the center of American political and media power and because they want some of the benefits that power can bestow. (1994: 81)

For Manheim, these visits and the (preferably pre-planned) accompanying media coverage are part of the diplomatic process. As he concludes from a series of case studies, the visiting 'leaders had an agenda of substantive policy objectives, and both saw the need to manage media portrayals of their respective visits. Communication strategies, in other words, are important means through which the goals of statecraft can be accomplished' (1994: 82). The imagery and ceremony contained in 'media events' can also be extremely powerful and politically useful ways of signalling dramatic change. If images of such events are carried across the globe, as were the images of Itzhak Rabin shaking hands with Yasser Arafat in Washington in 1993 after the signing of the declaration of principles, their political significance and repercussions are immense.

The White House setting and the ceremony for the signing of the declaration were replete with symbolism, and the expectations the event created were enormous. For the political speakers and the media this was a defining moment in time and a watershed in the relationship between 'old enemies'. It represented a break with a dismal past of hostility and enmity.

And so, isolated on the White House lawn, with President Bill Clinton on hand, the 'old enemies' were asked to sign the declaration on, as viewers were endlessly reminded, the same walnut table used by Menachim Begin and Anwar Sadat on a previous occasion to sign the Camp David agreement. When Rabin and Arafat shook hands – encouraged a little by President Clinton and overcoming a certain visible hesitancy – the declaration was symbolically sealed. That image of hands together was taken to signify that whole communities and established patterns of behaviour were now liberated from the shackles of the past. As Katz and Dayan observed, the

> live broadcasting of an event creates pressure on the event to succeed . . . the event must succeed, but it must succeed within a foreseeable time, that is, in full sight of the cameras. The emotion generated by the event can only be sustained if the ceremonial progress culminates in a cathartic conclusion. (1991: 191)

Other aspects of 'media events' are noteworthy. For example, the handshake between Rabin and Arafat may have taken place because media events 'liberate leaders to act more or differently than they otherwise might' (1991: 192). Also, the media connect the centre with the periphery, so permitting the international citizenry as television audience to participate actively in viewing historic moments of this sort. Katz and Dayan enumerate many other effects of media events ranging from effects on public opinion and on political institutions to effects on diplomacy, family, religion and collective memory and all of these can be read off from the brief example discussed here. The transmission of media events thus has repercussions on each of these areas as individuals, groups and nations are forced to reassess their relations with each other in the light of the actions taking place live in front of their eyes.

There are, however, three significant criticisms of media events both as a category of events and as events in themselves which run counter to the idea that they 'dissolve or de-emphasize social divisions, and bring members of a community together around shared values' (Hallin and Mancini, 1992: 121). First, as Hallin and Mancini point out, international media events offer a particular perspective on issues and problems. It reinforces 'hegemonic internationalism' where not everyone takes part on equal terms (1992: 132). One strong message emanating from international summitry and the signing of the declaration is the dominant and dominating presence of the USA as a world power. It holds the ring within which other things happen: other nations are less powerful and they acknowledge that in the presence of the USA at the same time as the symbolic significance of the USA increases. Second, 'media events' usually take place on the soil of the world's leading (and technologically advanced) nations. If they are to take place in other locations, such events need to involve leaders of world powers who will, in turn, attract media attention. Consequently, events taking place in other locations which may be considered locally or nationally significant cannot always cross the threshold which would ensure that images of their proceedings are broadcast internationally. In this respect, traditional domestic news values often impinge on the coverage, or lack of coverage, of events.

The third criticism is that international political media events often work as symbolic events because they are isolated from the very real problems which they are meant to resolve. The Rabin–Arafat handshake almost wishes away the real and deep divisions which existed (and exist) between the two communities. And so whilst live commentary of these events emphasizes their symbolic and diplomatic significance, it must also provide a reminder that there can be other contradictory interpretations of these events. In this respect, international political events may continue to be interpreted differently as they cross political nation-state boundaries: the Israelis celebrating the prospect of peace, the Palestinians moaning yet another sell-out to an American–Israeli brokered peace. The assumption of 'community' is thus not always borne out. Furthermore, journalists have to take on contradictory roles: as bringers of good news but also as coun-sellors of caution. Perhaps for these reasons, Hallin and Mancini conclude their analysis of the way summits were reported in three different countries by noting that media events have an ambivalent character: a mixture of 'internationalism and nationalism, of *communitas* and structure, of open-ness and exclusion'. They may be, in fact, no more than 'rituals of pacification' (1992: 135). The public was/is reassured that things are being done, if not behind the scenes then in front of our very eyes.

If the live broadcasting of media events forces political actors and the national and/or international citizenry to rethink their relations, the broad-casting (live or otherwise) of other images can also force actors to review their positions. Images of wars and atrocities, for example, can put pressure on political leaders to act (Gowing, 1994). Such images are unlike the images of 'media events' because they are not part of a controlled and packaged communication and they can intrude into the international political scene like unwelcome guests. Because of this, a great deal of effort is sometimes made to exclude the media on the grounds that they can disrupt diplomacy. Much of the negotiations leading up to the Rabin–Arafat meeting had taken place in secret in Norway. The reasons for that were many but high amongst them was the belief that had the media known about the negotiations they would not have proceeded as they did. The media would have confronted the negotiators with awkward questions at every stage of the negotiations; they would have sought to dissect the discussions; they would have brought in others/outsiders to debate points; they would, in other words, have placed the process of diplomacy under such an intense light that it would probably not have survived. By negotiating behind closed doors and in total secrecy, possible points of conflict and division could be bypassed more easily. Hence, a declaration could be agreed upon and signed. Sidestepping problems does not make those problems vanish; it merely postpones the point of confrontation, although the high expectations created by media events can often lead to bitter disappointment as the cracks open up and expose the real problems that had been papered over.

The degree to which the media may be considered unhelpful in the modern world of diplomacy and international politics emerged very clearly in a lecture on diplomacy and the media given in September 1993 by Douglas Hurd, the then British Foreign Secretary. In his speech, Douglas Hurd sought to draw a distinction between 'the reporter and the commentator' and 'the Minister and the serving officer'. Though his general thesis was that there was, on the whole, greater openness in diplomacy today than in the past, the two sides of government and media should become aware of essential differences. As he put it,

> the reporter and commentator have a different angle of vision and different preconception from those who decide and act. It is no use the Minister or serving officer assuming that reporters will see his problem his [*sic*] way. They will see it their way and act accordingly. It is no use resisting this or resenting it, but equally it would be wrong to be seduced by the apparent lure of favourable press comment. The relationship will be fruitful provided each side recognises the difference between the professions. The general should not fancy himself as a commentator or the commentator as a general or a Cabinet Minister. (1993: 9– 10)

The antipathy towards the commentator 'as interventionist' in the process of decision-making cannot be disguised. While the 'commentator' as interventionist seeks to force ministers into action – over ex-Yugoslavia, over Somalia, over Zaire, and so on – when ministers do take action, particularly if that action is disastrous, 'who would be the first to denounce the lack of judgement, the failure to foresee the recklessness of a disastrous misadventure?' (Hurd, 1993: 8).

It is possible that television has accentuated this problem inasmuch as events, atrocities, personalities and the like can now be seen more clearly, at close range and with an immediacy which would have been impossible with other media. But one should not exaggerate the significance of the media's alleged greater autonomy from government and politics, nor should one isolate the media's work from the actions of political actors themselves. In the case of Mr Hurd, though he was singling out reporting from Bosnia where reporters were all 'founder members of the "something must be done" school', political actors were able to resist those demands. They were not persuaded otherwise and their policies were not derailed by the television pictures, although one can imagine situations where they might have been. In a curious way, then, the example of Bosnia which runs through Mr Hurd's speech illustrates the powerlessness of the media to change the policy directions of political actors immersed in other struggles and pursuing other agendas.

This does not take anything away from the thesis that the media have become central to, and intrusive in, communication between national and political actors and their publics, nor that the media can play some part in the diplomatic process. The point to note is that the media's involvement in the diplomatic process can be complex: it can include bringing information to light, contributing new information, and persuading 'public opinion', rather than simply bringing about dramatic change in policies. Whilst Douglas Hurd may be correct in identifying different approaches to events as seen through the eyes of the 'commentator' and the 'minister', he may be misconstruing the intentions of the 'commentator'. After all, it is the duty of the reporter to report events seen and experienced; if political actors feel themselves under pressure 'to do something' could it not be because of their positive pursuit of alternative agendas or even their own sense of failure? To return to the example of Bosnia, Western governments did not actively and readily respond to the images of conflict and pain. This was both a failure of action and, more positively, a pursuit of a policy of non-intervention – often premised on national political considerations – justified on the grounds that the situation was complex, difficult, etc. A failure, in other words, on the part of political actors to act as political fixers, and therefore an implicit realization that their own power was severely limited. But instead of admitting their powerlessness or their inability to act or to resolve a problem, political actors often compound their failures by setting out a form of words which subsequently turns out to be empty. In such circumstances, to turn on the media or to restrict journalists to their own profession merely asks us to refocus our attention away from the politics of failure and the failure of politics. Interestingly, and sadly, Douglas Hurd's comments were made in 1993 and in defence of a NATO policy which had as a central feature 'the concept of operations for air strikes, if necessary'. At the time of writing (December 1995) the fighting in ex-Yugoslavia has just ceased and not, one should quickly add, as a direct outcome of any media intervention, although broadcast images and commentaries probably contributed to the willingness to find a solution to a sad state of affairs.

The difficulty of judging the precise contribution of the media arises from the general inability to pinpoint the different intensities of particular effects: who do images influence? what sort of influence is it? do images of conflict throw light on the issue? can images confuse the issue? can images give a one-sided account of atrocities, for example, by not focusing on other atrocities? These questions are fairly common in the general area of political communication (see Seymour-Ure, 1974) and are also relevant when reviewing the role of the media in the diplomatic process. As studies have shown, although the general influence of the media in the international context is taken for granted, more specific analyses of how that influence works and on whom is sadly lacking (see, for example, Yoel Cohen, 1986; Gowing, 1994; Berry, 1990; O'Heffernan, 1991; Serfaty, 1991). We are still a long way from being able to isolate the forces that bring about change and the processes by which such change does come about. Finally, none of these questions can be detached from more general ones pertaining to the 'adequacy' of the mass media as key institutions of communications in democratic systems.

Questions of 'adequacy' and 'media-centredness'

In his book, *Media Performance*, Denis McQuail set out a number of criteria for assessing the 'information quality in news'. These are 'factual-ness, accuracy and completeness' (1992: 205). None of these is straightforward: each can be subdivided to allow for a more in-depth analysis of a particular point. Thus, accuracy requires a comparison of news reports with 'reality', it requires an assessment of the credibility of news sources, audience assessment of accuracy, and so on. The same would be the case for 'completeness' where one could explore '*internal* complete-ness (all the essential facts of a given story) and *external* completeness (all the essential stories)' (1992: 210). One reason for developing these more detailed points for analysis is to allow for a better appreciation of the ways in which the 'information quality in news' can be examined.

Even using the bare essentials of this very complex and detailed schema, the many illustrations provided in this book permit us to conclude that the media's ability to offer 'adequate' coverage of events is severely con-strained, and that there are some fundamental questions which need to be asked about how well the media are/will be able to perform their tasks as media of, and for, political communication. The case study of the BAe–Rover affair (Chapters 1 and 2) highlighted a series of problems which the media faced: they were not always clear about the motivations of the main actors, they could not always interpret the financial dimension of the affair, and they rarely penetrated the many 'veils of secrecy' which cover govern-mental information. The 'arms to Iraq' controversy raises similar questions about the media's ability to 'tell the story', although in this case one also has to take into account some deliberately superb obfuscatory footwork on the part of the British government and Civil Service (Norton-Taylor, 1995). A very different case, that of the coverage of Parliament, Parliamentary select committees and Parliamentary reports (Chapter 3) once again shows up the unevenness in the coverage of these areas. The question of the meaning of 'specialization' in journalism (Chapter 4) has a bearing on many of these areas since it addresses directly the knowledge which jour-nalists bring to bear on their work. Finally, the examination of 'media events' in this chapter shows how the media can often become the accomplices of political actors, reproducing their discourses rather than retaining the distance which would allow them to be more critical of the set pieces they are 'invited' to cover.

Had these points applied only to one country, in this case Britain, one could perhaps have suggested that there were some peculiar factors which brought them to the fore. However, as has also been documented in the book, the lessons from America are not very different. Coverage of Congress has changed radically in recent years, and journalistic activity in America has also been criticized in not dissimilar ways. According to Kellner, 'Democracy has . . . clearly become subordinate to capitalism in the current [US] system of commercial broadcasting' (1990: 94), a point that underpins Roger Ailes' 'orchestra pit' theory of politics which runs like this:

> If you have two guys on a stage and one guy says, 'I have a solution to the Middle East problem,' and the other guy falls into the orchestra pit, who do you think is going to be on the evening news? (Roger Ailes quoted in Task Force, 1993: 69)

Moreover, if one were to look at commentaries on the 1992 presidential election campaign, one would be struck by the depth of dissatisfaction with the way the media, particularly television, played their role as agencies for political communication. There were criticisms of the way news organizations became obsessed with the scandals surrounding the private lives of candidates and paid considerably less attention to issues and debates (Hume, 1993: 13). An equally serious and very similar criticism of the news organizations was made with regard to the 1988 election by Kathleen Jamieson, who pointed out that the press focused on the strategy of campaigning, on statements made, especially statements made in political commercials, rather than on the substance of the campaign (Jamieson, 1992: xxii). There was concern about the 'gradual but indisputable blurring of the line between news and entertainment' giving rise to a situation where the candidates 'evaded the traditional press corps and went on the talk shows' (Kalb, 1993: 15). Such a trend raised important questions about how political actors would be, and could be, held accountable. A third criticism was that there was 'a trend towards an interpretive form of reporting that center[ed] on the journalist's view of political reality, not the candidate's'. Consequently, 'the candidate's words are noteworthy largely in so far as they illustrate the journalist's chosen theme, which typically centers on the election's contestual aspects' (Patterson, 1993: 102).

The sense of unease with the progress of election campaigns and with the quality of the coverage given to the whole electoral process comes out very clearly in all these comments. At the same time, however, the critics are fully aware of the continuing struggle between the media and political actors over control of the agenda and the communication process in general, and the way that this struggle to some extent determines the nature of the coverage. The more effort the political actor puts into ensuring that her 'message' gets through, the greater the effort on the part of the media to expose the manipulation. Consequently, newer ways are found to bypass media exposure, and so the cycle goes on. So the sense that 'something must be done about the nature of much modern political communication' is underpinned by the belief that there is an antithesis, an inherent conflict, between these two sets of institutions (see Blumler and Gurevitch, 1981), or between the 'commentators' and the 'minister'.

But this conflict – if it is a conflict rather than a series of more limited skirmishes – is only one of many factors that contribute to the nature of contemporary political communication. Many of the other factors have already been hinted at throughout this book. Prominent amongst these must surely be the greater commercial pressures under which media are currently operating locally, nationally and internationally. For example, a recent report on the regional and local press in Europe noted that 'in Western Europe, four out of five daily newspapers have disappeared in the last 80 years' (Musso, et al., 1993: 5). Issues of survival loom very large for the press as they do for broadcasters. Broadcasters in Europe have yet to fully adjust to the privatization and commercialization of broadcasting which have taken place since the mid-1980s. The effects of these are yet to be documented in detail but trends towards greater commercialization are already in evidence: public broadcasting services have been privatized or are under enormous threat, as in France and Greece respectively.

The impact of commercial pressures on news values also needs to be considered. News values lead to a situation where certain issues, events and personalities are considered worthy of comment and others not. A more commercial approach to the media would certainly push news organiz-ations to begin to define their roles much more carefully and to bring them into closer alignment with 'what the public wants'. For some, this amounts to a 'tabloidization' of news, news formats and news media; for others it is an abdication of the 'traditional' conception of news organizations and news media. Thus, one can point to the demise of the overtly 'party political press' and to the rise of the more commercially attuned press in Britain (Negrine, 1994; Seymour-Ure, 1991), in France (Kuhn, 1994) and in Germany (Humphreys, 1994), as well as to the changing relationship between political parties and news media. Others, as we have seen, use findings which pinpoint a decline in the coverage given to Parliamentary institutions as an indication of changing perceptions of what news media should and could do.

The significance of these two *related* factors – commercialization, and the changing perceptions of news – and the alleged greater autonomy of news organizations nowadays is best appreciated in David Swanson's analysis of 'media-centred democracies', and in the ways he seeks to connect the changing nature of journalism with its implications for modern political communication. According to Swanson, 'in the new professional culture [of journalism], traditional, ideological and political commitments are being replaced by a different conception of the values, social aims, and con-ventions that should guide news reporting'. The newer 'core values' include 'objectivity and neutrality' and the institutional need to develop 'conven-tions of reporting that are thought to make news interesting and attractive to audiences *most of whom after all do not have a great interest in day to day activities of the government and politics*' (1993: 6; my italics).

The contrast between these comments and those of Charles Curran on the role of the broadcaster (Chapter 1, p. 1) is quite striking, as is the view that audiences have no interest in government and politics. If Swanson is correct, then the news media can pursue a more commercial, more entertaining agenda without fear of jeopardizing their survival. Quite the opposite, in fact, for in an age of shifting alliances and weakening of political party ties and allegiances it is the overtly politically committed that is often most risk. So why bother with a *news* organization at all?

Or is it more likely that the media are confronting significant political change without any clear idea of how such change needs to be dealt with, and what new imperatives it imposes upon them? It may be, for instance, that 'audiences' do not have a great interest in government and politics as it is *presently* organized, constituted or reported? Or that its presentation *in the media* has itself created the current malaise, the current unhappiness with the standing of political actors (Garment, 1991)? The crucial point here is that although the media may be 'interjecting' their own independent views into the dialogue between political actors and public (Swanson, 1993: 6), they are doing so without a firm point of anchorage. Who are they meant to represent and whose interests are they upholding when they are so closely allied to political and economic centres of power? According to Patterson, 'with the demise of political parties, the media has been left to organize the political system, a role it is institutionally incapable of fulfilling effectively. "The press doesn't have the incentives or the account-ability or the values to provide political arrangements"' (quoted in Task Force, 1993: 27). They have, in the age-old phrase, 'power without (any obvious) responsibility'.

The relevance of this statement may be greater today than in the past if we are truly living in 'media-centred democracies' in which governments and politics are intertwined with the effective use of mass media. If all governmental and political communication has to be 'filtered' through the media, but a media system that is increasingly directed by its own institu-tional needs for survival and profitability, then the values which underpinned its traditional organization and purposes are clearly in need of drastic revision. Yet the new 'core values' do not necessarily provide the way forward since they expose the media's obvious lack of legitimacy and their contradictory posturings: neutral and objective but committed to the status quo! How to overcome these contradictory posturings and at the same time take on board new values and new duties and responsibilities remains an issue for the future of political communication.

Conclusion

This book has offered perhaps no more than another perspective on the rather knotty problems which lie at the heart of modern democratic systems: governments and political actors need to communicate, the media are means of communication – mass or otherwise – but their 'institutional needs' are very different. And if the Swanson and Blumler arguments concerning the state of modern political communication are correct, their institutional needs are becoming ever more divergent.

In these sorts of circumstances, it is hardly surprising to find commen-tators discussing calls for a revival of 'the public sphere' (see, for example,

Garnham, 1992, 1995; Keane, 1995; Curran, 1991). There ought to be an arena for the formation of public opinions, an arena for rational debate, but wishing these things is far from creating the conditions for their emergence. The real and central problem with advocating the idea of the public sphere is the impossibility of suspending the media in mid-air like some ever watchful, all-seeing eye surveying all and revealing everything. There is much that cannot be seen, and there is too much that needs to be taken in. Furthermore, who will weave the web which will suspend the media in mid-air, beyond all partisan influences?

Moreover, as the study of the announcement of pit closures amply demonstrates (Chapter 5), it was not a rational debate which brought about an about-turn in the government's policy but an emotional debate in tandem with a public in revolt. As with the poll tax (Deacon and Golding, 1994), public protest aided and abetted by a doubting media can have an impact. Does this suggest that rather than well-tempered discussion in the media, polities also need robust and committed positions advocated, and supported, by public and political action? Not less ideology and greater detachment, but more ideology and lesser detachment?

Unfortunately, the media in 'media-centred democracies' are all moving in the opposite direction: towards more 'objectivity', more 'neutrality', distancing themselves from governments and politicians, calmly offering contrasting viewpoints, 'interjecting' their own positions. Those in power have to meet the challenges set by the media. Both claim to be speaking on behalf of the public, the citizen, yet both are pursuing their own 'institutional needs' (or self-interests). Both are part of the problem of a lack of accountability in democratic systems, of a disillusioned citizenry, and of a host of other ills which critics can reel off. It follows that both are part of the solution. But so is the public on whose behalf they claim to act. It may be timely and appropriate, therefore, for the public to make its own demands of the media, and to channel its demands via the media to those who govern it. By contrast, 'media-centred democracies', 'the modern publicity process' and 'media events' continue to treat the public as an audience rather than a real participant in the democratic process. Its active participation in its own governance would surely force us to rethink the nature of political communication in contemporary societies.

References

Abu-Lughod, J. (1991) 'Going beyond global babble', in A. King (ed.), *Culture, Globalization and the World-System*. London: Macmillan. pp. 131–8.

Atkin, C. (1981) 'Communication and political socialization', in D. Nimmo and K. Sanders (eds), *Handbook of Political Communication*. London: Sage. pp. 299–328.

Barker, R. (1990) *Political Legitimacy and the State*. Oxford: Oxford University Press.

Barman, T. (1968) *Diplomatic Correspondent*. London: Hamish Hamilton.

Barnett, S. and Gaber, I. (1992) 'Parliamentary select committees on television', *Parliamentary Affairs*, 45 (3): 409–19.

Berry, N. (1990) *Foreign Policy and the Press: an Analysis of the New York Times' Coverage of US Foreign Policy*. New York: Greenwood Press.

Blumler, J. (1990) 'Elections, the media and the modern publicity process', in M. Ferguson (ed.), *Public Communication. The New Imperatives. Future Directions for Media Research*. London: Sage. pp. 101–13.

Blumler, J. and Gurevitch, M. (1981) 'Politicians and the press. An essay in role relationships', in D. Nimmo and K. Sanders (eds), *Handbook of Political Communication*. London: Sage, pp. 467–93.

Blumler, J., Dayan, D. and Wolton, D. (1990a) 'West European perspectives on political communication', *European Journal of Communication*, 5 (2–3): 261–4.

Blumler, J., Franklin, B., Mercer, D. and Tutt, B. (1990b) *Monitoring the Public Experiment in Televising the Proceedings of the House of Commons*. Published as the First Report from the Select Committee on the Televising of Proceedings of the House. Session 1989–90, vol. 1, HC 265–i. London: HMSO.

Blumler, J., McLeod, J.M. and Rosengren, K.E. (eds) (1992) *Comparatively Speaking: Communication and Culture across Space and Time*. London: Sage.

Bogart, L. (1972) *Silent Politics: The Polls and the Awareness of Public Opinion*. New York: J. Wiley.

Borthwick, R. (1993) 'On the floor of the House', in M. Franklin and P. Norton (eds), *Parliamentary Questions*. Oxford: Clarendon Press.

Bourdieu, P. (1979) 'Public opinion does not exist', in A. Mattelart and S. Siegelaub (eds), *Communication and Class Struggle: 1. Capitalism, Imperialism*. New York: International General. pp. 124–9.

Bower, T. (1991) 'Maxwell and the strong-arm of the law', *Guardian*, 9 December, p. 23.

Briggs, A. (1979) *The History of Broadcasting in the United Kingdom: Volume IV, Sound and Vision*. Oxford: Oxford University Press.

Briggs, A. (1995) *The History of Broadcasting in the United Kingdom: Volume V, Competition*. Oxford: Oxford University Press.

Buckingham, D. (1993) *Children Talking Television*. London: Falmer Press.

Burns, T. (1977) 'The organization of public opinion', in J. Curran, M. Gurevitch and J. Wollacott (eds), *Mass Communication and Society*. London: Edward Arnold. pp. 44–69.

Butcher, D. (1991) *Official Publications in Britain*. London: Library Association Publishing.

Butler, D. and Ranney, A. (eds) (1992) *Electioneering: A Comparative Study of Continuity and Change*. Oxford: Clarendon Press.

Calhoun, C. (ed.) (1992) *Habermas and the Public Sphere*. Cambridge, MA: MIT Press.

Cater, D. (1965) *The Fourth Branch of Government*. New York: Vintage Books.

Chomsky, N. (1989) *Necessary Illusions*. London: Verso.

Churchill, W. (1992) 'Where is the light at the end of the tunnel?', *Daily Mail*, 16 October, p. 8.

Cockerell, M. (1989) *Live from Number 10*. London: Faber and Faber.

Cohen, R. (1987) *Theatre of Power: The Art of Diplomatic Signalling*. London: Longman.

Cohen, Y. (1986) *Media Diplomacy*. London: Frank Cass.

Committee of Privileges (1990) Session 1989–90 Second Report *Premature Disclosure of Proceedings of Committee of Public Accounts*. HCP 476. London: HMSO. 18 July.

Committee of Public Accounts (1989) *Sale of Rover Group plc to British Aerospace plc*. Minutes of Evidence. Session 1989–90. HCP 57–i. London: HMSO. 4 December.

Committee of Public Accounts (1990) First Special Report *Leak of Confidential Memorandum on the Sale of Rover Group plc to British Aerospace plc* Session 1989–90, HCP 35–i, London: HMSO. 4 April.

Connell, R.W. (1971) *The Child's Construction of Politics*. Melbourne: Melbourne University Press.

Cook, T.E. (1989) *Making Laws and Making News Media Strategies in the US House of Representatives*. Washington: Brookings Institution.

Cornelius, A. (1988) 'British Aerospace aims to recoup outlay on Rover by sale of assets', *Guardian*, 20 September, p. 24.

Cowley, C. (1992) *Guns, Lies and Spies*. London: Hamish Hamilton.

Cox, G. (1983) *See It Happen: The Making of ITN*. London: The Bodley Head.

Curran, C. (1979) *A Seamless Robe: Broadcasting – Philosophy and Practice*. London: Collins.

Curran, J. (1990) 'The new revisionism in mass communication research: A reappraisal', *Media, Culture and Society*, 5 (2–3): 135–64.

Curran, J. (1991) 'Mass media and democracy: A reappraisal', in J. Curran and M. Gurevitch (eds), *Mass Media and Society*. London: Edward Arnold. pp. 82–117.

Dahl, R. (1989) *Democracy and its Citizens*. New Haven and London: Yale University Press.

Daily Express (1992a) 'The revolt of Middle England', 19 October, pp. 6–7.

Daily Express (1992b) 'The great coal U-turn', 20 October, pp. 1–2.

Daily Express (1992c) 'Months of talks . . . and hours of chaos', 17 October, pp. 6–7.

Daily Mail (1992a) 'Interest rates must be cut now', 16 October, p. 6.

Daily Mail (1992b) 'In step with miners. Tory stalwarts marching from all walks of life', 19 October, p. 2.

Daily Mail (1992c) 'Rumbles from the heartland of loyalty', 19 October, p. 9.

Daily Mirror (1992) 'Rotten to the core', 17 October, p. 1.

Daily Telegraph (1992a) 'Major facing his greatest crisis', 17 October, p. 1.

Daily Telegraph (1992b) 'Tory MPs experience the wrath of their constituencies', 19 October, p. 4.

Day, G. (1988) quoted in Trade and Industry Select Committee, *British Aerospace/Rover*, Minutes of Evidence, 11 May 1988. Session 1987–8, HCP 487–i. London: HMSO.

Deacon, D. and Golding, P. (1994) *Taxation and Representation*. London: John Libbey.

Delaney, T. (1982) 'Labour's advertising campaign', in B. Worcester and M. Harrop (eds), *Political Communications: The General Election Campaign of 1979*. London: George Allen and Unwin. pp. 27–33.

DNH (Department of National Heritage) (1994) *The Future of the BBC*. London: HMSO.

Dowse, B. and Hughes, J. (1972) *Political Sociology*. London: Wiley.

Elliott, P. (1981) 'Press performance as political ritual', in H. Christian (ed.), *The Sociology of Journalism and the Press* (*Sociological Review* Monograph 29). Keele University. pp. 141–77.

Entman, R. (1993) 'Framing: Toward clarification of a fractured paradigm', *Journal of Communication*, 43 (4): 51–8.

Ericson, R.V., Baranek, P.M. and Chan, J.B. (1989) *Negotiating Control: A Study of News Sources*. Milton Keynes: Open University Press.

European Commission, Decision of 13 July 1988 Part II, L25/92.

Financial Times (1992a) 'Miners look to public opinion to save them', 16 October, p. 10.

Financial Times (1992b) 'In the slough of despond', 17 October, p. 10.

Financial Times (1992c) 'Major abandons policy for crisis management', 17 October, p. 8.

Financial Times (1992d) 'Major summons emergency coal cabinet meeting', 19 October, p. 1.

Financial Times (1992e) 'The day's developments', 20 October, p. 12.

Franklin, B. (ed.) (1992) *Televising Democracies*. London: Routledge.

Franklin, B. (1994) *Packaging Politics*. London: Edward Arnold.

Franklin, B. (1995a) 'Parliament on the spike?' Paper given at the Political Studies Association, University of York, April.

Franklin, B. (1995b) 'Newspaper reporting of Parliament', Final Report, University of Sheffield.

Gamson, W. (1992) *Talking Politics*. Cambridge: Cambridge University Press.

Gandy, O. (1982) *Beyond Agenda Setting: Information Subsidies and Public Policy*. Norwood, NJ: Ablex.

Gans, H. (1980) *Deciding What's News*. New York: Vintage Books.

Garment, S. (1991) *Scandal. The Crisis of Mistrust in American Politics*. New York: Times Books/Random House.

Garnham, N. (1992) 'The media and the public sphere', in C. Calhoun (ed.), *Habermas and the Public Sphere*. Cambridge, MA: MIT Press. pp. 359–76.

Garnham, N. (1995) 'Comments on John Keane's "Structural transformation of the public sphere"', *The Communication Review*, 1 (1): 23–5.

Gavin, N. (1994) Review of W. Neuman, M. Just and A. Crigler 'Common Knowledge', *Media, Culture and Society*, 16 (4): 702–5.

George, A. (1995) 'Missiles and the media', *Guardian*, 9 June, p. 15.

Gerstlé, J., Keith, S. and Kaid, L. (1991) 'Commonalities, differences, and lessons learned from comparative research', in L. Kaid, J. Gerstlé and K. Sanders (eds), *Mediated Politics in Two Cultures: Presidential Campaigning in the United States and France*. New York: Praeger. pp. 271–82.

Giddens, A. (1990) *The Consequences of Modernity*. Cambridge: Polity Press.

Giddens, A. (1991) *Modernity and Self-identity*. Cambridge: Polity Press.

Goldie, G.W. (1977) *Facing the Nation. Television and Politics 1936–76*. London: The Bodley Head.

Golding, P. (1990) 'Political communication and citizenship: The media and democracy in an inegalitarian social order', in M. Ferguson (ed.), *Public Communication: The New Imperatives – Future Directions for Media Research*. London: Sage. pp. 84–100.

Golding, P. and Middleton, S. (1982) *Images of Welfare*. Oxford: Martin Robertson.

Golding, P. and Murdock, G. (1991) 'Culture, communications, and political economy', in J. Curran and M. Gurevitch (eds), *Mass Media and Society*, London: Edward Arnold. pp. 15–32.

Gowing, N. (1994) 'Real-time TV coverage from war: Does it make or break government policy'. Paper given at Turbulent Europe British Film Institute Conference, London, July 1994.

Graber, D. (1984) *Mass Media and American Politics*, 2nd edn. Washington, DC: Congressional Quarterly.

Guardian (1991) 'Labour says 33 pits to be axed', 13 September, p. 12.

Guardian (1992a) 'Shire toffs transformed into militants', 19 October, p. 3.

Guardian (1992b) 'Major calls crisis Cabinet', 19 October, p. 1.

Guardian (1995) *Media Guardian*, 'The global visage', pp. 16–17.

GUMG (Glasgow University Media Group) (1976) *Bad News*. London: Routledge and Kegan Paul.

Gunson, P. (1994) 'Noriega's heir wins Panama poll', *Guardian*, 10 May, p. 11.

Gurevitch, M. and Blumler, J. (1990) 'Comparative research: The extending frontier', in D. Swanson and D. Nimmo (eds), *New Directions in Political Communication*. London: Sage. pp. 305–25.

Gurevitch, M. and Blumler, J. (1993) 'Longitudinal analysis of an election communication system: newsroom observation at the BBC 1966–1992', *Osterreichische Zeitschrift für Politikwissenschaft*, 22 (4): 427–43.

Hall, S. and Jacques, M. (eds) (1989) *New Times: The Changing Face of Politics in the 1990s*. London: Lawrence and Wishart.

Hall, S., Critcher, C., Jefferson, T., Clarke, J. and Roberts, B. (1978) *Policing the Crisis: Mugging, the State and Law and Order*. London: Macmillan.

Hall, S., Held, D. and McGrew, T. (1992) 'Introduction', in S. Hall, D. Held and T. McGrew (eds), *Modernity and its Futures*. Milton Keynes: Open University Press.

Hallin, D. and Mancini, P. (1992) 'The summit as media event: The Reagan/Gorbachev meetings on US, Italian, and Soviet television', in J. Blumler, J.M. McLeod and K.E. Rosengren (eds), *Comparatively Speaking: Communication and Culture across Space and Time*. London: Sage, pp. 121–39.

Hansen, A. (1990) 'The construction of science in the mass media'. Paper presented to the International Association for Mass Communication Research Conference, Bled, Yugoslavia, 26–31 August.

Hansen, A. (1992a) 'What if there are multiple intentions? Journalistic practices and science coverage in the British press'. Paper presented at the annual meeting of the American Association for the Advancement of Science (AAAS), Chicago, 6–11 February.

Hansen, A. (1992b) 'Newspaper science: The press presentation of science and scientists'. Paper presented in the symposium: 'Promoting the public understanding of science'. Annual meeting of the Association for Science Education, Sheffield, 3–6 January.

Hansen, A. (1994) 'Journalistic practices and science reporting in the British press', *Public Understanding of Science*, 3 (4) (London, Science Museum): 111–34.

Hansen, A. and Dickinson, R. (1992) 'Science coverage in the British mass media: Media output and source input', *Communications*, 17 (3): 365–77.

Harris, R. (1991) *Good and Faithful Servant: The Unauthorized Biography of Bernard Ingham*. London: Faber and Faber.

Harwood, R. (1994) 'Bad news is no news', *Guardian*, 2 June, p. 14.

Held, D. (1989) 'The decline of the nation state', in S. Hall and M. Jacques (eds), *New Times: The Changing Face of Politics in the 1990s*. London: Lawrence and Wishart.

Hencke, D. (1989) 'Young did not get land valued before Rover sale', *Guardian*, 2 December, p. 1.

Hencke, D. (1994) 'Malaysia dam questions reveal extent of withheld Whitehall files', *Guardian*, 25 January, p. 5.

Hencke, D. and Cornelius, A. (1989) '£38 m secret Rover sweetener', *Guardian*, 30 November, p. 1.

Hennessy, P. (1990) *Whitehall*. London: Fontana Press.

Herbst, S. (1993a) 'The meaning of public opinion: Citizens' constructions of political reality', *Media, Culture and Society*, 15 (3): 437–54.

Herbst, S. (1993b) 'History, philosophy, and public opinion research', *Journal of Communication*, 43 (4): 140–5.

Hess, S. (1981) *The Washington Reporters*. Washington: Brookings Institution.

Hess, S. (1984) *The Government/Press Connection: Press Officers and Their Offices*. Washington: Brookings Institution.

Hess, S. (1986) *The Ultimate Insiders: US Senators in the National Media*. Washington: Brookings Institution.

Hess, S. (1993) 'Public opinion and the decline of legislative news in the United States'. Paper presented at the course on Parliament and Public Opinion sponsored by the Universidad Complutense de Madrid, El Escorial, Spain, 2–6 August.

Hill, D. (1993) 'Parting notes of the Labour reporter', Media Guardian, *Guardian*, 6 September, pp. 16–17.

Hilton, S. (1993) 'Galluping to the rescue of Boris', *Guardian*, 27 April, p. 24.

Himmelweit, H., Humphreys, P. and Jaeger, M. (1985) *How Voters Decide*. Milton Keynes: Open University Press.

Hume, E. (1993) 'Addendum', in 'Task Force: The Report of the Twentieth Century Fund Task Force on Television and the Campaign of 1992', *1-8000-President*. Washington: Brookings Institution. p. 13.

Humphreys, P. (1994) *The Press and Broadcasting in Germany*. London: Berg.

Hurd, D. (1993) 'The power of comment – government and the media'. London: Foreign and Commonwealth Office, 9 September.

Ingham, B. (1994) 'The Lobby system: Lubricant or spanner', *Parliamentary Affairs*, 47 (4): 549–65.

Inglehart, R. (1977) *The Silent Revolution*. Princeton, NJ: Princeton University Press.

Investors Chronicle (1989) 'British Aerospace: Tell-tale accounts', 15 December, p. 65. London.

Jamieson, Kathleen H. (1992) *Packaging the Presidency*. Oxford: Oxford University Press.

Jennings, M.K. and Niemi, R.G. (1985) *Generations and Politics: A Panel Study of Young Adults and Their Parents*. Princeton, NJ: Princeton University Press.

Jones, N. (1986) *Strikes and the Media*. Oxford: Blackwell.

Jones, N. (1994) 'Taming the spin doctors', *British Journalism Review*, 5 (4): 27–30.

Judge, D. (1992) 'Reports and surveys: The "effectiveness" of the post-1979 select committee system – the verdict of the 1990 Procedure Committee', *Political Quarterly*, 63 (1): 91–100.

Kaid, L. and Holtz-Bacha, C. (eds) (1995) *Political Advertising in Western Democracies*. London: Sage.

Kaid, L., Gerstlé, J. and Sanders, K. (eds) (1991) *Mediated Politics in Two Cultures: Presidential Campaigning in the United States and France*. New York: Praeger.

Kalb, M. (1993) 'Addendum', in 'Task Force: The Report of the Twentieth Century Fund Task Force on Television and the Campaign of 1992', *1-8000-President* Washington: Brookings Institution. p. 14.

Katz, E. and Dayan, D. (1991) *Media Events*. London: Sage.

Kaufman, G. (1994) 'The blank checks of government', *Guardian*, 30 December, p. 20.

Kavanagh, D. (1995) *Election Campaigning*. Oxford: Blackwell

Keane, J. (1991) *The Media and Democracy*. Cambridge: Polity Press.

Keane, J. (1995) 'Structural transformation of the public sphere', *The Communication Review*, 1 (1): 1–22. University of San Diego.

Kellner, D. (1990) *Television and the Crisis of Democracy*. Boulder, CO: Westview Press.

Kepplinger, H.M. and Köcher, R. (1990) 'Professionalism in the media world?', *European Journal of Communication*, 5 (2–3): 285–312.

King, A. (1992) 'Major suffers collapse in popularity', *Daily Telegraph*, 5 October, p. 1.

Köcher, R. (1986) 'Bloodhounds or missionaries: Role definitions of German and British journalists', *European Journal of Communication*, 1: 43–64.

Kuhn, R. (1994) *The Media in France*. London: Routledge.

Kynaston, D. (1988) *The Financial Times: A Centenary History*. London: Viking.

Lamb, B. (1992) 'The American experience: C-SPAN and the US Congress', in B. Franklin (ed.), *Televising Democracies*. London: Routledge. pp. 221–33.

Lang, G. and Lang, K. (1983) *The Battle for Public Opinion: The President, the Press, and the Polls during Watergate*. New York: Columbia University Press.

Lee, A. (1976) *The Origins of the Popular Press 1855–1914*. London: Croom Helm.

Lichtenberg, J. (ed.) (1990) *Democracy and the Mass Media*. Cambridge: Cambridge University Press.

Linklater, M. and Leigh, D. (1986) *Not with Honour: The Inside Story of the Westland Scandal*. London: Sphere Books.

Maarek, P. (1995) *Political Marketing and Communication*. London: John Libbey.

Maguire, J. (1990) 'More than a sporting touchdown: The making of American football in England 1982–1990', *Sociology of Sport Journal*, 7: 213–37.

Mair, P. (1995) 'Political parties, popular legitimacy and public privilege', *West European Politics*, 18 (3): 40–57.

Mancini, P. (1993) 'Between trust and suspicion: How political journalists solve the dilemma', *European Journal of Communication*, 8 (1): 33–52.

Mancini, P. and Swanson, D. (1994) 'Introduction', in P. Mancini and D. Swanson (eds), *Politics, Media and Democracy*. New York: Praeger.

Manheim, J. B. (1994) *Strategic Public Diplomacy and American Foreign Policy: The Evolution of Influence*. Oxford: Oxford University Press.

May, A. and Rowan, K. (eds) (1982) *Inside Information: British Government and the Media*. London: Constable.

McCrystal, C. (1993) 'Why desert us now?', *Independent on Sunday*, 13 June, p. 3.

McQuail, D. (1977) *Analysis of Newspaper Content*. Cmnd 6810–4, London: HMSO.

McQuail, D. (1992) *Media Performance*. London: Sage.

Milne, A. (1988) *DG: The Memoirs of a British Broadcaster*. London: Hodder and Stoughton.

Milne, S. (1995) 'Pit profit after sweetener', *Guardian*, 19 June, p. 2.

Moore, S.W., Lare, J. and Wagner, K.A. (1985) *The Child's Political World*. New York: Praeger.

Morley, D. (1990) 'The construction of everyday life: Political communication and domestic media', in D. Swanson and D. Nimmo (eds), *New Directions in Political Communication: A Resource Book*. London: Sage. pp. 123–46.

MRB Hellas (1993) *Media Trends 1993*. Athens: MRB Hellas.

Murdock, G.(1993) 'Communications and the constitution of modernity', *Media, Culture and Society*, 15 (4): 521–40.

Murphy, D. (1976) *The Silent Watchdog*. London: Constable.

Musso, P., Levasseur, L. and Souetre, P. (1993) *The Printed Press and Television in the Regions of Europe*. Report to the Council of Europe, June.

NAO (National Audit Office) (1989) *Sale of Rover Group plc to British Aerospace plc*. Report of the Comptroller and Auditor General, National Audit Oifce, Department of Trade and Industry. 21 November.

Negrine, R. (1982) 'The press and the Suez Crisis: A myth re-examined', *The Historical Journal*, 25 (4): 975–83.

Negrine, R. (1992) 'Parliamentary select committees and the media: A case study of the British Aerospace takeover of the Rover Group', *Parliamentary Affairs*, 45 (3): 399–408.

Negrine, R. (1993) *The Organization of British Journalism and Specialist Correspondents*. Discussion Papers in Mass Communication, University of Leicester.

Negrine, R. (1994) *Politics and the Mass Media in Britain*, 2nd edn. London: Routledge.

Negrine, R. (1995) 'Reporting British Parliamentary select committees: A case study in the communication of politics', in D. Paletz (ed.), *Political Communication Research*. Cresskill, NJ: Hampton Press. pp. 179–200.

Negrine, R. and Papathanassopoulos, S. (1990) *The Internationalisation of Television*. London: Pinter.

Neuman, W.R. and Fryling, A. (1985) 'Patterns of political cognition: an exploration of the public mind', in S. Kraus and R. Perloff (eds), *Mass Media and Political Thought: An Information-Processing Approach*. London: Sage. pp. 223–40.

Neuman, R., Just, M. and Crigler, A. (1992) *Common Knowledge*. Chicago: University of Chicago Press.

Nolan Committee (1994) (Committee on Standards in Public Life) *Committee on Standards in Public Life: Issues and Questions*. London.

Norton-Taylor, R. (1995) *Truth is a Difficult Concept: Inside the Scott Inquiry*. London: Fourth Estate.

O'Heffernan, P. (1991) *Mass Media and American Foreign Policy*. Norwood, NJ: Ablex.

Pallister, D. (1990) 'A war machine built by willing foreign hands', *Guardian*, 3 August, p. 3.

Palmer, M. and Tunstall, J. (1990) *Liberating Communications: Policy-making in France and Britain*. Oxford: National Consumer Council/Blackwell.

Parkin, F. (1971) *Class Inequality and Political Order: Social Stratification in Capitalist and Communist Societies*. London: MacGibbon and Kee.

Parsons, W. (1989) *The Power of the Financial Press*. Aldershot: Edward Elgar.

Patterson, T.E. (1993) 'Let the press be the press: principles of campaign reform', in 'Task Force: The Report of the Twentieth Century Fund Task Force on Television and the Campaign of 1992'. *1–8000–President* Washington: Brookings Institution. pp. 91–110.

Peacock Committee Report (1986) *Report of the Committee on Financing the BBC* (Chairman: Prof. A. Peacock). Cmnd. 9824. London: HMSO.

Pegg, M. (1983) *Broadcasting and Society 1918–1939*. London: Croom Helm.

Peters, J.D. (1993) 'Distrust of representations: Habermas on the public sphere', *Media, Culture and Society*, 15 (4): 541–72.

Pfetsch, B. and Schmitt-Beck, R. (1993) 'Communication strategies and the mass media in the 1990 German election campaign'. Paper presented at European Consortium for Political Research workshop on 'Party campaign strategies and mass communications techniques', 2–8 April, Leiden.

Philo, G. (1990) *Seeing and Believing*. London: Routledge.

Pilkington Committee Report (1962) *Report of the Committee on Broadcasting 1960*. (Chairman: H. Pilkington). Cmnd. 1753. London: HMSO.

Ploman, D. (1962) 'Public opinion and the polls', *British Journal of Sociology*, 13: 331–45.

Ponting, C. (1986) *Whitehall: Tragedy and Farce*. London: Sphere.

Price, V. (1992) *Public Opinion*. London: Sage.

Ray, J.L. (1995) *Global Politics*. Boston: Houghton Mifflin.

Robinson, J. and Levy, M. (1986) *The Main Source*. London: Sage.

Rose, Richard (ed.) (1974) *Lessons from America*. London: Macmillan.

Rush, M. (1990) 'Select committees', in M. Rush (ed.), *Parliament and Pressure Politics*. Oxford: Clarendon Press. pp. 137–51.

Sampson, A. (1991) 'Missile-bound media', *Guardian*, 15 November, p. 23.

Scammell, M. (1995) *Designer Politics*. London: Macmillan.

Schatz, H. (1992) 'Televising the Bundestag', in B. Franklin (ed.), *Televising Democracies*. London: Routledge. pp. 234–53.

Schlesinger, P. (1978) *Putting 'Reality' Together*. London: Constable.

Schlesinger, P. (1990) 'Rethinking the sociology of journalism: Source strategies and the limits of media-centrism', in M. Ferguson (ed.), *Public Communication: The New Imperatives – Future Directions for Media Research*. London: Sage. pp. 84–100.

Schlesinger, P. and Tumber, H. (1994) *Reporting Crime: The Media Politics of Criminal Justice*. Oxford: Oxford University Press.

Schlesinger, P., Tumber, H. and Murdock, G. (1991) 'The media politics of crime and criminal justice', *British Journal of Sociology*, 42 (3): 397–420.

Schou, S. (1992) 'Postwar Americanisation and the revitalisation of European culture', in K.C. Schroder and M. Skovmand (eds), *Media Cultures: Reappraising Transnational Cultures*. London: Routledge. pp. 142–60.

Schudson, M. (1991) 'The sociology of news production revisited', in J. Curran and M. Gurevitch (eds), *Mass Media and Society*. London: Edward Arnold. pp. 151–9.

Select Committee on Procedure (1990) *The Working of the Select Committee System*. Session 1989–90, vol. 1. HC 19–i. London: HMSO.

Serfaty, S. (ed.) (1991) *The Media and Foreign Policy*. London: Macmillan.

Seymour-Ure, C. (1968) *The Press, Politics and the Public*. London: Methuen.

Seymour-Ure, C. (1974) *The Political Impact of Mass Media*. London: Constable.

Seymour-Ure, C. (1977a) 'Parliament and government', in O. Boyd-Barrett, C. Seymour-Ure and J. Tunstall (eds), *Studies on the Press*. London: HMSO. pp. 83–158.

Seymour-Ure, C. (1977b) 'Science and medicine and the press', in O. Boyd-Barrett, C. Seymour-Ure and J. Tunstall (eds), *Studies on the Press*. London: HMSO. pp. 45–82.

Seymour-Ure, C. (1979) 'Parliament and mass communication in the twentieth century', in S. Walkland (ed.), *The House of Commons in the Twentieth Century*. Oxford: Clarendon Press. pp. 527–95.

Seymour-Ure, C. (1991) *The Press and Broadcasting in Britain since 1945*. Oxford: Blackwell.

Sharrock, D. (1990) 'Firm insists "gun" tubes do not link up', *Guardian*, 16 April.

Sigal, L. (1973) *Reporters and Officials: The Organization and Politics of Newsmaking*. Lexington, MA: DC Heath.

Smith, A. (1976) *The Shadow in the Cave*. London: Quartet.

Smith, A. (1991) *The Age of Behemoths: The Globalization of Mass Media Firms*. New York: Priority Press Publication/Twentieth Century Fund Paper.

Smith, A.C.H. (1975) *Paper Voices: The Popular Press and Social Change 1935–65*. London: Chatto and Windus.

Sreberny-Mohammadi, A. (1991) 'The global and the local in international communications', in C. Curran and M. Gurevitch (eds), *Mass Media and Society*. London: Edward Arnold. pp. 118–38.

Steed, W.H. (1938) *The Press*. London: Penguin Special.

Stevens, O. (1982) *Children Talking Politics*. Oxford: Martin Robertson.

Straw, J. (1993) 'The decline in press reporting of Parliament', mimeo paper, London, October.

Sun (1992a) 'Death of mines is criminal', Dear Sun, 19 October, p. 19.

Sun (1992b) '1,000 letters of hate for PM', 19 October, p. 19.

Sun (1992c) 'Send Roy stacks of your fax', 20 October, pp. 4–5.

Sun (1992d) 'Dig in for victory, Roy', 19 October, p. 5.

Sun (1992e) 'Pitmen win vote', 20 October, p. 4.

Swanson, D. (1981) 'A constructivist appoach', in D. Nimmo and K. Sanders (eds), *Handbook of Political Communication*. London: Sage. pp. 169–91.

Swanson, D. (1993) 'Political institutions in media-centred democracy'. Paper presented at the course on Parliament and Public Opinion sponsored by the Universidad Complutense de Madrid, El Escorial, Spain, 2–6 August.

Task Force (1993) The Report of the Twentieth Century Fund Task Force on Television and the Campaign of 1992. *1–8000–President*. Washington: Brookings Institution.

Thompson, J.B. (1990) *Ideology and Modern Culture*. Cambridge: Polity Press.

Tracey, M. (1978) *The Production of Political Television*. London: Routledge.

Trade and Industry Committee (1988a–d) *British Aerospace/Rover*. Minutes of Evidence, Session 1987–88, HCP 487-i to 487-iv. 11, 18 and 26 May 1988, and 2 November 1988. London: HMSO.

Trade and Industry Committee (1990) *Sale of Rover Group to British Aerospace*. Minutes of Evidence. Session 1989–90, HC 149–i and ii. Wednesday 17 January. London: HMSO.

Trade and Industry Committee (1991) *Sale of Rover Group to British Aerospace*. First Report. Session 1990–91, HCP 34. February 1991. London: HMSO.

Trade and Industry Committee (1992) *Exports to Iraq*. Minutes of Evidence. Session 1991–2, HCP 86i–86xv. London: HMSO.

Tuchman, G. (1978) *Making News: A Study in the Construction of Reality*. New York: Free Press.

Tunstall, J. (1970) *The Westminster Lobby Correspondents*. London: Routledge and Kegan Paul.

Tunstall, J. (1971) *Journalists at Work*. London: Constable.

Tunstall, J. (1977) *The Media are American*. London: Constable.

Tunstall, J. (1983) *The Media in Britain*. London: Constable.

Tunstall, J. and Palmer, M. (1991) *Media Moguls*. London: Routledge.

Turner, G. (1992) 'Ten vital questions that John Major must now answer', *Daily Mail*, 17 October, p. 6.

Walker, M. (1992) 'Major says sorry for Tory help to Bush', *Guardian*, 21 November, p. 14.

Waller, M. (1993) 'BAe agree to repay £57m for Rover sweeteners', *Times* (London), 28 May, p. 25.

Weir, S. (1995) 'Curse of the hidden hand', *Guardian*, 17 May.

Wernick, A. (1991) *Promotional Culture: Advertising, Ideology and Symbolic Expression*. London: Sage.

Windlesham, Lord (1966) *Communication and Political Power*. London: Jonathan Cape.

Worcester, R. (1994) 'Demographics and values'. Paper presented to 'The end of Fleet Street' conference, City University, London, 5 February.

Young, H. (1992a) 'Devious paths from the secrets maze', *Guardian*, 14 May, p. 18.

Young, H. (1992b) 'Of mires and ministers', *Guardian*, 24 November, p. 18.

Young, T. (1992) 'Little brother is watching you!', *Guardian*, 14 August, p. 27.

Index